Religion in Contemporary America

This book provides a fresh, engaging multi-disciplinary introduction to religion in contemporary America. The chapters explore the roots of contemporary American religion from the 1950s up to the present day, looking at the major traditions including mainline Protestantism, the evangelical-pentecostal surge, Catholicism, Judaism, African-American religions, and new religious movements. The authors ask whether Americans are becoming less religious, and how religious thought has moved from traditional systematic theology to approaches such as black and feminist theology and environmental theology. The book introduces religion and social theory, and explores key issues and themes such as: religion and social change; politics; gender; sexuality; diversity; race; and poverty. Students and instructors will find the combination of historical and sociological perspectives an invaluable aid to understanding this fascinating but complex field.

Charles H. Lippy held the LeRoy A. Martin Distinguished Professorship of Religious Studies at the University of Tennessee at Chattanooga, USA.

Eric Tranby is Assistant Professor of Sociology at the University of Delaware, USA.

Religion in Contemporary America

Charles H. Lippy and Eric Tranby

Routledge
Taylor & Francis Group

LONDON AND NEW YORK

First published 2013
by Routledge
2 Park Square, Milton Park, Abingdon, Oxon OX14 4RN

Simultaneously published in the USA and Canada
by Routledge
711 Third Avenue, New York, NY 10017

Routledge is an imprint of the Taylor & Francis Group, an informa business

British Library Cataloguing in Publication Data
A catalogue record for this book is available from the British Library

Library of Congress Cataloging in Publication Data
A catalogue record for this book has been requested

ISBN: 978-0-415-61737-6 (hbk)
ISBN: 978-0-415-61738-3 (pbk)
ISBN: 978-0-203-59111-6 (ebk)

Typeset in Sabon by
Saxon Graphics Ltd, Derby

Printed and bound in Great Britain by
TJ International Ltd, Padstow, Cornwall

Contents

Illustrations

Figures

Tables

Every effort has been made to trace copyright holders and obtain permission to reproduce material. Any errors or omissions brought to the attention of the publisher will be remedied in future editions.

Data sources

Chaves, Mark A. (2009) National Congregations Study, 1998 and 2006 (cumulative file). ICPSR03471-v2. Ann Arbor, MI: Inter-university Consortium for Political and Social Research (distributor), 2009-11-17. doi: 10.3886/ICPSR03471.v2.

Hartmann, Douglas, Joseph Gerteis, and Penny Edgell. (2003) American Mosaic Project Survey, 2003. ICPSR28821-v1. Ann Arbor, MI: Inter-university Consortium for Political and Social Research [distributor], 2010-12-16. doi: 10.3886/ICPSR28821.v1.

Pew Report Forum. (2007) Pew Forum's US Religious Landscape Survey, (online) 25 February 2008. Available at: http://pewforum.org/Datasets/Dataset-Download.aspx (accessed 1 Feburary 2012).

Pew Research Center. (2011) Pew Research Center's Political Typology Survey, (online) 4 May 2011. Available at: http://people-press.org/2011/05/04/beyond-red-vs-blue-the-political-typology/ (accessed 1 February 2012).

Smith, Tom W., Peter Marsden, Michael Hout, and Jibum Kim. (2011) General social surveys, 1972–2010 (machine-readable data file). Principal Investigator, Tom W. Smith; Co-Principal Investigator, Peter V. Marsden; Co-Principal Investigator, Michael Hout; Sponsored by National Science Foundation. NORC ed. Chicago: National Opinion Research Center (producer); Storrs, CT: The Roper Center for Public Opinion Research, University of Connecticut (distributor).

Preface

This idea for this book emerged shortly after Routledge published Lippy's survey text, *Introducing American Religion* in 2009. In addition to a general course on religion in American culture, many colleges and universities also had courses on contemporary trends in American religion or on current religious issues in their curricula. Sociologists taught most of them, sometimes in sociology programs and occasionally in religious studies departments. In addition, a few whose training was more in historical and cultural studies offered such courses.

Each brought different strengths to the classroom experience. Historians tended to emphasize the forces that propelled contemporary developments and trends, placing them in their larger cultural and social context. On the other hand, sociologists tracked those same trends by drawing on a host of empirical studies. Rarely were the two brought together. Sociologist Penny Long Marler, then teaching in a university religion department, suggested that having a text that presented the two perspectives would be valuable to all who took such courses, since the approaches were complementary.

Historical and cultural studies informed Lippy's previous work. So he set out to find a sociologist with interests in contemporary American religion to become part of a team that would join together to write a book that would use both approaches. Penny Edgell at the University of Minnesota put him in contact with Tranby. Shortly thereafter, the two began to work together to craft an outline for the book that follows. The collaboration has proved fruitful. On numerous occasions, each has challenged the unstated assumptions of the other, revealing that what historians might take for granted may not be so obvious after all. As well, what sociologists presume is common knowledge may be such for other social scientists, but not necessarily for those who look in humanistic terms at currents of social and cultural change.

What follows is an effort to have a conversation between sociology and religious history in looking at American religious life since the end of World War II. The first section introduces that conversation by discussing various sociological theories about religion and analyzing definitions of religion advanced by social scientists. We then look at how historians have examined American religious life, suggesting in the end that sociological and historical approaches each enrich and complement the other.

The second major section of the book continues the conversation by looking at major religious movements and traditions in the years since World War II, including mainline Protestantism, evangelicalism, Roman Catholicism, and Judaism. We interweave the discussion of those broader movements with consideration of some features of religious life and experience that are common to all – how religious belief and practice get transmitted from one generation to the next, how religion and political life intersect, and how issues related to sexuality and gender have an enduring imprint.

Then we move to examine many religious currents that too often seem on the margins – African American religious culture and some of the countless new religious movements that have taken hold in contemporary America. We then use the experience of one particular religious tradition, the Latter-day Saints or Mormons, as a lens through which to view the larger religious landscape. We also bring into the conversation in this section perspectives coming from sociologists and other social scientists on such matters as the relationship between religion and race (and ethnicity) in American religion as well as how religion operates as both an agent for social change and an agent to inhibit change.

The final section brings us to issues that are reshaping American religious life in the first quarter of the twenty-first century, from the fascination with "spirituality" as something distinct from religion, to fresh currents in religious thought, and then the "new pluralism" spurred by the growth of groups such as Buddhism and Islam. We end with a provocative consideration of what all this means for the character of the United States as a collective entity, wrestling with the question of whether the US is now a Christian nation or even a religious nation.

As we carried on our own conversation in writing and reviewing each other's work, we benefited greatly from the reviewers who helped refine the proposal for the project. The insights and questions offered by those who read the draft manuscript have made the final product even stronger still. We also owe thanks to many individuals who shared their wisdom with us. While writing, Lippy benefited from conversations with many other historians, especially John Corrigan, Amanda Porterfield, Grant Wacker, and Peter W. Williams. Tranby benefited from the loving support of his wife, Brianna, and two children, Elliott and Cara, the excellent research assistance of Samantha Zulkowski, the excellent work of Kai Lin in preparing the index, and many conversations with colleagues, especially Penny Edgell, Aaron Kupchik, Aaron Fitchelberg, and Phyllis Moen.

Both of us are grateful for the guidance and support of Lesley Riddle and Katherine Ong at Routledge. Our copy editor and the layout staff worked diligently to get everything in proper order. We also appreciate the way students who have taken our own courses have helped us shape what we have done here.

Now let the conversation begin.

Part I
Setting the stage

1 Defining and measuring religion
Classical views and theories

In this chapter

This chapter opens by providing definitions of the sociology of religion before examining the various ways in which sociologists define religion. We build on these definitions by exploring how classical theorists viewed religion in society, beginning with Karl Marx's famous claim that religion is the opiate of the people. Next we describe Max Weber's view of religion as a social force that drives major historical changes. Attention is then paid to Emile Durkheim's definition of religion. The chapter then turns to more recent theorists, describing Peter Berger's views regarding human nature and sacred experience. The chapter concludes by explaining how sociologists measure religion, before turning to a description of the contemporary American religious landscape.

Main topics covered

- The sociology of religion as the study of the human system of religion.
- The four key functions sociologists identify that religion serves in society.
- Karl Marx's claim that religion is an "opiate".
- Max Weber's contention that religious beliefs influenced the emergence of capitalism.
- Emile Durkheim's definition of religion which linked together religious beliefs, rituals, and moral community.
- Peter Berger's views of religion as a "sacred canopy" that imbues everyday life with meaning.
- Sociologists measure religion as religious identification/preference and religious participation/belief.

What is the sociology of religion?

The sociology of religion is the study of religion as a product and creator of human action. In other words, the sociology of religion is the study of the human system of religion. Across time and place, humans develop and modify belief systems, religious rituals, and religious communities in ways that are not "fixed" and that respond to broader social and cultural forces.

Religions are a human product because they are constantly being developed, changed, and modified. Christianity comprises the largest religious tradition in the contemporary US, with 78 per cent of the population claiming a Christian affiliation in 2007. It is also a diverse religious tradition with 217 distinct denominations in the US, according to the *Yearbook of American and Canadian Churches*. Even with this much diversity within the Christian tradition, there is the constant development of new denominations caused by the internal splitting of denominations, for example, as well as those resulting from the merger of several mainline Protestant denominations in the ecumenical movement, described in Chapter 4. There are also constant changes in denominational beliefs and rituals over time within existing denominations. Among the most prominent are the changes in Catholic ritual and belief associated with Vatican II, described in Chapter 6. In addition, there has been a general transition towards more contemporary and charismatic worship styles across US denominations.

The notion that religion is a human product that is constantly developing and being modified helps us understand the trends in the American religious landscape that are the central focus of this book. For example, as described in Chapter 16, in order to understand the trend toward more individualized forms of religious expression, we also need to understand how changing mass media forms have influenced the way that people explore and practice their religion. This broader picture of religion is possible only if we look beyond a narrow understanding of religion as dealing with God(s) or the supernatural. The sociology of religion is also the study of religion as a motivator for human action. Religion is a pervasive force in the US and around the world. Examples of religion as a motivator for human action are detailed throughout this book, but especially in Chapters 9, 10, 12, 15, and 19.

Box 1.1 Religion as a motivator for human action

Religion shapes how people behave and how they think about the world and their place in it.
  Examples include:

- Religion has been a force for both conservative and progressive social movements.
- Violence justified by religion has been the cause of many wars and even genocides.
- Political power is, and has been, distributed along religious lines.
- Religion shapes ideas about family life from birth to death.
- Religion shapes gender norms and roles and racial stereotypes.
- Religion shapes people's ideas about "who is like me" and "who is not like me."

How do sociologists define religion?

When defining any social phenomenon, sociologists rely on two types of definition. Substantive definitions examine religion as a type of philosophy, a system of belief, or an understanding of nature and reality. They also provide criteria for elements that make up the social phenomenon of religion. Substantive definitions often do not work well because they are almost always rooted in a particular time and culture and thus are not easily applicable to other times and cultures. Instead, sociologists generally believe that functional theories are the most universal and compelling. Functional definitions are those that describe the function of religion in society. Sociologists have identified four key functions that religion serves in society. These functions are common across very different religions and cultures.

Box 1.2 Functions of religion in society

1   Religion provides comfort to individuals.
2   Religion drives social change and helps people understand it.
3   Religion is a social act.
4   Religion is a brace against chaos.

First, religion provides comfort to individuals. There is much anecdotal and empirical evidence that religion provides comfort to individuals, especially in times of crisis. Sociological research shows that religious attendance and belief spike during times of personal and social upheaval, such as after divorces and deaths and during recessions and wars. Because religion provides a comfort and explanation for life events, religion often grants legitimacy to existing social arrangements. For example, as described in Chapter 15, civil leaders, such as kings, pharaohs, and popes were, and sometimes still are, considered to be God's representatives on earth. Moreover, verses in the Christian bible, such as Matthew 22:21, which says, in part, "render unto Caesar the things which are Caesar's," has been interpreted to mean that people should submit to state and civil authority. Women (see Chapter 10), African Americans (see Chapter 12), and immigrants (see Chapter 19) often turn to religion as a source of comfort in the face of inequality and discrimination.

Second, religion drives, and helps people understand, social change. There are numerous examples of this function cited in the chapters that follow, including the participation of the mainline Protestants (see Chapter 4), African American Protestants (see Chapter 11), and Catholics (see Chapter 6) in the civil rights movement. We see it also in the use of an engaged orthodox orientation, described in Chapter 5, to help evangelical Protestants grapple with major societal changes and also in the rise of new religious movements, especially Wicca, in response to the changing role of women in society, as described in Chapters 10 and 16. Many more examples, and the research that underlies them, are described throughout this book and are the central focus of Chapter 15.

Third, religion is a social act. As described later in this chapter, religion builds a community of people who share religious beliefs and rituals, integrate together within the group and also define the people outside of that community. The ways in which religion is communicated in social settings, including in the family, congregations, the media, and in popular culture is the focus of Chapter 8.

Fourth, religion provides a brace against chaos. In other words, religion provides humans with a sense that our lives are not mere aggregations of random events but are connected to some larger sacred order. For example, we often hear people say that some challenging or tragic event is "all part of God's plan for my life" or hear that the relatives of a person who died from a rare disease or violent act start an organization to prevent future deaths from the same cause in order to give that death a larger meaning in life. As described in Chapter 16, this sense of connection is a fundamental human condition, even among those who are not formally affiliated with a religion. This is, in many ways, the only function of religion that is exclusive to religion. Many other social institutions and phenomena provide comfort, drive social change, and are social acts; but only religion or religious and spiritual experiences can link our lives to a sacred purpose that is larger than ourselves.

The appropriate definition, whether substantive or functional, depends on the nature of the questions we wish to ask and answer about religion. All of these definitions assume that there is a universal something called religion that can be identified across cultures and in many people's experiences. As Talal Asad (1933–) points out, this assumption is a product of colonial western Christianity. The way we define and study religion is, in many ways, influenced by the study of comparative religions. Most earlier researchers in this field were western Christians who created definitions of religion based on their own religious practices and beliefs and then sought to find and define the thing they termed as religion in other cultures throughout history. Today, most researchers are more cautious about how they define religion and how those definitions shape the object and outcomes of their research.

In the sections that follow, we explore each of these functions in more detail by describing how the founders of sociology defined religion. The founders of sociology as an academic discipline considered the theorization and the study of religion to be foundational, one of the core forces in society. They believed that religion helped establish human communities and affected economic and other social behaviors in profound ways. Key examples include Max Weber's 1904 book *The Protestant Ethic and the Spirit of Capitalism* and Emile Durkheim's 1897 study of suicide and his 1912 book *The Elementary Forms of Religious Life*.

Box 1.3 Founders of sociology

The founders of sociology are usually considered to be Karl Marx, Max Weber, and Emile Durkheim. These thinkers set out to develop practical and scientifically sound methods of research to examine theories of the social world that were rooted in a specific historical and cultural context.

Karl Marx (1818–83) set out to develop scientifically justified systems of explanation for the development and effects of the industrial revolution and urbanization. He drew extensively on the philosophies of history and science. He was most interested in explaining the economic system of capitalism, human nature as it relates to labor and labor power, and the socioeconomic class structure.

Max Weber (1864–1920) was also interested in the development of capitalism and modernity, but emphasized the importance of understanding the cultural influences of the processes behind them, particularly religion. Weber's empirical methodology was based upon understanding the meaning and purpose that individuals attached to their actions. His analysis of the development of the authority of the state as embedded in bureaucracies is central to the modern study of organizations and political economy.

Emile Durkheim (1858–1917) established the formal academic discipline of sociology and set up the first European department of sociology in 1895. Durkheim believed that sociology was the science of the development and functions of social institutions and that the social sciences should adopt the scientific method as conducted in the natural sciences. His seminal monograph on the social causes of suicide is central to the modern study of criminology and social problems.

Other theorists who were important to the founding of sociology include: Auguste Comte, Charles Cooley, Karl Mannheim, George Herbert Mead, Vilfredo Pareto, Georg Simmel, Herbert Spencer, and Thorstein Veblen.

Religion as an opiate

Unlike other founders of the field of sociology, Karl Marx (1818–83) was only tangentially interested in religion. Ironically, his statement that "[religion] is the opium of the people" in the 1843 essay "Contribution to the Critiques of Hegel's Philosophy of Law" is one of the most famous, and infamous, social science quotes about religion. In this essay, Marx is concerned primarily with how German philosophers considered ideas as something apart and separate from those who created the ideas. He uses religion as an example of this process by arguing that because humans are led to believe that religion is handed down from an abstract, supernatural being, they forget that religion is created by human beings and is actually a reflection of human struggles and suffering. This understanding is the basis for the sociology of religion as the study of the human construction of religion and the ways that religion guides, and is shaped by, human experience and human efforts to understand and cope with the larger social and natural world.

Figure 1.1 Karl Marx, one of the founding fathers of sociology, famously stated in 1843 that "[religion] is the opium of the people"

Courtesy of the Library of Congress Prints and Photographs Division

Marx compares religion to opium to make the point that by uncritically and fully accepting religious teachings (along with philosophy), people replace concrete reality with an abstract, supernatural reality, much like the way opium replaces actual sense experience with an abstract feeling. In particular, Marx argues that religion serves different functions for different classes of citizens. The poor working class uses religion to explain and give meaning to the hardships that they face in life – in other words, to provide comfort. For the upper, capitalist classes, religion is a tool that they use to mask their control over the poor working class. This understanding influenced later sociological ideas that religion generally acts as a conservative force in society, an idea elaborated on in Chapter 15. Although Marx does not believe that religion should be abolished, he does believe that in an equal society, one with few socioeconomic differences among people, religion would be unnecessary.

Marx's ideas influenced much later work. In particular, Max Weber (1864–1920) posited that religions developed theodicies, or systems of belief that explain negative aspects of human life and society, to show why some people suffer and why some people do not. Theodicies are also discussed in more detail in Chapter 15. Additionally, Georg Simmel (1858–1918) argued that faith or complete belief in God or in the doctrines of religion is at the center of each religion and is an essential part of broader society. He argues that faith plays a key role in reinforcing the stability of social institutions of all types. For example, faith in government means that citizens are less likely to revolt, while faith in religious institutions means that believers will be less likely to abandon their belief.

Box 1.4 Georg Simmel's main features of religion

In his 1905 essay "A Contribution to the Study of Religion", Simmel argues that religion is an evolving social institution situated in ongoing social interactions and that religion should not be seen as a static entity situation in history or antiquity. He also asserts that not every value or belief came from religion but rather that values and beliefs evolved from other areas of society, such as customs and laws, and were, then, adopted into religious institutions. In particular, three main features within society have been adopted into religious institutions: faith, unity, and dependence. Faith is at the center of religious institutions, religion provides unity among its members, and binds individuals to the universal.

Religion as a creator of social change

In his most famous work, the 1904 *The Protestant Ethic and the Spirit of Capitalism*, Max Weber posits that changes in religious beliefs allowed capitalism, as a cultural and economic form, to develop. Weber's book introduced a line of research he worked on until his death. Weber considered religion to be one of the core forces of society. He was interested in the effect of religion on economic activity and social inequality. He also was fascinated by the differences between eastern and western civilizations and societies.

Weber began by noting that Protestant countries, such as England, Germany, and the US, were the centers of economic power in the modern world and had more highly developed capitalist economies. He concluded that it must therefore be the case that the origin of modern capitalism is, at least in part, the result of the rise of Protestantism. In particular, the Calvinists and other austere Protestant sects differ theologically from other religions because they adopted the doctrine of predestination. Predestination is the belief that those who are to be saved by God have already been chosen and no actions on earth can change whether they are saved or not. Calvinists began to search for signs that assured them that they were among this elite class. A strong work ethic and zeal for a secular profession became key signs that Calvinist Protestants thought showed God has chosen them for salvation.

Protestants living according to this ethic were likely to accumulate money over time. However, Protestant doctrine condemned the use of accumulated wealth to purchase luxuries as wasteful and discouraged excessive donations of money to churches or the poor. Instead, accumulated wealth was supposed to be reinvested into business and professions because a thriving and successful business or profession was a sign of salvation.

Over time, the Protestant ethic spread from its base in the more austere sects of Protestantism to encompass whole communities and take the form of the spirit of capitalism. For Weber, the spirit of capitalism is the expectation that individuals should increase their wealth and capital through success in a vocation and that this gain is not to be used for enjoyment, but should be invested into the vocation as a sign of competence and proficiency. Thus, the Protestant ethic spurred the development of modern capitalism.

In later works, Weber linked religion to other social forces, including the absence of capitalism in China and India. He also claimed that what he called "salvation religions," such as Christianity and Islam, are reinforced by unequal social relationships. These, in turn, he thought explained the cultural differences between the East and the West. In sum, Weber believed that religion was a major creator of social change and was a motor of historical and cultural change. In short, religion is a powerful explanation, and tool for, social change. This function of religion is a constant theme of this book, explored in detail in Chapter 15

Religion as a social act

Emile Durkheim (1858–1917) in his last work, *The Elementary Forms of Religious Life*, set out to describe religion at its most primitive, or elementary state, in order to better understand the functions of modern forms of religion. Durkheim believed that exploring so-called "primitive" religions would highlight similarities among modern religions that are often hidden by their complexities. In other words, Durkheim saw primitive religions as prime cases to study because they were *simple* cases.

Based on his study of various elementary religious systems around the world, Durkheim defined religion as "a unified system of beliefs and practices relative to sacred things, that is to say, things set apart and forbidden – beliefs and practices which unite into one single moral community called a Church, all who adhere to them." Let's unpack this definition. First, note that any notion of God(s) or the supernatural is missing. For Durkheim, any definition that incorporates the concept of the supernatural neglects two categories of religious facts: religions such as Buddhism and Jainism have an absence of "spiritual beings," but are still considered among the great religions; and religions contain rituals (practices) that are independent of the supernatural, such as the isolation of women who are menstruating in ancient Judaism.

There are three key elements in Durkheim's definition: beliefs, practices or rituals, and community. Religions create an absolute duality between the sacred and the profane. Although the nature of the sacred varies from religion to religion, all religions define the nature of the sacred as something that must be protected and kept away from the profane (or that which is not sacred). Rituals are rules of conduct for what can and cannot be done in the presence of the sacred or with objects that represent the sacred. Rituals are distinguished from other forms of action because they are specifically oriented towards religious belief. Examples of religious rituals, often in the form of precautions, abound across religious traditions. In many Christian traditions, communion bread and wine must be consumed and not discarded. In religions in which animals or food are sacrificed, the rituals associated with sacrifice are distinguished from typical butchering practices. In many religions, certain classes of people, such as menstruating women or the uninitiated, are banned from attending services or participating in certain rituals to avoid bringing the profane into the presence of the sacred. As a final example, Hindus abstain from eating the meat of cows, because cows are sacred to them.

Although beliefs and rituals define religion as separate from other social institutions, the key function of religion is to build a moral community for all those who share common beliefs and rituals. Thus, for Durkheim, religion is fundamentally a social act that builds a religious community. Religious beliefs and rituals do this by integrating together into a community all those who adhere to those beliefs and rituals. They also allow this community to distinguish itself from all others who do not share those beliefs and rituals. The implication of this understanding of religion for racial inequality and for religious diversity is explored later in Chapter 12 and Chapter 19. In addition, religious community also provides a foundation for the rest of social life because it provides social networks and a basis for shared action. For example, religion may have an impact on political behaviors, the focus of Chapter 9.

Box 1.5 Religion according to Auguste Comte

August Comte (1798–1857) is most famous for being the first to define and use the term "sociology." However, he did discuss religion in his work "A General View of Positivism" and is known for attempting to develop a religion of humanity that influences the current secular humanist movement. Comte describes religion as a state of harmony among the individual, society, and nature. Comte argued that religion's main focus is to bring order to human life and general harmony among humankind. Religion, then, becomes a source of unity unique to humankind since other animals do not have a social nature. For Comte, religion must deal with different parts of life: thought, activity, and feeling. Religion does this by having a belief system, a set of principles to govern action, and a set of habits that inspire emotions.

Other classical sociologists recognized that religion is a social act. Georg Simmel (1858–1918) argued that religion provides a sense of unity among its members because, unlike most institutions within society, religion allows individuals to come together and obtain goals without competition. He also noted that members often feel unified against those who do not share in their same beliefs. Auguste Comte (1798–1857) argued that religion's main role was to bring order and harmony to human life. In sum, for Durkheim and others, religion is a social act that serves to strengthen human community by defining both who is inside and who is outside a person's moral community.

Religion as a brace against chaos

More recently Peter Berger (1929–), in his 1967 book *The Sacred Canopy*, defines religion as a brace against chaos. His central thesis is that it is human nature to impose order on our experiences, to seek meaning in day-to-day events, and thus to deny the possibility that our lives are full of chaotic and random events over which we hold little control. Berger uses a Greek word, *nomos*, to describe the order that people prefer to chaos. Humans are inherently scared of the unknown, so they stabilize everyday life by using concepts of time, schedules, laws, and norms to impose order and make events more predictable.

Religion has an even larger role to play in stabilizing chaos. For Berger, religion is "the human enterprise by which a sacred cosmos is established" and the "the audacious attempt to conceive of the entire universe as being humanly significant." Berger sees religion as a human construct that is meant to give meaning and order to the whole of the universe by giving human experience a larger and deeper meaning. Religion defines what is sacred and protects people from the chaos of meaninglessness. For example, many religious individuals will uses phrases such as "it's in God's hands" or "it was fate" in order to explain events such as the death of a loved one or the loss of a job. Religion, then, separates the sacred (a transcendental, supernatural realm) from the profane (the earthly realm) and provides a sacred canopy that assures followers of a larger cosmic order.

Berger was not the first to describe religion as providing followers with a brace against chaos and with assurances of a larger cosmic order. Georg Simmel argued, in a *Contribution to the Study of Religion*, that religion creates a sense of dependence such that "the individual feels himself bound to a universal, to something higher, out of which he came, and into which he will return, and from which he also expects assistance and salvation, from which he differs and yet identical with it." In other words, religion provides humans with a universal higher purpose that imbues day-to-day life with meaning. As described in Chapter 16, this general sense of a connection to a higher power exists even among those who are spiritual, but claim no religious affiliation. This understanding propelled Clifford Geertz (1926–2006), the renowned cultural anthropologist, to see religion as a cultural system that worked to establish powerful, pervasive, and long-lasting conceptions of the general order of existence.

Berger also describes how religion justifies the socially defined reality. For society to continue making order out of chaos, he asserts any particular group must have a common definition of social order. Religion is particularly effective at doing this, and, for Berger, is the ultimate form of social control because it constructs social reality as being related to the ultimate, or cosmic, reality. In particular, when you depart from the established order in society, you are only violating society's notions of right and wrong. However, when you depart from the established religious order, you are disrupting the fundamental essence and order of the entire universe. With such dire consequences for social deviance, adherence and conformity are strongly established. Religion is key to maintaining consensus about the social order within a group. Accordingly, religion has been used as an instrument of legitimation of, and justification for, political power throughout history, as described above and in Chapter 15. Berger argues that this legitimation is effective because it imbues constantly changing social institutions with a semblance of inevitability and firmness.

How do sociologists measure religion?

In addition to defining religion, sociologists are interested in measuring how religious Americans are. New measurements of religious preference, participation, and belief are constantly being developed. Broadly, measures of religiosity can be broken down into two categories: religious identification/preference and religious participation/belief.

Religious identification and preference measures religiosity by assessing which religions and denominations Americans are members of, affiliate with, or prefer. The earliest measures utilized the self-reported membership of religious bodies. These measures are published in the *Yearbook of American & Canadian Churches*, published annually since 1916 by the National Council of Churches USA and its predecessors. Based on these reports, 60 per cent of Americans are members of churches, a figure that has been relatively stable over time. However, these reports likely underestimate the number of Americans who are religious. This results in part because not all religious bodies count members in the same way. In addition, some religious bodies are not included in the yearbook, some new religious movements have no defined membership, and some people who attend religious services sporadically or attend multiple houses of worship may not be counted.

More recently, sociologists have defined religious identification by asking respondents of nationally representative surveys to identify the religion and denomination or church they prefer. These data are easier to collect than membership data, and they allow people to define their own religious identity. This approach thus corrects some of the problems with the membership data. However, Americans are likely to over-report or overestimate their religiosity because they can report a religious identification even if they never or rarely participate in any church, denomination, or religion.

Most recently, religion scholars and sociologists have begun to classify the religion and denomination or church that respondents prefer into denominational families or religious traditions. The most common scheme is RELTRAD (for religious tradition), proposed by Steensland, Park, Regnerus, Robinson, Wilcox, and Woodberry in 2000. This scheme reduces the vast religious complexity in American society, especially among the Christian traditions, in manageable and historically meaningful ways. The religious traditions in this classification are: Mainline Protestants, Evangelical Protestants, Black Protestants, Catholics, Jews, Other, and the Unaffiliated. The collapsing of denominations in this manner is supported by the common orthodoxy, history, and orientation of the various denominations and religions within each tradition, as described throughout the rest of the book (especially in Chapters 4, 5, 6, 7, 11, 13, 14, 16, and 18). It is also supported by research that suggests that most denominational differences no longer matter to most individuals or denominations, as evidenced in the ecumenical movement and the fact that many individuals freely switch from one denomination to another.

Box 1.6 Religious traditions and denominations in the US

Mainline Protestant: United Methodist Church, Disciples of Christ, United Church of Christ, Episcopal Church, Evangelical Lutheran Church, American Baptist Church, Presbyterian Church.

Evangelical Protestant: Charismatic, Brethren, Church of Christ, Church of God, Evangelical Covenant Church, Evangelical Free Church, Holiness, Pentecostal, Seventh-Day Adventist, Assemblies of God, Holiness, Missouri Synod Lutheran, Churches of the Nazarene, Southern Baptists, Full Gospel, Apostolic, many non-denominational.

Black Protestant: African Methodist Episcopal Church (AME), African Methodist Episcopal Church of Zion (AMEZ), Christian Methodist Episcopal Church (CME), predominantly black Baptist churches, and some Pentecostal and Churches of God in Christ congregations.

Catholic

Jewish: Reform, Conservative, Orthodox, Hasidic.

Other: Buddhist, Hindu, Muslim, Mennonites, Amish, Orthodox Church, Jehovah's Witness, Mormons/Latter-day Saints.

Unaffiliated: Atheist, Agnostic, Nothing in Particular.

Another way to measure religiosity is to measure religious participation and religious beliefs. Religious participation is measured using self-reports of how frequently a person attends religious services. While widely used, this measure has been the subject of intense debate because evidence from audit studies (studies that directly observe the rate of religious service attendance) finds that actual attendance rates are approximately one-half of those found through surveys. This overestimation of religious service attendance on surveys likely results from both a problem of lower response rates among the nonreligious on surveys and over-reporting of attendance due to the pressures of social desirability among those who are religious. Many surveys also ask people about their religious beliefs, since beliefs can be distinct from either participation or affiliation. Common questions include the strength of persons' belief in God, the importance of religion in their daily lives, the frequency of prayer or meditation, belief in the afterlife and specific conceptions of the afterlife, and how literally one should interpret religious texts.

What is the American religious landscape?

According to the 2007 US Religious Landscape Survey of 35,000 Americans, conducted by the Pew Forum on Religion & Public Life, the majority of Americans (78.6 per cent) claim a Christian religious affiliation, with the Protestant denominations making up just over 50 per cent of the population. Among Protestant denominations, the evangelical Protestant denominations are the largest, followed by the mainline groups, and then Black Protestants. Jews, Muslims, Hindus, and Buddhists are all relatively small religious groups, although their visibility and influence surpasses their relative size. Finally, the religious unaffiliated make up 16 per cent of the population, with the majority of those people reporting that they are "nothing in particular" when it comes to their religious preference.

According to the same survey, religious attendance and beliefs are prominent features of many Americans' lives. For example, 39 per cent of Americans report attending religious services at least once a week. A full 92 per cent of Americans believe in God or a universal spirit, with the majority of those people expressing absolute certainty in that belief and also claiming that one can have a personal relationship with God or the universal spirit. A large majority of Americans believe in an afterlife and pray or meditate at least weekly. Slim majorities report that religion is very important in their life. Finally, American religious belief appears to be non-dogmatic, with 70 per cent of Americans believing that many religions, and not just their own, can lead to eternal life and that there is more than one true way to interpret the teachings of their religion.

In the next two chapters, we focus on contemporary sociological theories of religion (Chapter 2) and on the methods that historians use to understand developments in religion (Chapter 3). In Parts 2, 3, and 4, we carefully examine the groups, traditions, and movements that dominate contemporary American religious life by focusing on the social, historical, and cultural context across the religious landscape. We also examine issues, themes, and theories that cut across groups, traditions, and movements, relying on a wealth of sociological research and data.

Table 1.1 Religious affiliation in the United States, 2007

Religious Tradition	%
Evangelical Protestant	26.3
Mainline Protestant	18.1
Black Protestant	6.9
Catholic	23.9
Mormon	1.7
Other Christian	1.7
Jewish	1.7
Buddhist	0.7
Muslim	0.6
Hindu	0.4
Unaffiliated	16.1
Other faiths	1.1
Don't know/refused	0.8

Source: US Religious Landscape Survey, Pew Forum on Religion & Public Life (2007)

Key points you need to know

- The sociology of religion is the study of religion as a product and creator of human action.
- Across time and place, humans develop and modify belief systems, religious rituals, and religious communities in ways that are not "fixed" and that respond to broader social and cultural forces.
- Sociologists have identified four key functions of religion that are common across very different religions and cultures.
- Karl Marx said that religion was the opium of the people because he believed they forget that religion is created by human beings and is a reflection of human struggles and suffering.
- Max Weber believed that changing religious beliefs allowed capitalism, as a cultural and economic form, to develop because the Protestant ethic spread across communities and turned into the spirit of capitalism.
- For Emile Durkheim, the primary function of religion was to build a moral community for all those who shared the beliefs and rituals that make up religion.
- According to Peter Berger, religion is important because it separates the sacred from the profane and provides a sacred canopy that assures followers of a larger cosmic order.
- Sociologists measure how religious Americans are by assessing religious identification/preference and religious participation/belief.
- The majority of Americans claim a Christian identity and the majority of those are Protestant.
- Attendance at religious services and a belief in a God or universal spirit are common features of American's lives.

Discussion questions

1 What is the sociology of religion?
2 What are the four functions of religion identified by sociologists?
3 In what ways is defining religion a product of western Christianity?
4 What did Karl Marx mean when he said "religion is the opium of the people"?
5 According to Marx, how do members of different social classes use religion in different ways?
6 Why did Weber think that religion is the motor of history?
7 What is the doctrine of predestination? How did it influence some Protestant sects to invest wealth into vocations?
8 According to Durkheim, what is the relationship between the sacred and the profane?
9 In Durkheim's view, how does religion create human community?
10 In what ways do humans try to give order and meaning to their lives, according to Berger?

11 In what ways did Berger claim that religion has been used to legitimate political power?
12 Which of the four theories of religion described in this chapter do you find most convincing? Why?
13 What do you think is the best way to measure religion?

Further reading

Asad, T. (1993) *Genealogies of Religion: Discipline and Reasons of Power in Christianity and Islam*, Baltimore, MD: The Johns Hopkins University Press.

Berger, P. (1967; 2nd edn 1990) *The Sacred Canopy: Elements of a Sociological Theory of Religion*, New York: Anchor Books.

Bergesen, A. (1984) "Swanson's Neo-Durkheimian Sociology of Religion," *Sociological Analysis*, 45: 179–84.

Comte, A. (1851) *Auguste Comte and Positivism*, trans. G. Lenzer (1998), New Brunswick, NJ: Transaction Publishers.

Durkheim, E. (1912) *The Elementary Forms of Religious Life*, trans. K. Fields (1995), New York: Free Press.

Maduro, O. (1977) "New Marxist Approaches to the Relative Autonomy of Religion," *Sociological Analysis*, 38: 359–67.

Marx, K. (1844) "Contribution to the Critique of Hegel's Philosophy of Right: Introduction," trans. R Tucker (1978) *The Marx–Engels Reader*. New York: Norton.

Parsons, T. (1944) "The Theoretical Development of the Sociology of Religion: A Chapter in the History of Modern Social Science," *Journal of the History of Ideas*, 5: 176–90.

Simmel, G. (1905) "A Contribution to the Study of Religion," *American Journal of Sociology*, 11: 359–76.

Taves, A. (2009) *Religious Experience Reconsidered: A Building-Block Approach to the Study of Religion and Other Special Things*, Princeton, NJ: Princeton University Press.

Weber, M. (1904) *The Protestant Ethic and the Spirit of Capitalism*, trans. S. Kalberg (2002), London: Roxbury Publishing Company.

2 Contemporary views and theories of religion

In this chapter

This chapter explores some of the contemporary views and theories of religion developed by sociologists. It begins with a description of secularization theory and sketches positions of proponents and opponents of the notion that American society has become more secular. It next turns to exploring an opposing set of views that use economic theories to examine the trends in religious belief and affiliation religion in the American experience. It then turns to critiques of both secularization theory and economic theories. The chapter concludes with other views and theories of religion that might better explain religion in contemporary America, including those that focus on congregational and religious subcultures and how people live their religious lives.

Main topics covered

- Debates about whether society is becoming more secular.
- Proponents of secularization theory believe that religion is becoming increasing irrelevant in society.
- Opponents of secularization theory point to continued religious vitality.
- Economic theories of religion use the concept of a "free market" to explore why religious vitality is strong in the US.
- Critics of economic theories of religion argue that religion in the US does not follow "free market" principles.
- Institutional theories of religion describe how denominations and congregations operate in different ways to serve the needs of members.
- Subcultural theories of religion focus on how local religious communities create a culture for their members.
- Individual approaches to religion focus on individual religious lives.

Is society becoming more secular?

For much of the twentieth century, a major question in the sociology of religion, and in many media accounts of religion, has been whether society is becoming more secular, or non-religious, and the consequences of secularization, if it exists. In other words, is America losing religion? In particular, sociologists have been interested in the fate of religious institutions and authority and the conditions under which mainstream religious institutions either decline or thrive in the modern world. Debates about secularization are controversial, and the resolution to them depends on a variety of factors, including how secularization is defined, how the process of secularization is defined, and the period of time and geographic area considered.

A fundamental part of secularization theory is that it occurs as part of the process of modernity. Modernity, as a process, began as part of the industrial revolution in the eighteenth century. Key features of modernity include an increasing division of life and labor, increasing regulation of the world through the bureaucratic state, the growing explanatory power of science, the rise of capitalism, and increasing urbanization and industrialization. In its most basic and oldest formulation, secularization theory argues that the growth of modern institutions limits the power of religion in the areas of work, science, public life, and the government. Thus, the social significance of religious values and institutions is reduced and will be replaced by nonreligious values and institutions.

Box 2.1 Defining modernity

Modernity is:

- Division of life and labor

  An increasing division of labor, division of life into distinct spheres, and a division of social life into public and private spheres.

- Increasing regulation of the world through the bureaucratic state

  Increased regulation of public and private life through policies, procedures, administrative rules, and science.

  Called "Rationalization" by Weber.

- Explanatory power of science

  Including the increasing role of medicine, engineering, and physics in our day-to-day lives and the increasing ability of evolutionary biology and astronomy to explain the origin of things.

- Rise of capitalism

  The economic system in which the means of production are privately owned and operated for profit in a competitive "free" market environment.

- Industrialization and urbanization

  The process of centering work into large scale institutions like factories and life into large-scale cities. This is thought to reinforce a cultural pluralism focused on tolerance and acceptance.

The founding figures of sociology, such as Max Weber, as well as many of the sociologists of religion in the mid twentieth century (including Bryan Wilson, Peter Berger, and Thomas Luckmann) took for granted that society is becoming more secular as it becomes more modernized, that religion was in decline, and that it may completely disappear. For these scholars, the process of secularization works as a cycle in which religion loses significance because of the rise of modernity, leading to fewer people thinking and acting religiously, which, in turn, further reduces religion's influence in society; this cycle would repeat until religion essentially disappears. These scholars alternatively lamented and relished the "fact" of religious decline.

Though always controversial, secularization theory remained the dominant sociological theory for understanding religion until the late twentieth century. Sociologists outside of the religion subfield often still treat secularization as a simple fact, something given. However, since the 1970s there has been increasing evidence that religious vitality is staying roughly constant or even growing (presented in the following section), along with key episodes of religious politicization across the globe, such as the rise of fundamentalism documented in Chapter 15, including the tight connection between conservative politics and evangelical Protestantism in the US or even the establishment of religious governments, such as the Islamic Republic of Iran. In particular, Chapter 5 documents how the evangelical surge was driven, in part, by a response to the perceived secularization of society. These events led many sociologists of religion to reject the notion that religion will disappear as a socially significant phenomenon. Some jettisoned secularization theory altogether, and proponents are revising it around a more limited and specific set of descriptive claims.

Mark Chaves and Robert Wuthnow describe secularization as the declining scope and power of religious *authority* at all levels of society. At the societal level, there has been a decline in religious authority over other social institutions. For example, as detailed in Chapter 9, freedom of religion is defined in the constitution of the US and has been increasingly, although with some variation, refined and expanded through legal decisions. Additionally, violating the practices and norms of one religion has no legal consequences for those who do not practice that religion. At the institutional level, religious organizations and congregations have become more secularized. In particular, there have been internal changes in churches so that they act more like businesses (for example, the ecumenical movement described in Chapter 4) to be more competitive in the religious "marketplace" described below. Moreover, Wuthnow demonstrates that young adults are less attached to religious institutions as the sole, or best, authority on religious beliefs and practices. At the individual level, the authority of religious leaders, doctrines, and traditions over individuals has declined, leading to changes in what individuals actually believe and what they do when it comes to their faith. As discussed in Chapters 8 and 16, increasing numbers of people, and especially young adults, define themselves as having no religious affiliation. However, many of those same people continue to define themselves as spiritual and engage in non-institutionalized forms of religion.

Critiques of secularization theory

Many sociologists of religion reject secularization theory. For example, Roger Finke argues that secularization theory does not stand up to the empirical evidence because it does not provide explanations for why evangelical and more orthodox denominations or religions are growing, why the rise in urbanization and industrialization does not reduce church adherence, or why religious diversity appears to strengthen, not weaken, religious involvement and church adherence. Others, including Rodney Stark, R. Stephen Warner, and Phillip Gorski, utilize evidence from major surveys and historical evidence to show that there continue to be high levels of religious vitality in the US and across the world and that religion does not appear to be shrinking. Although the percentage of the population reporting no religious affiliation has risen as a percentage of population in recent years, 83.1 per cent of the population continue to report a religious affiliation. In addition, as shown in Fig. 2.1, the percentage of the population reporting that they attend church weekly has stayed between 20 per cent and 25 per cent since the early 1970s. In addition, as shown in Fig. 2.2, the percentage of the population that believes in a life after death, that regards the Bible as the inspired word of God, and that prays once per day has not significantly increased or decreased over the last twenty to thirty years.

What are we, then, to make of these large-scale trends in religion and what do they mean for secularization theory? It is clear that at least some versions of secularization theory are correct in that religious authority, especially the power of religious institutions, has clearly declined in scope and power in the US. On the other hand, there are clearly high degrees of religious involvement and belief in the US that have not shown a significant decline over time. These empirical realities have led some to reject secularization theory and to adopt a new theoretical framework to describe the conditions under which mainstream religious institutions either decline or thrive in the modern world. This framework includes economic theories of religion.

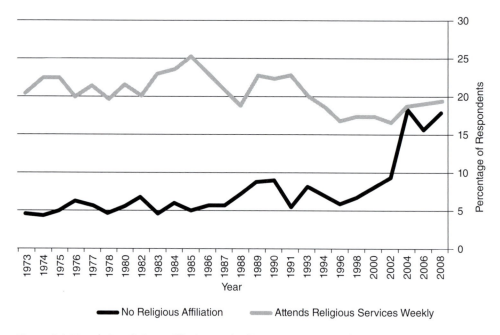

Figure 2.1 Trends in religious affliation and religious service attendance

Source: General Social Survey (GSS)

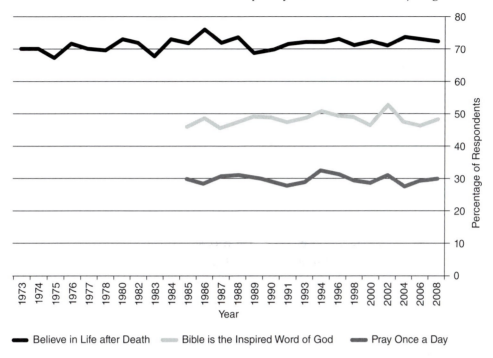

Figure 2.2 Trends in religious beliefs

Source: General Social Survey (GSS)

Economic theories of religion

Economic theories of religion claim that where there is religious freedom, religion operates according to free market principles and individuals are free to choose between competing religious institutions and experiences in order to satisfy their needs. Economic theories of religion have been most rigorously advanced by Roger Finke, Rodney Stark, and Laurence Iannaccone. Although there are a variety of ways in which economic theories apply to the religious context, the three reviewed here include the ideas that religion operates as a free market, that strict religious denominations and congregations have the highest rates of participation and commitment, and that a free religious market produces high degrees of religious freedom.

A key assumption of economic theories of religion as advanced by Finke and Starke (2005) is that the religious "economy" of the US consists of a free market made up of religious consumers and a set of religious institutions seeking to serve the market of religious consumers. In the marketplace of religion, such institutions compete to attract and retain consumers. The relative success of any religious institutions in the free marketplace of religion depends on a variety of factors. These factors include the members of the congregation and how committed they are to the religion and congregation, the ability of the leaders of the congregation to attract new members and convince existing members to stay, the doctrines and orthodoxy of the congregation, denomination, and religion, and the effectiveness of the conversion or evangelization techniques of the congregation or institution. According to these theories, because religious institutions compete in free religious markets, they will be highly motivated to attract and retain members in order to maintain their viability. They will use a variety of strategies to do this, including creating comprehensive programs to serve many needs or creating highly specialized groups, congregations, or denominations to serve particular populations in society, having highly trained and charismatic leaders and services, and focusing conversion efforts on those most likely to be attracted to the institution. Some examples of these strategies are detailed in Chapters 4, 5, and 8.

Another influential researcher, Laurence Iannaccone (1994), finds that in a free religious market, strict religions and institutions are stronger. In this context, "strict" means demanding that members believe in an exclusive truth, conform to member expectations, and maintain distinctiveness from the broader society; "strong" means members have high rates of participation, demonstrate high levels of commitment, and report getting many benefits from their participation. Strict churches are stronger because they minimize the "free-rider" problem. Free-riders minimize their own efforts to gain the most benefit with the least amount of work. Many social groups, including religious ones, are social commodities, meaning that individuals receive benefits from membership in the group rather than individual effort. The free-rider problem exists in all social groups but can be particularly prevalent in religion. For example, a church member who does not contribute time or energy to the life of the church can receive the same benefits in the form of the religious experience and social support as one who contributes much time and energy. Strict churches mitigate the free-rider problem by demanding more time, more exclusive and restrictive beliefs, and more distance from society than other churches. In other words, strictness screens out those people who would normally "free-ride," thus increasing the rewards of being in the group because all members contribute significant time and energy while also receiving the benefits from participation in the group.

A weaker, but related, version of the "strict is strong" thesis argues that the more individuals are required to invest their time and energy into their religious life, the higher their level of commitment and participation. In other words, low-cost, low-effort religion doesn't give people any reason to participate. Those who subscribe to this theory see this as a primary reason for the waning of the mainline Protestant

---

Box 2.2 Limits to strictness

Strictness only makes religious institutions stronger because the benefits of membership outweigh the costs of membership. When the costs of strictness become too high, it will weaken a religious institution. For example, churches that require members to cut off contact with family and friends who are not members of the church are unlikely to experience large-scale growth because that cost is probably too high for many potential members. Thus, religious institutions and churches must manage a dynamic strictness in which they maintain a tension between themselves and society. The aim is to create enough distinctiveness from society in general to minimize the number of free-riders. At the same time they must continually adjust to social change in order not to become too deviant and raise the cost of strictness too dramatically.

denominations and the rise of the evangelical Protestant denominations described in Chapters 4 and 5.

A final core assumption of economic theories of religion is that a religious free market generates a high degree of religious diversity within that marketplace. In this context, religious diversity means a variety of religions, denominations, and congregational styles being available to religious "consumers" in the area. The free religious market generates religious diversity because it is relatively easy to develop new religions and new churches. Therefore, a large variety of religious institutions can develop to cater to the special needs and interests of specific segments of the religious marketplace. Moreover, religious leaders and institutions are constantly developing new organizational strategies, congregational styles, communication, education, music, and evangelical strategies in order to attract and retain adherents. There are competing findings regarding the consequences of religious diversity, with some research finding that religious diversity increases religious involvement and other research finding no link between religious diversity and involvement.

Critiques of economic theories of religion

Economic theories of religion are not without their critics. These theories are largely critiqued for their inability to account for known religious behavior. For example, as we shall see in Chapter 15, an individual's choice of religious institutions is deeply socially embedded, such that most people keep the religion they grew up in or adopt the religion of their significant other. If they do switch religious institutions, people are more likely to switch to a closely related congregation, denomination, or religion. Therefore, it appears that the fundamental assumption of economic theories of religion, that of a free religious marketplace in which individuals are free to choose their own religion, may be flawed. Additionally, economic theories of religion have been criticized for assuming that being religious has a strong effect and singular social action. In fact, as we shall emphasize in Chapter 15, the relationship between religion and social action is complicated and multi-directional.

Economic theories of religion are also challenged on other grounds. For example, Iannaccone's definition of strong religious institutions is criticized because it applies only to contemporary Protestant denominations. It is hard to see how this definition of strength would apply to Christian denominations that are both engaged in the community and have committed members, such as African American Protestants, or to individually oriented religions, such as Buddhism and Hinduism. More broadly, economic theories of religion have been criticized for being ethnocentric – in other words applying only to the northern hemisphere and only to Christianity with little explanatory capacity for non-Christian or non-Western religions and religious experiences.

Critiques of large-scale theories of religion

Secularization theory and the economic theories of religion discussed above are large-scale theories that attempt to describe societal-level trends in religious affiliation and belief. Many scholars, including Wendy Cadge and David Smilde, have criticized these theories for focusing disproportionately on the Protestant denominations, especially white evangelical Protestants, and neglecting Catholic, non-Christian, and particularly non-Western religious experiences and practices. This focus is understandable, given the growth and power of white evangelical Protestantism described in Chapter 5 and the focus of secularization and economic theories on growth and decline. However, it has led researchers to extend these claims to the broader study of religion in unwarranted and unsupported ways.

Both theories have alternatively emphasized only the voluntary, positive, and social aspects of religious belief *or* religion's role as a source of inequality, conflict, or division. Instead, the research described throughout the following chapters shows that religion can be both at the same time. For example, Chapter 16 demonstrates that religion is both a force for positive social behaviors and social change *and* a source of conflict and division. Chapter 9 describes the ways in which religion in the contemporary US can reinforce existing patterns of racial inequality, but also how racially integrated congregations can challenge such patterns. This, and other research, highlights the power of religion to create social solidarity within the religious congregation or institution but generate divisions with those outside of the religious group.

Finally, the focus of both secularization theory and economic theories of religion on societal-level trends in religious affiliation and belief has framed sociologists' understandings of religion in ways that are not useful for explaining many contemporary developments in religion. These theories tend to ignore, or treat dismissively, the turn towards spirituality in contemporary America. We describe this trend in Chapter 16 and the popular media trends that reinforce it in Chapter 8. Both theories also largely ignore the powerful role that religion plays in shaping political attitudes and behaviors (the focus of Chapter 9), as a force for social change (the focus on Chapter 15), or as source of national identity and unity (Chapter 19). Finally, both theories ignore the relationships of power and inequality that are embedded in contemporary religion, issues that we explore throughout the balance of this volume, especially in Chapters 10, 12, 17, 18, and 19. To counter the large-scale nature of secularization theory and economic theories of religion, and as a way to overcome some of the limitations of these theories, sociologists of religion have developed theoretical and empirical frameworks that operate at the institutional (organizational), subcultural, and individual levels.

Institutional theories of religion

Institutional theories of religion focus on the local religious institution, congregation, or community as the unit of analysis. Some scholars focus on the institution because religion in the US is defined by a set of dominant organizational forms, most often the congregation, which have normative routines organized around core tasks, regulatory structures, and provide common experiences and explanations for life events. Congregations are usually the focus of institutional theories and approaches to religion because local congregations have become the core organizational form as denominations have declined as the primary center of religious identification.

Penny Edgell Becker finds that local congregations all engage in the core tasks of worship and religious education, but they vary in the degree to which they facilitate civic engagement, social activism, and the fostering of close-knit, caring networks of support. In particular, she finds four ways of approaching congregational life. One model, the house of worship model, focuses on providing members with an intimate, individualized worship experience and religious training. Second, the family model is focused on creating close-knit communities focused on supportive relationships. Third, the community model stresses supportive relations fostered by shared values, a commitment to social activism, and providing policies and programs to serve a variety of needs. Finally, the values taught in the leader model are more tightly tied to denominational doctrines and congregations are generally less concerned with engaging in activism.

Box 2.3 Conflicts in congregational life

Penny Edgell Becker (1999: 2) describes a conflict that started with a new pastor at Hope Episcopal, one of the twenty-three congregations in which she conducted interviews about what kind of congregation it was and was going to become:

> As I talked to more people in this church, I would come to understand, while the trouble began when the new pastor came, it was essentially a fight between two groups of lay leaders and core members. One group seemed to take for granted that their church is primarily about having a place of worship, about long-term friendships and family-like attachments, about people who know you and your family and could be counted on for help in times of crisis. Most of these people valued a traditional approach to doctrine and ritual practice ... For others, the church is primarily about providing leadership in the community, about interpreting doctrine and ritual tradition in light of contemporary social reality and current members' needs, about taking a stand on issues like AIDS and gay and lesbian rights. For this group, the church is about service and witnessing to the community about the virtue of tolerance and the importance of diversity ... The new pastor's arrival triggered a series of conflicts, opportunities for people to articulate, and thus defend and sharpen, their different underlying assumptions about "who we are" and "how we do things here."

Institutional theories of religion provide a more nuanced understanding of religious change, especially decline, than large-scales theories. For example, Robert Wuthnow does not attribute the steep decline in religious affiliation among young adults, described in Chapter 15, to secularization or other profound changes in religious belief. Instead he argues religious institutions have declined as a source of religious authority among young adults because they have failed to adapt their ministries to the radically altered transition to adulthood in the contemporary US, including longer periods of education, delayed or absent marriage and childbearing, and difficulty in starting a career.

Subcultural theories of religion

Christian Smith and Nancy Ammerman, in separate books on American evangelicalism and fundamentalism, describe how religious subcultures are important for creating identification, meaning-making, and political engagement in the US. Religious subcultures create common explanations for the world, a sense of meaning, and a sense of social unity within a diverse society in which people have very different sets of beliefs, values, and lifestyles. For example, the evangelical subculture creates a distinct religious identity based on orthodox evangelical theology, conservative moral values, and group-based religious practice, as detailed in Chapter 5.

Religious subcultures engage in what Ammerman calls "world construction" and "world maintenance" among fundamentalist groups. As described in Chapters 5 and 15, fundamentalists work to separate themselves from the world and believe in dispensational premillennialism (see definition in Chapters 5 and 15) and biblical literalism. Fundamentalists create a world in opposition. They view the modern world as chaotic so they create order by maintaining that God has a plan for all his followers. This is a common function of religion, described as "the sacred canopy" by Berger, as we noted in Chapter 1. Fundamentalists take these beliefs further than many by believing that God is in full control of their lives and nothing they do to the outside world matters. In this sense, fundamentalist beliefs function as a coping mechanism against the unknown and create a sense of permanence and stability in a modern society built on rapid changes. Conversely, fundamentalist beliefs also give adherents a sense of power over their lives by providing rules, work within the church, and the feeling of superiority over others who are not saved.

More broadly, sociologists have found that religious subcultures create cultural "tools" or ideas, symbols, and metaphors that individuals use to understand and interact with the broader social world. We describe the use of religious tools in shaping attitudes about, and preferred solutions to, racial inequality in Chapter 12. In addition, religious tools are often use by successful social movements, including the civil rights movement (Chapters 11 and 15). Religious subcultures also shape social boundaries around gender and sexuality (Chapter 10) and national religious identity (Chapter 19) in ways that either challenge or reinforce patterns of social inequality.

Individual theories of religion

The most recent trend in the study of religion is developing theories and approaches focused on individual religious lives. This approach has been called "lived religion" by Meredith McGuire (2008) or "everyday religion" by Nancy Ammerman (2007). These scholars argue that sociologists of religion have been much too concerned with religion as an organization and must reassess assumptions about individual religious lives. The focus of this research is on how individual people attend to matters of religion at a particular time and context in their own lives. Although these scholars acknowledge that religions are often organizations that routinely try to shape the spiritual boundaries of their members, they realize that individual members assert their own distinct beliefs, which may differ from official ones, and shape their own religiosity. This research distinguishes the actual experience of religious persons from an institutionally defined set of religious beliefs and practice. The focus of this research is on how religiosity and spirituality are practical, experienced, and expressed by ordinary people in their day-to-day lives. Scholars of this approach use in-depth interviewing and ethnographic observation to describe individual stories. As we shall note in the next chapter, in recent years historians have also given greater attention to lived religion.

Box 2.4 Complex religious lives

An example from one of Meredith McGuire's (2008: 10) interviews highlights the complexity of individuals' spiritual lives, as represented in the practice of keeping a home altar, as well as how researchers in this approach conduct interviews:

> I interviewed Laura, during an early 1990s study of middle-class Latinas in Texas, using a set of questions on religion and spirituality that was carefully phrased to avoid use of the term "religion". Our effort was added by the fact that these interviews were usually in women's own homes, so early in the conversation we asked if the interviewee kept an *altarcito* – a home altar … common in Mexican American homes. As Laura showed us her altar and talked about what she had chosen to place on it, she described a rich inner life, built on personally selected images and practices, borrowed eclectically from a wide range of cultural resources. Her home altar held several traditional items, including a family heirloom … , pictures of several deceased or distant loved ones … There were numerous and prominent nontraditional items as well: amethyst crystals used in healing meditations, Asian incense and a Tibetan prayer bell, a large colorful triptych of Frida Kahlo, and a modern representation of the Virgin of Guadalupe …

Importantly, individual approaches to religion provide an important contrast to large-scale and many institutional theories of religion because they examine the practices and beliefs of individuals in non-dominant and disempowered groups. This approach challenges the privileging of traditional religious authority in large-scale and institutional approaches to religion. By doing so, this paradigm has been very fruitful for understanding even large-scale trends in religious identification. For example, the research and insights regarding hybrid spiritualities described in Chapter 16 come, in part, from individual theories and approaches to the sociology of religion. Research by Courtney Bender and others on magic, pagan, occult, or paranormal rituals and experiences finds that these non-dominant religious expressions are common, overlap with more traditional forms of religious activities in many people's lives, and serve the four functions of religion described in the previous chapter.

By way of conclusion, in this chapter we described contemporary theories and approaches to the study of religion in society. We began by considering the claims of proponents and opponents of secularization theory. We next explored an opposing set of theories that use economic theories to examine the fate of religion in the American experience. Finally, we described theories that focused on smaller-scale religious phenomena, including religious institutions and organizations, religious subcultures, and how individuals integrate religion into their lives. In many of the chapters that follow, we focus on specific themes that sociologists and historians have explored in the sociology of religion. This research builds on the theories and approaches described in this and the previous chapter. In the next chapter, we explore the approaches historians have used to understand religion in American society.

Key points you need to know

- Secularization theory argues that as modern institutions grow in significance, the power of religion and religious institutions is reduced and may eventually disappear.
- As evidence emerged that religion is not disappearing, proponents of secularization theory emphasized the declining scope and power of religious authorities at all levels of society.
- Opponents of secularization theory argue that there continue to be high levels of religious vitality in the US and that religion does not appear to be shrinking.
- Economic theories of religion argue that the religious economy of the US:
  - consists of a free market made up of religious consumers and a set of religious institutions seeking to serve the market of religious consumers;
  - in a free religious market, strict religions and institutions are stronger;
  - a religious free market generates a high degree of religious diversity.
- Opponents of economic theories of religion argue that these theories cannot account for known religious behavior and that these theories focus on white Protestant religious expression.
- Both large-scale theories of religion have been criticized for focusing on white Protestant Christianity, taking a one-sided view of religion, and being unable to explain contemporary trends in religion.
- Institutional theories of religion focus on the local religious institution, congregation, or community as the unit of analysis.
- Local congregations all engage in the core tasks of worship and religious education, but they vary in the degree to which they facilitate civic engagement, social activism, and the fostering of close-knit, caring networks of support.
- Religious subcultures are important for creating identification, meaning-making, and political engagement in the US.
- Individual theories of religion focus on individual religious lives as distinct from institutionally defined beliefs and practices.

Discussion questions

1 Is America becoming more secular? How do you define secular?
2 What are the two strands of revised secularization theory?
3 What are the core ideas of economic theories of religion?
4 Do you feel free to choose your own religion and religious beliefs? Why or why not?
5 If economic theories of religion are true, are liberal religious groups going to disappear over time?
6 Why are strict churches thought to be strong in economic theories of religion?
7 Can secularization theory or economic theories of religion apply to non-Christian or non-Western settings?

8 Why do institutional approaches to religion focus on local congregations?
9 How are individual theories of religion different from other theories of religion?
10 Why do you think so much sociological research on religion is focused on orthodox religious groups, such as evangelicals and fundamentalists?

Further reading

Ammerman, N. (1987) *Bible Believers: Fundamentalists in the Modern World*, New Brunswick, NJ: Rutgers University Press.

—— (ed.) (2007) *Everyday Religion: Observing Modern Religious Lives*, Oxford: Oxford University Press.

Bender, C. (2010) *The New Metaphysicals: Spirituality and the American Religious Imagination.* Chicago: University of Chicago Press

Berger, P. (1967; 2nd edn 1990) *The Sacred Canopy: Elements of a Sociological Theory of Religion*, New York: Anchor Books.

Bruce, S. (1993) "Religion and Rational Choice: A Critique of Economic Explanations of Religious Behaviour," *Sociology of Religion*, 54: 193–205.

Cadge, W., Levitt, P., and Smilde, D. (2011) "De-centering and Re-centering: Rethinking Concepts and Methods in the Sociological Study of Religion," *Journal for the Scientific Study of Religion*, 50: 437–44.

Chaves, M. (1994) "Secularization as Decreasing Religious Authority," *Social Forces*, 72: 749–74.

—— (1995) "On the Rational Choice Approach to Religion," *Journal for the Scientific Study of Religion*, 34: 98–104.

Edgell, P. (forthcoming) "Cultural Sociology and New Approaches to the Study of Religion," *Annual Review of Sociology.*

Edgell Becker, P. (1999) *Congregations in Conflict: Cultural Models of Local Religious Life*, New York: Cambridge University Press.

Finke, R. (1992). "An Unsecular America," in S. Bruce (ed.), *Religion and Modernization*, Oxford: Oxford University Press.

Finke, R. and Stark, R. (2005) *The Churching of America, 1776–2005: Winners and Losers in our Religious Economy*, rev. edn, Camden: Rutgers University Press.

Gorski, P. (2000) "Historicizing the Secularization Debate," *American Sociological Review*, 65: 139–67.

Iannacconne, L. (1994) "Why Strict Churches are Strong," *American Journal of Sociology*, 99: 1180–211.

—— (1998) "Introduction to the Economics of Religion," *Journal of Economic Literature*, 36: 1465–96.

Lechner, F. (1991) "The Case Against Secularization: A Rebuttal," *Social Forces*, 69: 1103–20.

McGuire, M.B. (ed.) (2008) *Lived Religion: Faith and Practice in Everyday Life*, Oxford: Oxford University Press.

Smith, C. (1998) *American Evangelicalism: Embattled and Thriving*, Chicago: University of Chicago Press.

Stark, R. (1999) "Secularization, R.I.P.," *Sociology of Religion*, 60: 249–74.

Warner, R.S (1993) "A Work in Progress toward a New Paradigm for the Sociological Study of Religion in the United States," *American Journal of Sociology*, 98: 1044–93.

Wuthnow, R. (2007) *After the Baby Boomers: How Twenty- and Thirty-Somethings are Shaping the Future of American Religion.* Princeton, NJ: Princeton University Press.

3   The changing faces of history

In this chapter

In the first two chapters, we looked at how sociologists understand both the nature and function of religion. Here we turn attention to how historians look at religion and religious developments. We will look first at what history actually tries to do. Then we will explore how historians looked at developments in American religion, emphasizing religious institutions – churches, synagogues, temples, and the like – and religious groups such as denominations and the traditions that shaped them. Then we will turn to how historians broadened their perspective to look at the larger social and cultural context in which those institutions and traditions existed. Next we will examine how emphasizing context allowed historians to broaden their focus. Here we shall move beyond institutions and groups to ordinary people, exploring what men and women actually did and thought. We will also look at how material culture, from styles of architecture for religious buildings to objects found in the home, reflects particular understandings of religion. Finally, we will show how our understanding of religion in contemporary America becomes more complete when we bring history and sociology into conversation with each other.

Main topics covered

- What history tries to tell us.
- How and why historians looked to religious traditions and institutions – and their leaders – to understand religion in America and the ways in which it developed and changed.
- Ways in which placing institutional developments in social, cultural, and intellectual context led to emphasizing themes and broad movements that affected all traditions and institutions.
- The deeper understanding that resulted when historians looked at ordinary people, not just religious professionals and leaders.
- What examining material culture adds to our understanding of religion.
- How the shift towards personal spirituality and an increasingly pluralistic religious ethos added new dimensions to understanding historical developments.
- The ways in which history and sociology complement each other to help us understand more fully what is going on with religion in contemporary America.

What is history anyway?

Although people often think historians dwell on "the past" and try to figure out what happened in some earlier time, historians are actually keenly interested in the present. But the tools or ideas they use to look at the present presume that what persons are doing and thinking today represents a stage in an ongoing process of development. The renowned English playwright William Shakespeare in *The Tempest* (Act II, Scene 1) wrote an oft-repeated statement about history: Antonio observes that "what's past is prologue." This phrase highlights the way historians link the past and the present. What is happening in the world around us today emerges from the confluence of everything that came before. So historians believe that we can better understand the present by exploring what came earlier, seeing those events and forces as paving the way for what is going on in the world around us today.

Another analogy comes from human life itself. Although adults are quite different from the babies they once were, there is a relationship between them. Genetics plays one part, of course. But we also know that there are other influences. They include ethnicity, place of birth, socioeconomic opportunities, education, how families function in raising children, personality type, and a host of others. These provide each individual with unique life experiences that shape who they become in the process of moving from infancy through childhood and adolescence and then into adulthood. In other words, there is both continuity and change as one looks at individual lives. The same is true for the life of a people, a nation, even a region within a nation. Historians, of course, are not the only ones interested in these matters; they also propel much sociological analysis and interpretation.

But sociologists and historians may approach their common interests from different vantage points. Sociologists often tend to be more concerned with measuring what people of a particular ethnic-religious heritage think about controversial moral issues like abortion or what approach they take to raising their families, including transmitting some sort of religious identity to children. They may measure responses at different times and places for purposes of comparison. Historians seek to sort through the total process of change and continuity when looking at any one episode, moment, or figure. They look at everything from written records, if they exist, to archeological remains for cultures that no longer survive. In other words, they comb whatever evidence they can find to chart the ongoing process of development in human society, on the assumption that a clearer understanding of the past will illuminate the present. The past is indeed prologue, but the final chapters of the story have yet to be written.

This understanding reveals another feature of traditional historical inquiry. Historians until recently have concentrated on institutions and traditions that claim to be religious. They have also tended to look at religious professionals, such as clergy or theologians, for clues about religious belief and practice. By contrast, sociologists have traditionally been more concerned with what religion does in human life or in the life of a culture. As we saw in Chapter 2, this endeavor may entail accepting some things as having religious dimensions that might not at first glance always seem to be religious. As we shall see, in recent years, there has been more coming together of these two approaches.

The triumph of faith: telling religion's story through institutions and traditions

In the 1890s, a professor of church history at New York's Union Theological Seminary named Philip Schaff (1819–93) undertook to organize a series of books that would tell the story of religion in America. Already renowned for his own multi-volume history of Christianity, the Swiss-born scholar who was educated in Germany brought together a cadre of writers, each of whom traced the historical development of his own denomination in the US. Several principles that informed this project represented shared convictions among historians who looked at religion in America.

Among those convictions were the belief that although human actors, especially in the form of religious leaders, played a central role, divine providence – what believers called God – ultimately determined the course of religious history, which for Schaff and his associates was a steady story of progress and growth. These historians also believed that the heart of religion lay in organized groups or institutions, denominations like the Presbyterians and Methodists, each of which had a unique quality contributing to the overall portrait of American religious life. Virtually all of them were convinced that the American environment itself also played a key role, particularly in there never having been a single denomination or tradition officially established or sanctioned by the government. This freedom was coupled with a commitment, understood in slightly different but compatible ways from one denomination to the next, to basing belief and practice on the Bible. Consequently, most believed that the larger Protestant heritage, because of its presumed emphasis on the Bible, carried a divine destiny to dominate American life.

They thus told their story not only from the perspective of the denominations, institutions, and traditions they represented, but also from the vantage of their own faith commitments. The past that was prologue to the present in which they wrote and the future to which they pointed had its grounding in the ancient creeds of Christendom and then especially in the Protestant Reformation of the sixteenth century. The variant interpretations of the creeds and the different twists on Protestant doctrine, along with differences in how churches should be organized and administered that often reflected the politics of the period in which they emerged, led to the denominations that these historians studied. In Chapter 4, where we talk about trends in mainline Protestantism, echoes of this understanding of history come through in the use of denominational labels (Methodist, Episcopal, Baptist, etc.), although we do not tell the story of any single one of these denominational institutions exclusively.

A similar perspective held true at the time for those writing about the Roman Catholic experience in America. Pre-eminent among them were John Gilmary Shea (1824–92) and Peter Gilday (1884–1947), both of Irish immigrant heritage. Echoing official doctrine emphasizing Catholic belief, Shea and Gilday anticipated the eventual triumph of Catholic truth even in an American context dominated by Protestants – telling their story through events like councils of American Catholic bishops, parish and diocesan history, and the efforts of key church leaders such as John Carroll, the first American Roman Catholic bishop, and John England, a bishop who strengthened American Catholic identity by founding a periodical that circulated widely throughout the US. Like Schaff and other Protestant historians, Catholic writers such as Shea and Gilday reflected the optimism of the progressive era, assuming that growth and expansion meant increasing acceptance of their understanding of religious truth. For

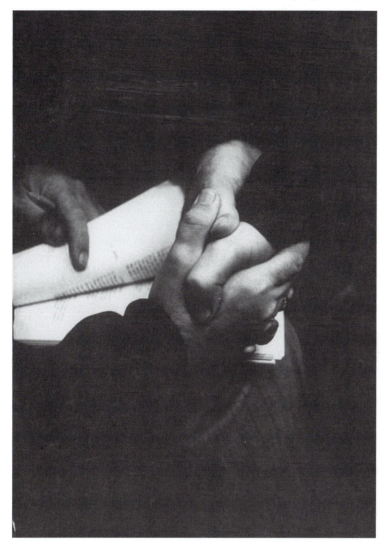

Figure 3.1 The 1957 merger of two denominations to create a new one, the United Church of Christ, illustrates the importance of institutions in understanding American religion and the emphasis on common understanding shared by denominations

Courtesy of Time & Life Pictures/Getty Images

Catholic historians, even the vitriolic anti-Catholicism sometimes marked by violence became a stepping-stone to eventual triumph. Guilday sought to secure serious study of American Catholic life when he helped organize the American Catholic Historical Association in 1919.

Another term that describes the historical approach exemplified by scholars such as Schaff, Shea, and Gilday is apologetic. In this context apology means something very different from the standard understanding of its being a statement expressing regret. Here apology is closer in purpose to a legal brief, an argument making a case to prove a point. For Schaff and his associates, history was an apology or an argument to demonstrate the superiority of Protestant forms of Christianity and their eventual dominance over other expressions of Christianity. For Shea and Gilday, history as apologetic meant demonstrating the superiority of Roman Catholic belief and practice and Catholicism's ultimate triumph. Christianity's roots in the Roman Empire provided the sacred past that was prologue to Roman Catholicism's present and future.

Expanding historical horizons: the contribution of "secular" historical method

By the end of the nineteenth century, however, other currents suggested that the study of religious history would soon move in new directions. In 1893, the American Historical Association met in Chicago in conjunction with the World's Fair celebrating the four hundredth anniversary of Columbus' "discovery" of the New World. Among those speaking at the conference was Frederick Jackson Turner (1861–1932), whose presentation on "The Significance of the Frontier in American History" redirected the course of historical studies in the US for a generation. For Turner, the frontier represented not only geographical space to be conquered, but also a psychological key to American uniqueness. In adapting to the frontier, Americans, in his view, had forged the institutions and national character that set them apart. This idea also had a profound impact on how analysts told religious history. Hence it was the frontier, already past when Turner gave his landmark address, that became a prologue to a different understanding of the present.

William Warren Sweet (1881–1959), who became the major figure nurturing the study of American religious history as a distinct field while teaching at the University of Chicago, used Turner's thesis as the key to understanding the whole of American religion. Sweet, like his predecessors, still saw groups and institutions as paramount, but he argued that the Protestant bodies best adapting to frontier conditions, such as the Methodists and Baptists, were those destined to flourish and dominate, and that the fierce independence of the frontier spirit helped account for the emergence of new groups that were distinctively American, groups such as the Disciples of Christ and the Church of Jesus Christ of Latter-day Saints or the Mormons.

But Sweet also paved the way for historians to move in new directions. For example, he began to look at common features among groups that flourished on the frontier. So, for example, he looked at phenomena such as revivalism and camp meetings that were not exclusive to any one denomination, recognizing that what cut across boundaries might sometimes better explain developments than looking from the more narrow perspective of a single group or denomination. Undergirding Sweet's approach – and Turner's – was a conviction that what distinguished Americans, regardless of their ancestral backgrounds in various European (or African) cultures, was a pragmatism, or a penchant to do whatever was practical and necessary in order to prosper.

In turn, other historians began rethinking religious developments with an eye to placing them in a broader social and intellectual context. Literary historian Perry Miller (1905–63), for example, focused on Puritan theology in the seventeenth and eighteenth centuries, claiming that its growth in colonial America, itself a frontier wilderness, not only determined its content, but also revealed the brilliance of Puritan thinkers in crafting systems of belief whose impact endured even in the twentieth century when Miller wrote, undergirding the ideology of American independence and democracy and sustaining a country committed to high moral standards as a nation.

Box 1.3 The historical study of American religion in the early twentieth century

By the beginning of the twentieth century, historians of religion began to rely more on the tools and approaches used by "secular" historians. Consequently, they concentrated less on institutions and denominations and also began to attribute developments to social and cultural forces more than to divine intervention. Here is how historian Henry W. Bowden described the shift:

> Some historians continued to produce narrowly focused, denominational apologetics. Others [began] to tackle denominational surveys of increased scope, but ... still highlighted core Protestant groups ... Attempts to align religious history with secular chronology and themes had more far-reaching consequences ... [R]eligious historians ... learned that new rigors concerning documentary evidence required a shift in their ... approach. It became increasingly difficult to invoke divine guidance as a factor in history, and ... new generations of investigators gradually abandoned references to providential causation. In its place they conformed to secular interpretive themes current among historians of social and political topics.
>
> (From Henry Warner Bowden, "The Historiography of American Religion," in *Encyclopedia of the American Religious Experience*, ed. Charles H. Lippy and Peter W. Williams (New York: Scribners, 1988), vol. 1, p. 5)

The work of Miller and others like him helped us understand that religious thought or theology, even if reflecting a faith commitment on the part of believers, must be understood as part of the larger history of ideas, what we call intellectual history. Our discussion of contemporary religious thought in Chapter 17 builds on this understanding that larger intellectual currents shape the way religious thought takes expression.

Recasting religious history in this way also brought interaction with sociology, not just with intellectual history and political history. H. Richard Niebuhr (1894–1962), influenced by the renowned sociologist Max Weber discussed in Chapters 1 and 13, in 1929 published his *Social Sources of Denominationalism*. Religious groups – denominations and their offshoots – remained primary in Niebuhr's analysis, but he made a strong case that differences in belief or differences in theology among groups, even if important in an earlier era, counted for less in the American context than the socioeconomic standing of adherents. In other words, Niebuhr added an economic dimension to historical appraisal, insisting that the particular style of a religious group reflected the economic standing of those attracted to it. He insisted that the way a group structured its belief system echoed the socioeconomic status of members, not any ultimate truth. Here, he also revealed an appreciation for Marx's notion that religion served as an opiate for the masses, also discussed in Chapters 1 and 13, for Niebuhr believed that persons from the lower socioeconomic classes, those whom he called "the disinherited," compensated for their lack of economic standing by identifying with religious groups that promised divine reward, however perhaps not until the hereafter, for faithfulness in the present life. In time, historians and sociologists alike modified Niebuhr's understanding and recognized that the relationship between religion and socioeconomic standing is more complicated, but any student of religious life must take its basic ideas into account.

From institutions to themes: religious history as social history

By the mid twentieth century, historians of religion in America were expanding their horizons even more. Some began to look for larger themes that might include many denominations and institutions in their scope, moving away from presuming a faith commitment or to seeing divine Providence as a primary factor and placing religious developments in the broader context of social history or the history of societies and culture as collective entities. Although many historians retained ties to theological schools, more and more of those who studied religious developments came from colleges and universities with broader academic aims than preparing persons for professional ministry in particular denominations.

Among seminary-affiliated historians who moved to uncover broad themes and trends that looked beyond individual denominations and institutions were Winthrop Hudson (1911–2001) and Robert T. Handy (1918–2009). Hudson, for example, looked at the whole of American religious history, concluding that the absence of a state church grounded in the First Amendment to the US Constitution was a vital theme that was prologue to the story of all American religious life and every religious group. He spoke of the "voluntary principle" to highlight how choosing to affiliate (or not to affiliate) with any organized religious group was a matter of personal choice, something one did voluntarily. Consequently, religion in the US operated in a way akin to the free market; each group had to persuade or convince persons of the benefits of affiliating. Those that were most effective in doing so succeeded. Of course, Hudson understood that other factors played a role – from upbringing to ethnicity. But his point was that larger themes, not narrow institutional history, held the key to better understanding. In subsequent chapters, when we talk about such trends as people switching their allegiance from one denomination to another or to none at all, we indirectly reflect the theme Hudson emphasized about religion's being a matter of voluntary choice.

For Handy, what stood out was the move among many Protestant denominations in the nineteenth century to minimize differences and emphasize commonalities in order to leave an enduring imprint on all American culture, not just on religious life. This desire for a Christian culture in the past was what shaped the present religious world, albeit in complex ways. Although he still told the story largely through agencies and leaders from the denominations, Handy also demonstrated that broader historical realities – in this case the increasing religious pluralism in American life – doomed Protestantism's hopes to craft an enduring Christian culture. Indeed, Handy repeatedly trumpeted what he called the "pluralistic style" of American religion, a matter we shall probe more fully in Chapters 18 and 19.

Perhaps the last major historian to craft a grand narrative of American religion built around a recurring theme was Sydney Ahlstrom (1919–84). His monumental *A Religious History of the American People* (1972), although still oriented towards denominations and traditions, emphasized the multiple ways the colonial Puritan heritage – his prologue to the present in which he worked – infiltrated virtually the whole of American religion – even when there were efforts to start new religious movements. But Ahlstrom, like Handy and Hudson, understood that religious history had to be placed in the larger context of the political, social, and intellectual developments occurring in American culture at any particular moment. No longer could one attribute religious developments to the intervention of divine providence. In all of the later chapters where we examine the historical underpinnings of religion in contemporary America, we assume the importance of this larger political, social, and intellectual context and emphasize that context rather than attributing religious developments to divine intervention.

Alongside these historians and their associates, then, were social historians intent on seeing how religious developments dovetailed with, reflected, or sometimes challenged prevailing currents in the larger society, For example, by the mid twentieth century, historians in general had become more sensitive to social currents such as urbanization and industrialization, moving more and more beyond a more narrow political history. Their work also influenced the study of American religious history. Aaron I. Abell (1903–65), who taught history at Notre Dame, explored how urbanization and issues of social justice that came to the fore in the decades of rapid urbanization and industrialization following the Civil War shaped the American Catholic experience, as much as Catholic belief itself shaped how those social questions were framed. In Chapter 6, where we examine currents in contemporary Catholicism more closely, we are heirs to the work of persons like Abell because a sensitivity to concerns like those he probed was a critical factor in moving Catholicism from being a religion of immigrants who lived on the fringes of society to being a key component of American religious life. In other words, we place religious developments in contemporary America in their larger social and cultural context. Religious history remains a part of social and intellectual history.

The ever-expanding horizons of social history

If the past is prologue to the present and the future, those who write about the past are also creatures of their own time and place. Hence the questions they ask and the materials they explore often reflect the world in which they live and work as much as they reveal a desire to understand how current trends came to be. By the 1950s and 1960s, historians were becoming more attuned to the need to look at race, for example, especially both the history of slavery and the distinctive history of African Americans. The civil rights movement helped propel this awareness and, as we shall see in subsequent chapters, had significant impact on religion.

In turn, the civil rights movement formed the backdrop for the women's movement, what some call "second-wave feminism" of the 1960s and 1970s. Historians, including those who wrote about religion, became all too keenly aware that even as they moved away from the denominational triumphalism of an earlier day, they still refracted their stories through the prism of white male experience. Women's history as a subfield of history emerged. All these endeavors meant looking to a more complex past, one in which gender and race made a difference and in which racism and sexism had dominated. Doing so involved retelling the story of American religion up to the present and refracting it through different prisms.

Box 3.2 How the search for women's history created a "new" past

In the wake of the civil rights movement and events such as Vatican II, women in the 1960s began to take a fresh look at religious history, which had until then been told from a white male perspective. Although much of what historians discovered was negative and involved the subordination and subjugation of women, especially when looking at American religious history they also found a "usable" past. In the introduction to her history of women and religion in America, Susan Hill Lindley noted:

> Scholars have found that women have been disruptive and submissive, challenging and supportive. They have been slaves, preachers, missionaries, reformers, critics, and the pillars of home and morality ... There are the individuals and movements who stepped out of their culturally assigned subordination in society, family, and church ... The other side is equally important, as researchers have lifted up and valued "ordinary women and what they did: the Puritan "goodwife" with her quiet but critical contributions to the colony's survival; the Jewish or Polish Catholic immigrant mother preserving for the next generation a religious and ethnic heritage; the black women keeping the church going through their cleaning, cooking, fundraising, and teaching so that it could be a center and haven for the community
>
> (From Susan Hill Lindley, *"You have Stept Out of your Place"*:
> *A History of Women and Religion in America*,
> Louisville, KY: Westminster John Knox, 1996, p. x)

An early effort to rethink the story from the African American perspective came with Joseph R. Washington, Jr.'s *Black Religion: The Negro and Christianity in the United States* (1964). Soon a fertile new subfield had emerged, as we shall note in Chapters 11 and 17, propelled in part by the theological initiatives such as James Cone's *Black Theology and Black Power* (1967) and historical works such as Albert Raboteau's *Slave Religion: The "Invisible Institution" in the Antebellum South* (1978). Historian Rosemary Skinner Keller (1934–2008) and theologian Rosemary Radford Ruether (1936–) spearheaded several multivolume works to bring women's experience to the foreground, from the colonial period through to the close of the last century. Most prominent was their co-edited three-volume *Encyclopedia of Women and Religion in North America* (2006).

Topics such as race and gender helped move the historical study away from institutions such as denominations and churches or synagogues, organizational bodies such as councils of bishops or general conventions, and even religious professionals such as clergy and theologians. This shift suggested that looking at the past through the eyes of ordinary people, even those on the margins, might shed new light on the shape of contemporary religion. Some historians referred to this as "popular" religion as a way of suggesting that it emerged from the people themselves, not necessarily from official pronouncements of denominational bodies and their leaders or even from the larger tradition. Of course, sometimes new religious movements, some of which we discuss in Chapter 13, resulted from these popular impulses, adding an institutional layer to them. Often they remained more amorphous, reflecting the spirituality that we analyze in Chapter 16, with its individualistic orientation. Those studying this aspect of American religious history have more recently come to call the subject of their research "lived religion" to denote that it takes in everything that persons do and think when they are going about the business of being religious as they understand it; in other words, it zeroes in on what they are doing when they "live" their religion. We noted how sociologists have talked about lived religion in Chapter 2. In addition, historians began to pay attention to dimensions of popular culture or mass culture that carried religious significance.

Those who emphasized popular religion or lived religion helped kindle new conversation between historians and sociologists, anthropologists, and ethnographers. The reason is simple: lived religion drew historians away from their earlier focus on institutions, traditions, and religious professionals. In other words, they had to ask the same questions social scientists asked about what religion actually was and how it was expressed in human life. Recall some of the definitional understandings of religion discussed in Chapter 2. Several offered insight to historians when they began to look beyond what was "obviously" religious to what ordinary people did, thought, and believed when they were trying to give meaning to what they experienced in day-to-day life.

Historian Peter Williams (1944–), for example, drew on a multidisciplinary approach in his appraisal of popular religious currents that he believed reflected how people reacted to the modernization process. Robert Orsi (1953–), looking particularly at Roman Catholics who fused ethnic and religious impulses, found ethnographic analysis helpful. As we shall see in Chapter 6, how Catholics see themselves as being Catholic for decades has had less to do with official church teaching, doctrine, and practice, and much more to do with how individuals create a personal world of meaning that taps not only what is overtly Catholic but also a host of other phenomena. In addition, historians who emphasized lived religion became increasingly candid about how the historian's own lived experience shaped analysis, gradually abandoning the idea that historians were merely dispassionate observers who recounted only "facts" as if they existed in a vacuum.

Another shift in historical understanding that resulted from looking more at lived religion than institutional religion was an emphasis on material culture. Historian Colleen McDannell, for example, in her *Material Christianity: Religion and Popular Culture in America* (1995) and the edited two-volume *Religions of the United States in Practice* (2001), demonstrates how vernacular art (works designed for home use) and objects found in such domestic space often reveal more about the religious sensibilities of real people than pronouncements of church councils or policies promulgated by denominations. Likewise, both Peter Williams and Jeanne Halgren Kilde have looked at the architecture of structures used for religious purposes, showing that the design and use of such space tell us more about how religion is both received and perceived by people than doctrine and creed. Material culture becomes critical to broader historical interpretation.

One example will illustrate how these broader approaches to historical inquiry have changed our understanding of the past. As we shall see, particularly in Chapter 4, analysts in the 1950s often talked about a "revival" of religion in the US. To use a

Box 3.3 The historian and lived religion

David D. Hall is among those historians who have insisted that the study of lived religion is central to understanding not only contemporary religious life, but also the past that created it. Here is how he described the ways lived religion has changed how historians understand religion:

> Lived religion … directs us to religion as experienced … [T]his approach makes room for the personal and private in the midst of (or as alternatives to) the bureaucratic and the institutional. [It] requires historians to rethink the utility of large-scale constructions such [as] "mainstream," "liberalism," "evangelicalism," and "secularization" that have little resonance among ordinary people and rarely coincide with the complexities of everyday practice or experience. Nor does the concept support overly rigid assertions of identity or tradition. To seek lived religion is to find it in unexpected places: habits of dining, bathrooms and hospital beds, street festivals, the "gospel blues," and cyberspace.
>
> (From David D. Hall, "Lived Religion," in *Encyclopedia of Religion in America*, ed. Charles H. Lippy and Peter W. Williams, Washington: CQ Press, 2010, pp. 1282–83)

Figure 3.2 Home altars or religious shrines like this one are part of what analysts call "lived religion" or how ordinary people express their spirituality in very personal ways

© Stephanie Maze/CORBIS

word like "revival" implies that there had been a decline at some point prior to this new spurt of interest. Regarding the past as prologue, historians began to probe the past to see if they could discern times of decline and reasons for it, convinced that doing so would illuminate the religious revival of the 1950s.

Among those historians was Robert Handy, whose work on Protestant efforts to create and sustain a Christian culture we have already mentioned. Handy focused on the time of the Great Depression, when the national – indeed global – economy was in tatters, unemployment was widespread, and many familiar patterns of life were disrupted as a result. Still concentrating on institutions, Handy went to membership and attendance records of congregations of all sorts, as well as evidence of monetary support for organized religion among adherents. Not surprisingly, given the economic catastrophe of the Great Depression, he found that support dropped significantly, as did attendance and participation – the latter continuing on into the years of World War II when millions were engaged in overseas military activities. So Handy spoke of a "religious depression" that accompanied the economic one, and just as the economy revived thanks to World War II and the needs generated by a peacetime culture, he said, so too religion began to revive.

Colleen McDannell, however, with her eyes focused on material culture and lived religion found a different story to tell, a different past that was prologue to the 1950s. Analyzing hundreds of photographs, artifacts of material culture, taken of homes and domestic space during the Depression, McDannell found an extraordinary number of religious items. By looking closely at what was portrayed and the prominence of religious objects, McDannell argued that a vital current of religion continued to flourish in ordinary life during the Depression, even if attendance at religious services and contributions to religious groups declined. In other words, the location of vital religion had shifted more to domestic space than public space that carried a religious label. We will see the interweaving of popular culture and religion and also of material culture and religion especially when we examine the resurgence of evangelicalism in Chapter 5 and the many faces of individualized personal spirituality in Chapter 16.

History and sociology in conversation

This example is indicative of broader movements in both sociology and history by the early twenty-first century. Sociologists, although still interested in defining precisely what functioned as religion in the lives of people, were trying to flesh out the larger social and cultural context in which those definitions made sense. They were crossing into the territory of historians. In addition, sociologists who used survey data to measure what people claimed to believe and to practice had little choice but to take their responses at face value when they identified with a particular religious group or tradition or with none at all. But those labels also had a past that was prologue to their use at any contemporary moment. Unpacking that past brought history and sociology into conversation.

Meanwhile, as historians expanded their range of vision beyond the realm of institutions and traditions, beyond the world of churches, temples, and synagogues, they discovered other religious impulses – what analysts from many disciplines have called spirituality, although there are other designations – and that looking to ordinary people, to those left out (women, ethnic communities, and such), a different past emerged. Historians were learning from sociologists.

In the early twenty-first century, the arena where these two disciplines revealed that they were complementary perhaps emerged from trying to understand what has been called the "new pluralism." When historian Robert Handy noted that Protestant hopes for a Christian America were shattered by the historical realities of pluralism in the nineteenth century, he did not envision the day when Islam and Buddhism would be among the faster-growing religious traditions in the US. For him pluralism was still primarily the variety of expressions of Christianity mixed with the various strands of Judaism. Sociologists, too, struggle to make sense of how the changing face of pluralism is altering not only personal religious consciousness, but how religion relates to a range of social issues from abortion to homosexuality.

If the texture of religion in contemporary America makes anything clear, it is that history and sociology both benefit from ongoing conversation, with each strengthening the analysis offered by the other.

Key points you need to know

- History and sociology in the past have had different starting points in trying to understand religion.
- For many years, historians looked primarily at institutions and traditions as providing the backdrop for current religious developments.
- Another generation of historians emphasized broad themes and issues that affected all institutions and traditions, moving their analysis closer to social and cultural history.
- Historians found a more complex past when they moved to the forefront groups often marginalized, from women to various ethnic communities.
- Other ventures that brought history and sociology closer together emerged when analysts began exploring popular religion or lived religion and drew on material culture and popular culture, not just the usual religious institutions and belief systems.
- Today history and sociology are engaged in a complementary quest to discover exactly where religion is located in contemporary society and what historical forces led to the beliefs and practices of ordinary people.

Discussion questions

1   What different questions do sociologists and historians bring to any conversation about religion in contemporary America?
2   What do historians mean when they say that the past is the prologue to the present?
3   What is the value of emphasizing the story of religious institutions and traditions when examining the past?
4   Why did historians come to believe that looking at common themes, such as the impact of the frontier, represented a better way to link the past with the present?
5   What did the history of religion gain as scholars drew more and more on tools used in the analysis of social and cultural history?

6 How does looking at the religious life of ordinary people and using items from material culture enhance historical understanding of religious developments?
7 What are the advantages of history and sociology being in conversation with each other in looking at religion in contemporary America? Are there any drawbacks to doing so?

Further reading

Ahlstrom, S.E. (1970) "The Problem of the History of Religion in America," *Church History*, 39: 224–34.

Bowden, H.W. (1991) *Church History in an Age of Uncertainty*, Carbondale, IL: Southern Illinois University Press.

—— (1971) *Church History in the Age of Science: Historiographical Patterns in the United States, 1876–1918*, Chapel Hill: University of North Carolina Press.

Clark, E.A. (2004) *History, Theory, Text: Historians and the Linguistic Turn*, Cambridge, MA: Harvard University Press.

Hall, D.D. (ed.) (1997) *Lived Religion in America: Toward a History of Practice*, Princeton, NJ: Princeton University Press.

Maffly-Kipp, L.F., Schmidt, L., and Valeri, M. (eds.) (2006) *Practicing Protestants: Histories of Christian Life in America, 1630–1965*, Baltimore, MD: The Johns Hopkins University Press.

Orsi, R.A. (2005) *Between Heaven and Earth: The Religious Worlds People Make and the Scholars who Study them*, Princeton, NJ: Princeton University Press.

Tweed, T.A. (ed.) (1997) *Retelling U.S. Religious History*, Berkeley: University of California Press.

Williams, P.W. (1989) *Popular Religion in America: Symbolic Change and the Modernization Process in Historical Perspective*, Englewood Cliffs, NJ: Prentice-Hall.

Part II

Mainline religions in historical and sociological context

4 Mainline Protestantism
The erosion of cultural dominance

In this chapter

This chapter explores trends within mainline Protestantism since World War II. It looks first at the presumed surge of interest in religion immediately after the war. Then it examines how currents evident in the 1960s challenged groups long accustomed to prominence in American life. Attention then turns to the interplay of religion and social forces since the 1970s; most contributed to membership decline in mainline Protestant groups and whittled away at their impact on the larger society. Finally, the chapter looks at changes in worship and the institutional life of mainline Protestant denominations, concluding with a discussion of internal debates over homosexuality that continue to threaten mainline influence.

Main topics covered

- How the years just after World War II suggested that mainline Protestantism was flourishing.
- Ways in which the postwar "baby boom" affected mainline Protestantism.
- The impact of the ecumenical movement, revivalism, and the civil rights movement on mainline denominations.
- Early signs of mainline Protestantism's eroding membership and cultural influence.
- How mainline Protestantism tried to stem that loss.
- Debates over homosexuality within mainline Protestantism.

Mainline Protestants and the "religious revival" of the 1950s

After America celebrated the end of World War II in 1945, religious life appeared to enter a boom time. Since the Great Depression of the 1930s, organized religion had faced countless challenges. Meager financial resources provided little opportunity to build, renovate, or expand church facilities, while service in the military took millions away from their homes. One result was a drop in church membership and attendance. For a decade and a half after the war, the picture looked very different.

As military personnel returned home, re-entering the domestic work force, they began to settle down in communities where they found employment. That effort often involved relocating to a new area. The US birth rate steadily rose, resulting in the "baby boom" generation, those born between 1946 and 1964 (when the number of new births dipped for the first time in the postwar era).

With population growth and mobility, every major city sprouted suburbs that witnessed construction not only of millions of new homes, but also of buildings to accommodate social and cultural institutions such as schools, churches, and synagogues, and places to shop and spend leisure time. Benefiting from this seemingly limitless growth were the religious denominations popularly called mainline Protestant – Presbyterians, Methodists, Episcopalians, some Baptist groups, Congregationalists (United Church of Christ), Lutherans, Reformed Church in America, and Disciples of Christ. These groups had long dominated American religious life, both in terms of the numbers who identified with them (somewhere between 20 per cent and 25 per cent of the nation's population in 1950) and their deep influence on American culture. As late as 1993, more than 40 per cent of the members of the US Congress were affiliated with mainline Protestant groups, a figure that dropped to about 33 per cent just over a decade later.

Box 4.1 Defining mainline Protestantism

Mainline Protestant denominations:

- have colonial roots, reflecting the earliest waves of European immigration to the US;
- emphasize both personal spirituality (such as questions of salvation) and engagement with social problems;
- dominated American religious life until the last third of the twentieth century, but now account for only about 15 per cent of the population;
- are strongest in northeastern and midwestern US and some areas of the south;
- have disproportionately influenced American culture in such areas as government or holding public office and founding educational institutions, especially colleges and universities;
- usually include predominantly white groups such as the American Baptist Churches in the USA, Christian Church (Disciples of Christ), Episcopal Church, Evangelical Lutheran Church in America, Presbyterian Church in the United States of America, Reformed Church in America, United Church of Christ, and United Methodist Church.

Historian James Hudnut-Beumler has noted the significant increase in expenditures for new church buildings as suburbs mushroomed. Denominations not only spent more money to create larger physical plants to meet the needs of young suburban families, they also channeled a larger proportion of their resources into the "bricks and mortar" dimension of religious life. At the same time, mainline Protestants became increasingly enamored with business methods to measure success and to organize their ministries. For Hudnut-Beumler, this passion for adapting business approaches demonstrated how deeply William Whyte's image of the "organizational man" penetrated postwar society.

Paralleling suburban growth and the erection of new buildings to house an array of religious programs was a theological movement called ecumenism. The word "ecumenism" comes from the same Greek root that gives us the word "economy" but technically denotes an efficient household. In 1950, an agency formed early in the twentieth century to coordinate Protestantism's response to rapid urbanization and industrialization changed its name from the Federal Council of Churches to the National Council of Churches. The latter was associated with the World Council of Churches, an international group established in 1948. All fostered cooperation and coordination of ministry among member denominations. Working together was more efficient, echoing the emphasis on efficiency in business. But it reflected a deeper theological conviction, namely that mainline denominations shared a common heritage in Protestant Christianity transcending the differences in belief and practice separating them. Commonality had a visible symbol in 1958 when President Dwight D. Eisenhower participated in ceremonies around the laying of the cornerstone of New York City's Interchurch Center, home to the National Council of Churches and other ecumenical and mainline Protestant groups

Some ecumenical endeavors led to denominations with a common ancestry but some differences based on ethnicity merging together. In 1957, for example, two groups that shared a congregational approach to church authority and theological

Figure 4.1 US President Dwight Eisenhower participated in ceremonies in 1958 celebrating the building of the Interchurch Center in New York City. Bringing many religious groups together to have offices under one roof illustrates the ecumenical movement and its emphasis on cooperation rather than competition

roots in Calvinist strands of Puritanism and pietistic religiosity merged to form the United Church of Christ (UCC). The Evangelical and Reformed Church, one of those coming into the UCC, traced its history to German immigrants, while the Congregational Christian Churches looked back to New England settlers for antecedents. Just over thirty years later (1988), three Lutheran denominations, each of which reflected the ecumenical merger of groups with distinctive ethnic backgrounds (Norwegian, Finnish, Swedish, German, and so on) formed the Evangelical Lutheran Church in America.

Theologically, all ecumenical endeavors echoed the belief that Christians had much in common with each other even if ethnicity or differences in practice separated them. Ecumenicity also related to the suburbanization of religion. As people flocked to the suburbs, churches scrambled to build structures to serve their religious needs. But not every group could go to every suburb. Often local councils of churches patterned after the National Council of Churches coordinated expansion on the suburban frontier. Working together, mainline Protestants assured the success of a particular congregation by minimizing competition for members.

An unintended consequence was the homogenization of mainline Protestantism. If distinctive beliefs and ways of organizing (e.g. whether to vest authority in bishops or in the congregation) once characterized each denomination, cooperation and mergers muted differences. Population mobility exacerbated this trend. When earlier generations of Protestants relocated from one place to another, they tended to seek out a religious group affiliated with their former denomination. Suburbanization and ecumenicity changed that. Denominational switching became the norm, not the exception. Folks simply affiliated with the church closest to them or the one with the most appealing programs, regardless of denominational label.

Nonetheless, in the 1950s, mainline Protestant denominations enjoyed significant numerical growth. Some saw their growth rate equal or exceed the growth rate of the population as a whole; some did not. Two examples illustrate this trend. In 1950, the Methodist Church and the Evangelical United Brethren Church, which merged in 1968, together reported around 9.7 million members; a decade later, that figure soared to just over 10.6 million, an increase of more than 9 per cent, one of the lower rates among the mainline. During the 1950s, the Episcopal Church added some 850,000 adherents to the 2.5 million on record in 1950, a growth rate of nearly 38 per cent. During that decade, the US population increased by slightly more than 18 per cent. Other mainline bodies reported similar growth. To casual observers, mainline Protestantism was experiencing unprecedented gains.

Another sign of the presumed postwar return to religion among Americans, especially mainline Protestants, came with the surge of interest in religious revivals, particularly those associated with Billy Graham (1918–). Graham came to public attention in 1948 when he led a revival in Los Angeles lasting several weeks. Then came crusades, as Graham called his revivals, in London in 1954 that ran twelve weeks and in New York City's Madison Square Garden in 1957 that spanned four months.

Graham's operation was built on standard organizational and business principles. Before he visited a city, his team secured the sponsorship and endorsement of local mainline Protestant leaders. Graham's evangelistic work thus furthered the impression that mainline Protestantism was flourishing as never before. Support from multiple denominations – sometimes with local leaders seated together on the platform on a

Figure 4.2 Evangelist Billy Graham attracted hundreds of thousands to his evangelistic crusades or revivals beginning in the mid 1950s, giving support to the perception that the nation was experiencing a great surge of interest in religion after the end of World War II

Courtesy of Time & Life Pictures/Getty Images

crusade's opening night – added to the perception that mainline Protestants were pretty much alike. If their leaders gave their common blessing to Graham, denominational beliefs and practices could not vary much.

Popular culture buttressed the perception that mainline Protestantism was flourishing. The ministry of Norman Vincent Peale (1898–1993) provides one example. A one-time Methodist who spent most of his career at New York City's Marble Collegiate Church, affiliated with the small mainline Reformed Church in America, Peale effectively blended self-help psychology with faith in his "positive thinking." His book, *The Power of Positive Thinking*, made the bestseller lists when it appeared in 1952, remaining there more than three years. Peale and the American Foundation for Religion and Psychiatry that he co-founded offered a practical approach to faith and even business success. Practitioners of positive thinking crafted a mental image of what they desired – whether physical health, marital happiness, or success in one's vocation – and then acted as if the end result had been attained. Peale insisted that prayer was part of the process, but detractors saw the approach as a simplistic way of ignoring or even manipulating the realities of life.

Other signs of the expanding influence of religion in postwar America came in the public sector. In 1954, Congress added the phrase "under God" to the Pledge of Allegiance to the American flag. Although composed in 1892, the pledge received Congressional sanction only in 1942. The modification in the 1950s came at the height of Cold War tension between the US and the presumably godless communist empire symbolized by the Soviet Union and its allies. The phrase marked the nation as a bastion of goodness and righteousness. Two years later, spurred by the same concern to affirm American goodness, Congress adopted the phrase "In God We Trust" as the official national motto. The words appeared on some coinage first in the Civil War era and gradually had been put on all coins. The 1956 Congressional action extended the practice to paper currency as well.

By the end of the 1960s, the apparent religious boom yielded to decline, a pattern continuing into the twenty-first century. Sociologists Penny Long Marler and Kirk Hadaway have shown that membership in mainline bodies peaked in the mid 1960s at around 28.2 million, but dropped steadily thereafter. By 2003, for example, they estimate mainline membership at around 20.8 million, a net loss of more than 25 per cent. During that time, the US population grew by more than 50 per cent, from around 194 million to 294 million. In retrospect, close analysis finds the embryonic stages of decline in the 1950s, lurking beneath the surface growth.

Challenges confront the mainline

By the mid 1950s, challenges came to the mainline. Foremost were those emanating from the civil rights movement, with its beginning in the 1955 Montgomery, Alabama, bus boycott. The civil rights movement raised profound questions about all authority through its direct confrontation with legalized segregation. Peaceful sit-ins and demonstrations questioned the morality and justice of laws that declared one race inferior to another. Denominations with congregations separated by race, including those of mainline Protestantism, seemed complicit in the injustice of segregation. Not until 1964, for example, did the Methodist Church dismantle an administrative structure organized around racial separation.

With the Rev. Martin Luther King, Jr. (1939–68) and his Southern Christian Leadership Conference in the forefront, Protestant, Catholic, and Jewish clergy called for an end to legalized segregation. Many mainline Protestant pastors took positions that contrasted with views held by parishioners. Lay folk claimed that pastors let political activism trump spiritual nurture. As ministers walked in protest demonstrations, their flocks began to walk with their feet, leaving churches that seemingly favored political and social engagement over faith. In his 1969 book *The Gathering Storm in the Churches*, sociologist Jeffrey Hadden warned of impending mass defection from the mainline if pastors focused on social rather than spiritual concerns. Issues of how religion and race are related and how religious forces interact with social movements receive further scrutiny in Chapters 12 and 15.

The civil rights movement stirred cognate efforts among others long consigned to the margins of Protestant life. Civil rights concerns helped give birth to second-wave feminism and its calls for the ordination of women, for inclusion of women in leadership positions at all levels, and for ending use of exclusively male language to describe God. Here, too, moves began in the 1950s, despite scattered examples of women ordained by Congregationalists (UCC) and Disciples of Christ in the nineteenth century. In 1956 the Methodist General Conference first authorized the ordination of women to professional ministry. That same year, northern Presbyterians moved to ordain women to the ministry of Word and Sacrament. Other groups followed, often experiencing much contention. The first Lutheran body ordained women in 1970, and the Episcopal Church in 1974 had to deal with retired bishops who ordained women priests in what was called an irregular rite. As the role of women changed, some predicted the demise of mainline Protestantism. Convinced that because Jesus was male and called twelve male disciples and because some New Testament passages prohibited women from speaking in church or instructing men, they saw the movement undermining not only tradition, but also the authority of scripture. If tradition and scripture crumbled, so, too, would all mainline Protestantism. Similar fears propelled those who recoiled at gender-inclusive language in new translations of the Bible and revised orders for worship.

Box 4.2 The challenges of the 1960s

Many social movements and calls for social change in the 1960s challenged the dominant influence of mainline Protestantism and contributed to its gradual decline. Among them are:

- the civil rights movement;
- second-wave feminism;
- the antiwar movement of the Vietnam era;
- a drop in the birth rate after the baby boom ended and use of artificial methods of contraception became more common;
- theological movements such as situation ethics;
- Supreme Court cases restricting devotional religious activities in public schools and expanding abortion rights.

Added to the maelstrom were theological currents in the 1960s that talked about the "death of God" and a "secular" Christianity. Harvard theologian Harvey Cox, for example, insisted that life in the "secular city" reflected a Christianity come of age, shorn of its supernatural trappings. Confirmation that mainline Protestantism had drifted away from the faith came in the fascination with "situation ethics" that seemed to deny absolute right and wrong, allowing individuals to determine moral conduct based on personal appraisal of circumstances. Some critics felt that a dangerous liberal spirit had overtaken mainline Protestantism. Liberalism made individuals the final arbiter of all truth, replacing certainty in faith and practice with ambiguity

By the end of the 1960s, some noticed that although mainline Protestant denominations were beginning to lose members, conservative groups with their firm insistence on absolute truth grounded in scripture were growing. National Council of Churches analyst Dean M. Kelley, for example, attributed the early signs of decline in the mainline to the liberal ethos with its lack of firm authority and certainty. He credited the growth of conservative bodies to their insistence on absolute standards of belief and practice.

Decisions of the US Supreme Court provided additional fodder for those convinced that American life was unraveling in the 1960s. In 1962 and 1963, the court ruled that devotional prayer and Bible reading in public schools violated the principle of separation of church and state. Other court decisions in the 1960s and 1970s chipped away at restrictions on teaching evolutionary theory or requiring instruction in both "scientific creationism" and evolutionary theory. Public schools once reflected the dominant mainline Protestant piety undergirding American culture. They now seemed bastions of a secular humanism that left students adrift, with no sense of truth or falsehood, right or wrong. Religious issues involving public education will receive more attention in Chapter 9.

Americans also had to come to terms with medical advances that at first glance seem little connected with religion. In 1960, artificial means of contraception took a leap forward with the introduction of "the pill." Advocates saw "the pill" as enhancing responsible family planning. Critics believed it promoted sexual promiscuity and reflected dangers symbolized by rampant feminism and situation ethics; now persons could freely engage in sexual activity with little fear of unwanted pregnancy. Mainline Protestants tended to sanction use of "the pill," although they did not condone promiscuity. More conservative Protestant groups and the Roman Catholic Church remained opposed, arguing that contraception interfered with God's using every act of sexual intercourse as an opportunity to create new life.

After the postwar baby boom, the ability to control family size struck many mainline Protestants as providing a better way to care for the children they had. Marler and Hadaway have shown that by the end of the 1960s, the decline in the birth rate among mainline Protestants exceeded the natural drop that followed the baby boom. Mainline Protestants stopped reproducing in numbers sufficient to replenish their ranks as members aged and died. In other words, decline was inevitable once the birth rate plummeted. Compounding the issue was *Roe v. Wade*, the 1973 Supreme Court case that expanded access to abortion. Some saw the decision as acknowledging the rights of women; others feared it would become a way to control the birth rate that sanctioned killing unborn children. We explore religious issues linked to abortion in Chapter 9.

At the same time, analysts have found that baby boomers broke with previous trends in terms of religious behavior. Researchers had long noted that many raised in a religious environment retreated from active engagement in organized religion at some point in the life cycle, most notably in late adolescence and early adulthood. They returned at another stage, particularly when they had families for whom they wished to provide religious nurture. The baby boom generation, moving into adulthood in the 1960s, was different. Religious institutions, particularly those of mainline Protestantism, did not retain even vestiges of loyalty among many, who became what sociologist Wade Clark Roof called "a generation of seekers." Some turned to new religious movements that flourished in the counterculture of the age that we will explore in Chapter 13. Others pursued private, personal religious journeys, a phenomenon we shall discuss in Chapter 16. Regardless of in which direction boomers went, instead of returning to traditional forms of religion after some spiritual exploration, they often remained alienated. Their exodus from mainline Protestantism seemed permanent. How religion is transmitted from one generation to the next in contemporary American life will inform some of our discussion in Chapter 8.

Adding to boomers' discontent with the status quo was the national malaise regarding US military engagement in Vietnam. The antiwar movement of the 1960s and early 1970s only exacerbated the challenge to authority launched by the civil rights movement. When priests and nuns broke into government offices to destroy draft board records and when rabbis and ministers marched in the streets protesting against American policy, the gathering storm begun in the civil rights era intensified. Mainline Protestant denominations found themselves caught between a patriotic impulse to support the government and a need to minister to those who neither endorsed nor accepted policies that sustained brutal fighting in southeast Asia.

Mainline Protestant bodies had long buttressed some expressions of nationalism. Most applauded when "In God We Trust" became the national motto and "under God" inserted into the Pledge of Allegiance. Millions assumed that divine Providence guided American history and destiny, even if Americans constructed multiple ways to acknowledge that Providence. In the wake of national anxiety and the first clear signs that mainline denominations were losing members, sociologist Robert Bellah sought to shore up the religious foundations of national identity when he wrote about a "civil religion" that existed alongside organized religious institutions, a religious impulse linking the American people to a God working through historical events. Bellah worried that this civil religion, this ambiguous bond between religion and nationalism, was collapsing. Like mainline denominations, American civil religion was also in decline. Other ways of understanding the ways in which religion related to politics and the public sector come under examination in Chapter 9.

Reaction and response: mainline Protestantism's continuing dilemma

How did the mainline respond? Efforts to reverse the decline had to take into account a growing suspicion of commitment to all social institutions as the baby boomer generation came of age. It was not only mainline Protestant denominations that experienced decline; so too did fraternal orders and lodges such as the Masons and the Order of the Eastern Star. Political parties counted a smaller percentage of the population as members; the numbers of those claiming no political affiliation swelled. Even commitment to traditional social institutions such as marriage seemed to dwindle as divorce rates moved steadily higher. There was, it seemed, a national reluctance to become committed to any kind of social institution. Could mainline Protestantism remake itself to appeal to those wary of all institutions and unwilling to commit to them?

Early efforts involved revamping worship. A broad-based liturgical renewal movement marked many Christian bodies in the 1960s; many jettisoned forms, language, hymns, and other modes of expression thought outmoded if not archaic. Leaders looked to popular culture for ways to revitalize worship, make it more appealing, and extend its relevance into the future. Hymn writers such as Ruth Duck (1947–) and Brian Wren (1936–) crafted new texts sensitive to inclusive language concerns and issues raised by women. Their work found its way into mainline Protestant hymnals, but did little to stem the numerical decline of such denominations.

Others looked to ways to refashion what churches, congregations, and worship encompassed. In 1975 Bill Hybels (1952–) started what became Willow Creek Community Church in suburban Chicago. Using sophisticated survey methods, Hybels and his associates determined that the formality of much mainline worship apparatus, from "Sunday clothes" to pipe organ music, seemed artificial to boomers and the generations following them. Greater informality, use of drama and contemporary entertainment forms, and downplaying overt Christian symbols that seemed relics of a bygone era harmonized the "contemporary Christian worship" of Willow Creek with postmodern culture. Even sermons, though grounded in biblical texts, addressed topics from choosing a mate to balancing budgets, practical issues real people confronted daily. Some churches, like Willow Creek, attracted thousands to services often held at times other than the traditional Sunday morning hours, becoming known as megachurches. They also had a significant impact on the evangelical resurgence of the later twentieth century to be discussed in Chapter 5.

Many megachurches spurned denominational affiliation. However, the appeal of contemporary worship was such that by the beginning of the twenty-first century, many mainline congregations offered at least one "contemporary" service to attract those disenchanted with traditional worship. Some adapted the megachurch emphasis on supplementing worship with scores of small groups that focused on everything from parenting skills to exercise and weight loss to meet the presumed needs of a constituency uninterested in deep questions of faith. The greatest successes, even as the megachurch gave way to what advocates called the emerging church or a home-based approach, came with independent congregations. Experimentation in structure and worship failed to halt mainline decline.

Box 4.3 Debates over homosexuality

Mainline Protestant denominations have experienced wrenching internal division over homosexuality. Representative of the reluctance to accept homo-sexual persons at all levels of church life is the following statement, taken from the Social Principles of the United Methodist Church, first adopted in 1972, as it appeared in the denomination's 2008 Book of Discipline:

> The United Methodist Church does not condone the practice of homosexuality and considers this practice incompatible with Christian teaching. We affirm that God's grace is available to all. We will seek to live together in Christian community, welcoming, forgiving, and loving one another, as Christ has loved and accepted us. We implore families and churches not to reject or condemn lesbian and gay members and friends. We commit ourselves to be in ministry for and with all persons.
>
> (www.archives.umc.org, accessed 1 October 2010)

Much different is the stance taken by another mainline group, the United Church of Christ, as evidenced in the following resolution on same-gender marriage adopted by its 2005 General Synod:

> WHEREAS equal marriage rights for couples regardless of gender is an issue deserving of serious, faithful discussion by people of faith, taking into consideration the long complex history of marriage and family life, layered as it is with cultural practices, economic realities, political dynamics, religious history and biblical interpretation ...
>
> THEREFORE LET IT BE RESOLVED, that the Twenty-Fifth General Synod of the United Church of Christ affirms equal marriage rights for couples regardless of gender and declares that the government should not interfere with couples regardless of gender who choose to marry and share fully and equally in the rights, responsibilities and commitment of legally recognized marriage ...
>
> (www.ucc.org/lgbt/statements.html, accessed 1 October 2010)

Complicating efforts to reinvigorate mainline Protestantism were fresh disagreements over sexuality. In most cases, the issue was no longer the role and status of women as in the 1960s. Instead, what caused contention was homosexuality. That issue took many forms. Mainline Christians found themselves divided over whether homosexuality should be classified as a sin, despite the mounting evidence from scientists and psychologists that same-gender attraction was inborn. Those wary of full inclusion of gays and lesbians in churches believed biblical passages, from the Levitical code in the Hebrew scriptures to statements in the Christian New Testament attributed to Paul, condemned homosexual practice, though not necessarily homosexual persons. For them, accepting homosexual identity as legitimate undermined biblical authority and plunged the church deeper into an abyss of uncertainty.

Within mainline denominations, groups such as Integrity (Episcopal) and Affirmation (United Methodist) advocated on behalf of full inclusion of gays and lesbians in the church. Several moved to recognize gay clergy. The United Church of Christ led the way, accepting gay and lesbian clergy in 1980. By 2011, the Episcopal Church, the Evangelical Lutheran Church in America, and the Presbyterian Church (USA) had also approved policies allowing for ordination of homosexuals, although not without contention and controversy. The maze of issues surrounding gender and sexuality in contemporary American religious culture will be a major focus of Chapter 10.

By the second decade of the twenty-first century, debates over the role of homosexuals threatened the cultural hegemony of mainline Protestantism. Sharp disagreements over this issue added to the sense of decline already provoked by the loss of the baby boom generation as active members, the earlier anxiety caused by the civil rights movement, fierce dissension over inclusive language and the status of women, and contention over how to conduct worship in a postmodern age. Together, these forces suggested that the impact of mainline Protestantism on American religious and public life would continue to dwindle and its ranks continue to shrink.

Key points you need to know

- Demographic changes in the years after World War II affected mainline Protestantism, bringing numerical growth, expansion of church facilities, and a sense that religion was flourishing.
- The ecumenical movement, mass revivalism, and figures such as Norman Vincent Peale fostered a spirit of cooperation and shared identity among mainline Protestants.
- The Cold War threat of "godless communism" strengthened the idea that the US was a religious, righteous nation.
- Mainline Protestantism began to decline both in influence and membership during the 1960s.
- Contributing to that decline were a drop in the birth rate among mainline adherents and the failure of mainline churches to retain participation of baby boomers as they moved into adulthood.
- The mainline attempted to recover by experimenting with new approaches to worship and new ways of organizing congregations in order to meet the perceived needs of persons unaffiliated with churches.
- Internal dissent over homosexuality continued to plague the mainline.

Discussion questions

1   What evidence suggests that the US experienced renewed interest in religion in the first decade and a half after World War II ended?
2   In retrospect, why do those signs of growth indicate that the religious surge may have been superficial, not a reflection of increased religious commitment?
3   What is the ecumenical movement? How did it impact mainline Protestantism?
4   What social movements of the 1960s challenged mainline Protestantism?
5   Why did the mainline begin to lose members and cultural influence?
6   How did mainline Protestantism try to reverse the decline?
7   How and why are debates over homosexuality within mainline denominations similar to and different from the earlier debates over civil rights and the role of women in the churches?
8   Do you think that mainline Protestantism in the US will continue to decline? Why or why not?

Further reading

Bellah, R.N. (1975) *The Broken Covenant: American Civil Religion in Time of Trial*, New York: Seabury Press.

Bellah, R.N., Madsen, R., Sullivan, W.M., Swidler, A., and Tipton, S.M. (1985) *Habits of the Heart: Individualism and Commitment in American Life*, Berkeley: University of California Press.

Cox, H. (1965) *The Secular City: Secularization and Urbanization in Theological Perspective*, New York: Macmillan.

Fletcher, J. (1966) *Situation Ethics: The New Morality*, Philadelphia: Westminster.

Hadaway, C.K. and Marler, P.L. (2006) 'Growth and Decline in the Mainline', in C. H. Lippy (ed.) *Faith in America: Changes Challenges, New Directions*, vol. 1, Westport, CT: Praeger.

Hadden, J. (1969) *The Gathering Storm in the Churches*. Garden City, NY: Doubleday.

Hardesty, N.A. (1987) *Inclusive Language in the Church*, Atlanta: John Knox.

Hoge, D.M., Luidens, D.W., and Johnson, B. (1994) *Vanishing Boundaries: The Religion of Protestant Baby Boomers*, Louisville, KY: Westminster John Knox.

Hudnut-Beumler, J. (1994) *Looking for God in the Suburbs: The Religion of the American Dream and its Critics, 1945-1965*, New Brunswick, NJ: Rutgers University Press.

Kelley, D.M. (1972) *Why Conservative Churches Are Growing: A Study in Sociology of Religion*, New York: Harper and Row.

Lippy, C.H. (ed.) (2006) *Faith in America: Changes, Challenges, New Directions*, 3 vols, Westport, CT: Praeger.

Redman, R. (2002) *The Great Worship Awakening: Singing a New Song in the Postmodern Church*, San Francisco: Jossey-Bass.

Rogers, J. (2009) *Jesus, the Bible, and Homosexuality: Explode the Myths, Heal the Church*, rev. edn, Louisville, KY: WestminsterJohnKnox.

Roof, W.C. (1993) *A Generation of Seekers: The Spiritual Journeys of the Baby Boom Generation*, San Francisco: HarperSanFrancisco.

Sargeant, K.H. (2000) *Seeker Churches: Promoting Traditional Religion in a Non-Traditional Way*, New Brunswick, NJ: Rutgers University Press.

Scanzoni, L.D. and Mollenkott, V.R. (1994) *Is the Homosexual My Neighbor? A Positive Christian Response*, rev. edn, New York: HarperOne.

York, T.W. (2003) *America's Worship Wars*, Peabody, MA: Hendrickson.

5 The evangelical surge

In this chapter

This chapter analyzes how evangelicalism came to dominate white Protestantism in the US as the influence of mainline denominations declined. It looks at how recent evangelicalism and fundamentalism differed from their earlier expressions in American religious life, acting in the public sector to change American society. Next, attention turns to what made evangelicalism plausible in American life. Then the chapter tracks the rise of Pentecostalism, noting why students of American religion believe that Pentecostalism's impact on American religious culture will increase.

Main topics covered

- Early fundamentalism's retreat from American culture.
- What brought evangelicalism to life by the 1960s.
- Ties between evangelicalism/fundamentalism and the "religious right" in American politics.
- Why evangelicalism succeeded.
- How Pentecostalism began to eclipse fundamentalism by the early twenty-first century.

A new style of evangelicalism

In 1950, mainline Protestants outnumbered evangelicals. Exact numbers are elusive, but some estimates suggest that just over 8 per cent of all church members in 1950 could be called evangelicals. By 2010, the picture looked very different. A survey conducted by the Pew Forum on Religion and Public Life indicated that by 2010, even with historically African American denominations omitted, evangelicals made up 26.3 per cent of the total American population, not just those religiously affiliated. Mainline Protestants could claim only 18.1 per cent. Some growth came from a higher birth rate among evangelicals; some came from efforts to attract persons who had no religious affiliation. Only a few switched from mainline denominations. What led to this evangelical surge?

The story of evangelicalism's rise is striking because in the 1920s, pundits wrote obituaries for evangelicalism, especially its fundamentalist expression. In the celebrated "Monkey Trial" in Tennessee in 1925 that convicted John Scopes of breaking a state law banning the teaching of evolutionary theory in the public schools, defense attorney Clarence Darrow (1857–1938) made fundamentalism's biblical literalism seem anachronistic.

News writers, such as the *Baltimore Sun*'s H.L. Mencken (1880–1956), ridiculed fundamentalism, making it appear anti-intellectual. Consequently American fundamentalists retreated from the public eye, avoiding active engagement in public affairs. Society for them became a place fraught with evil and temptation. Evangelicalism's message of personal conversion sought to rescue folk from the clutches of such evil and render them pure, set apart from a dirty world. At the same time, evangelicals founded networks of institutions to sustain their vision, including schools and colleges, publishing houses, radio stations, and a host of periodicals.

This retreat from the public square did not mean that all evangelicals or even all fundamentalists were hostile to the larger world. Some saw signs that all was not lost. After all, mainline Protestants, despite their more liberal views, still exercised a kind of cultural hegemony. Public school children still recited prayers and often heard the scriptures read. With this veneer of righteousness cloaking public life, an evangelical world flourished beneath the surface. Most evangelicals applauded the efforts to pit a righteous America against godless communism symbolized by the Congressional action of the 1950s that inserted the phrase "under God" in the pledge of allegiance and placed "In God We Trust" on all coins and currency. For evangelicals, these were not hollow gestures but revealed an enduring religious substratum buttressing national life.

Figure 5.1 The Scopes Trial in 1925, pictured here, symbolized the conflicting perspectives between American Protestants called fundamentalists and those who wanted to affirm new scientific currents, like the theory of evolution

---

Box 5.1 Defining key terms

Sometimes words like "evangelicalism" and "fundamentalism" are used interchangeably although they are not exact synonyms. It is also not always clear how Pentecostalism is related to, but yet different from, fundamentalism. Here are some guidelines:

- *Evangelicalism* usually refers to a Protestant movement rooted in the eighteenth century revivals called the Great Awakening. It emphasizes individual inner experiences of conversion, sometimes filled with emotion. It also takes the Bible seriously as the primary guide for belief and practice.
- *Fundamentalism* is a subset of evangelicalism that emerged in the late nineteenth century in response to new theological ideas and changes in American culture that were thought to be undermining orthodox Christianity and biblical authority. This movement wanted to return to the basics (fundamentals) of Christian belief. Fundamentalists stress the divinity of Jesus, the historical reality of supernatural events recorded in the Bible, and belief in the death and resurrection of Jesus as the only path to salvation.
- *Pentecostalism*, another subset of evangelicalism, developed parallel to fundamentalism. Most Pentecostals share fundamentalism's core beliefs, but also emphasize "gifts of the Spirit" (especially glossolalia or speaking in tongues) to confirm their salvation. These gifts, described in the New Testament book of Acts, first appeared on the Day of Pentecost.

An early sign of evangelicalism's renewal came in 1942 when the National Association of Evangelicals (NAE) formed in St. Louis, MO. It welcomed denominations, local congregations, and individuals as members. The NAE was committed to making an evangelical understanding of Christianity relevant to the times and as credible as the liberal belief style associated with mainline American Protestant denominations. It also countered the American Council of Christian Churches, an aggressively fundamentalist group founded a year earlier that spurned association with non-fundamentalists; cooperation could taint their quest for salvation.

The popular, expanding ministry of Billy Graham provided another hopeful sign. As noted before, Graham's crusades usually secured backing from mainline groups, as well as evangelical ones. Graham's message, however, was quintessentially evangelical. In his fiery preaching, Bible held aloft in his hand, Graham exhorted listeners to make an intense personal commitment to Christ, the only hope for happiness in this life and glory in the life to come.

But Graham and others, such as the NAE's first president, the Boston pastor Harold Ockenga (1905–85), and Carl F.H. Henry (1913–2003), a theologian and college friend of Graham and another of the founders of the NAE, were concerned. They sensed that the more liberal tone of mainline Protestantism had garnered greater intellectual plausibility than evangelicalism. Liberal views also undergirded most universities and the Protestant theological schools that trained pastors. They believed a more orthodox evangelical perspective could command intellectual respect, a respect lost because a stridently separatist and theologically bland fundamentalism was popularly regarded as synonymous with evangelicalism. Henry addressed these concerns in his first book, *The Uneasy Conscience of Modern Fundamentalism*. He rejected both the optimism of liberal thought and the separatism of extreme fundamentalism, while insisting that Christian belief must have a strong biblical base.

In 1956, Henry became the founding editor of *Christianity Today*, backed by Graham and supported by the NAE. The journal offered commentary on political, societal, and ethical issues from an evangelical, but rigorously intellectual perspective. By 2010, the journal's circulation approached 150,000; its readership likely nearly double that figure. Additional efforts to shore up the intellectual credibility of a resurgent evangelicalism meant founding theological schools that could compete with those of the mainline or even more liberal independent seminaries in terms of curriculum, faculty, and academic stature. Fuller Theological Seminary, established in California in 1947, joined the more theologically conservative Dallas Theological Seminary, which opened in Texas in 1924. Stridently fundamentalist schools also flourished. Among the most well known remains Bob Jones University, established in Florida in 1927, relocated to Cleveland, TN, in 1933, and then to Greenville, SC, in 1947. Denominationally unaffiliated, it epitomizes the separatist fundamentalist school.

By 1960, evangelicalism had penetrated American religious life. The events of the 1960s that contributed to the decline of mainline Protestantism proved the reverse for evangelicalism.

Evangelicalism's ascendancy

The social movements of the 1960s invigorated American evangelicalism. Historian Joel Carpenter talked about the "reawakening" of the fundamentalist strand of evangelicalism. *Newsweek* proclaimed 1976 as "the year of the evangelical" following the election of Southern Baptist Jimmy Carter to the presidency that November. Carter had talked freely about his faith during the campaign, using the "born again" language familiar to evangelicals.

What brought about this revitalization of a religious style consigned to the fringe of Protestant life for half a century? For some, the Supreme Court decisions of the 1960s restricting devotional religious activities in public schools ominously signaled the decay of those core values thought central to American life. A decade earlier, those values received confirmation when "In God We Trust" became the national motto. A creeping secularism was dismantling the moral fiber of the nation, also evidenced in increased attention given to teaching science as the "space race" got underway when in 1957 the Soviet Union launched Sputnik, the first satellite.

Recall the concern accompanying the so-called sexual revolution of the 1960s, the women's movement, the introduction of new means of artificial birth control, and a fascination with situation ethics. Calls for "women's liberation" challenged women's roles as homemakers and wives dutifully subordinate to their husbands, and the increased stridency of gay, lesbian, and transgender Americans for full acceptance convinced many evangelicals that marriage and family life were endangered. Evangelicals railed against the proposed Equal Rights amendment to the US Constitution and harshly criticized moves to extend marriage rights to homosexuals. Most failed to see that other challenges to the family, such as a rising divorce rate, affected evangelicals in roughly the same proportion as the larger population. Adding to these fears were the challenges to legal authority implicit in both the civil rights movement and the Vietnam War protest movement. As ministers and rabbis, priests and nuns took to the streets calling for change, more evangelicals saw all social authority collapsing.

Box 5.2 What brought evangelicalism to life?

Several social, political, and religious forces worked in tandem to revitalize evangelicalism after World War II. Among them were:

- a new appreciation of the supernatural to counter the rationalism and naturalism of science and technology;
- fears of moral collapse in American culture resulting from the sexual revolution, situation ethics, the introduction of the birth control pill, the end of devotional religious exercises in the public schools, and movements such as women's liberation and gay liberation;
- the sense that social protest, epitomized by the civil rights movement and the antiwar movement of the Vietnam era, joined with theological relativism to denigrate respect for authority;
- a conviction that mainline Protestantism condoned these dangerous cultural shifts or was helpless to stop them.

For two generations, evangelicals had remained on the sidelines, believing a religious veneer still covered the culture. With that veneer stripped away, all that was righteous crumbled. There were "culture wars," as analyst James Davison Hunter put it, as opposing sides battled to control the nation's soul. It was time for evangelicals to save not only individual souls, but also the soul of the nation.

Many evangelical congregations started "Christian schools" where prayer and Bible reading were integral and moral values inculcated. Many had only white students, reflecting anxiety about newly integrated public schools. Another educational initiative followed the 1961 publication of *The Genesis Flood* by John C. Whitcomb (1924–) and Henry M. Morris (1918–2006). A growing number of evangelicals presented "creation science" as an alternative to Darwinian evolutionary theory. Morris started what became the Institute for Creation Research at a small Christian college in California. Later moving to Texas, the institute once offered undergraduate and graduate degrees in creation science. As efforts grew to introduce instruction in creation science, lawsuits followed. In the 1960s and 1970s, courts repeatedly struck down efforts to include creation science in school curricula. Both the efforts and their defeat provided fodder for evangelicals, particularly fundamentalists who saw the Genesis creation narrative as scientific fact, not a statement of religious truth. By the end of the twentieth century, some spoke of intelligent design, although a federal district court in Pennsylvania in 2005 found intelligent design a religious notion, and teaching it a violation of the separation of church and state.

Evangelicals also used communications media and techniques from popular culture to promote their vision of the ideal society. As early as the 1920s, evangelicals took to the radio waves. By the late 1930s and 1940s, Charles E. Fuller (1887–1968) stood at the forefront, becoming one of the first religious figures to buy commercial airtime. At its peak, his "The Old-Fashioned Revival Hour" reached more than ten million listeners each week.

When television eclipsed radio as the most popular medium for home entertainment, evangelicals quickly adapted. For example, Marion G. "Pat" Robertson (1930–) established the Christian Broadcasting Network (CBN) in 1961 in Virginia. Robertson in turn launched the careers of two well-known religious television personalities, Jim Bakker (1940–) and his then-wife Tammy Faye Bakker (1942–2007). Mastering the variety and talk show format, the Bakkers took their program to the Trinity Broadcasting Network, before establishing their own evangelical empire near Charlotte, NC. Charges of tax fraud and sexual misconduct effectively ended the careers of these Assemblies of God evangelists. But their approach in presenting the evangelical message in a lively, entertaining way became widely imitated, remaining a staple of evangelical communication in the early twenty-first century.

Print media also took the evangelical message to a wide audience. Evangelicals penned novels emphasizing conversion as the sole hope for both individuals and society. The wildly popular *The Late, Great Planet Earth*, written by Hal Lindsey (1929–) with the assistance of Carole C. Carlson, appeared in 1970, becoming an instant bestseller. By 1990, more than twenty-eight million copies had been sold. Lindsey and Carlson also collaborated on *Satan Is Alive and Well on Planet Earth*, published in 1972. In 1973, a film version of *The Late, Great Planet Earth* appeared. All reflected the fundamentalist approach to history Lindsey absorbed while studying at Dallas Theological Seminary. Assuming a literal interpretation of scripture and a strident supernaturalism, the novels divided history into epochs or dispensations, with the last ending in the final confrontation between good and evil and the physical Second Coming of Christ. The name for this theological approach is premillennial dispensationalism.

Bookstores added "Christian fiction" and "Christian romance" sections, with "Christian" almost always denoting an evangelical, if not fundamentalist, posture. Even so, the success of a series of sixteen novels co-authored by evangelical writers Tim LaHaye (1926–) and Jerry B. Jenkins (1949–) was astounding. All sixteen focus on those "left behind" following the rapture or taking of believers into the heavens that premillennial dispensationalism sees as signaling the end times. The series urged readers to be "born again," the evangelical code for a conversion experience, to avoid being "left behind" to face the cataclysmic horrors expected to accompany the apocalyptic end of time. The first of the novels appeared in 1995; within fifteen years, total sales for the series exceeded sixty-five million.

Historians who looked at other aspects of material culture for clues about evangelicalism's growing popularity found other evidence. For example, in the 1990s, millions of teenagers and young adults sported plastic bracelets carrying the letters "WWJD." They stood for a question: "what would Jesus do?" Although few knew that the question was the subtitle of a bestselling late-nineteenth-century novel by Charles M. Sheldon, *In His Steps*, those who wore them carried a visual, material reminder of their personal evangelical religious commitment. Of course, the bracelets also served as a way for evangelicals to recognize kindred spirits; one could assume that another wearing the same bracelet shared common beliefs and moral values.

New approaches enrich evangelicalism

Evangelical hopes soared when the born-again Jimmy Carter became president in 1977, but the most conservative – particularly fundamentalists – became disenchanted when Carter's administration did not move to end legalized abortion, return prayer and Bible reading to the schools, or otherwise promote so-called traditional values. The cultural divide over abortion widened in the late 1970s. When the Supreme Court issued *Roe v. Wade* in 1973, few evangelicals took notice. Some Southern Baptist leaders believed it supported individual choice, a longstanding Baptist principle of faith, and removed intrusion into private matters. Many evangelical pastors, such as Jerry Falwell (1933–2007) dismissed abortion as a religious concern only to Catholics, insisting that they sought to save individual souls, not to dictate government policy.

The evangelical mood gradually shifted, in part because of prodding from evangelical theologian Francis A. Schaeffer (1912–84), an American with a ministry based in Switzerland. Schaeffer urged evangelicals to become politically active, castigating those who consigned personal faith and societal life to separate spheres. A popular lecturer on campuses and a widely read author, Schaeffer saw abortion as evidence that secular humanism had captivated western civilization. For him, abortion not only sanctioned the murder of unborn children but also promoted sexual license by allowing for the termination of unwanted pregnancies.

Schaeffer's influence penetrated into evangelical circles, prompting Jerry Falwell in 1979 to found Moral Majority. A religiously conservative political action body, Moral Majority condemned the women's movement, abortion rights, and homosexuality. It also worked to elect officials whose views reflected this posture. Falwell insisted that Moral Majority cemented Ronald Reagan's victory over Jimmy Carter in the 1980 presidential election. Reagan mastered evangelical rhetoric on issues such as abortion, but did not expend political capital promoting evangelical goals. Soon other similar groups entered the fray. Pat Robertson, for example, attempted a presidential run in 1988. When that proved unsuccessful, he steered supporters into the Christian Coalition that concentrated on grass-roots political activity. Falwell disbanded the Moral Majority in the late 1980s and the Christian Coalition receded from public view, but ties between evangelicalism and conservative politics, often identified with the Republican party, continued.

New approaches to congregational life, noted in Chapter 4, also enriched evangelicalism. Many independent pastors followed Falwell's steps, building both a local and national presence through televising their services. The Willow Creek Community Church model inspired many evangelical congregations to downplay or shed denominational affiliation while marketing their ministry to those alienated from organized religion. Like Willow Creek, the Calvary Chapel movement, begun in California by Chuck (Charles W.) Smith (1927–), has scores of affiliated congregations, as does the Association of Vineyard Churches, started by John Wimber (1934–97). Wimber joined evangelicalism with Pentecostal expression when he talked about how believers could experience the "signs and wonders" of spiritual power through a deepening faith. Both Calvary Chapel and Vineyard congregations may represent new evangelical denominations in embryonic form. The role of the megachurch in American religious life receives more examination in Chapter 8.

Not all pioneers of new ways to structure ministry came from those eschewing denominational affiliation. Willow Creek's founding pastor, mentioned earlier, had ties to the mainline Reformed Church in America. The Willow Creek church itself, however, makes little mention of that identification. Such also held true for one of the earliest megachurch endeavors, the Crystal Cathedral in California. Robert H. Schuller (1926–), who in 1955 started that congregation, likewise received ordination in that denomination.

In 1980, Rick Warren (1954–) launched the Saddleback Church in California. Since then, it has become another model for the evangelical megachurch, thanks to Warren's bestselling books about "purpose-driven" lives and churches. Warren and Saddleback had connections with the Southern Baptist Convention, but downplayed them in order not to alienate those who found denominational labels negative. Warren's stature led Barack Obama to invite him to give the invocation at the 2009 presidential inauguration, much to the consternation of non-evangelicals.

Other evangelicals regarded the megachurch as a deterrent to spirituality. The institutional apparatus associated with a church claiming perhaps more than 10,000 members eclipsed individual faith development. Brian McLaren (1956–), a one-time English professor and pastor, is among those who sought yet another model, one attuned to the postmodern ethos. Some have called this model the "emerging" church; while others talk of the "emergent" church. Both avoid large-scale institutional structures, often preferring "house church" or small home gathering as the locus for

Figure 5.2 Robert Schuller, standing here in front of the Crystal Cathedral in California, was a pioneer in developing the megachurch as a new approach to spread evangelical styles of Protestant Christianity

Courtesy of Joan Adlen/Getty Images

worship. Both see the spiritual quest resulting in engagement in society. Some remain attached to larger congregations, but many have no denominational ties or connections with larger bodies.

In addition, the devastating economic recession of the first decade of the twenty-first century affected many megachurches. Many had large operating budgets. The recession brought a drop in financial support from members and regular attendees, as well as from those who participated in a megachurch's ministry through television, special interest groups, or some other activity. In late 2010, for example, the Crystal Cathedral, with the daughter of founding pastor Robert Schuller at the helm, filed for bankruptcy protection. Its plight, some analysts thought, was an omen for other megachurches that were overextended financially.

Division within the evangelical ranks

Evangelicalism's growth assured that this Protestant style would have enduring influence in American culture, but the social forces that caused dissension within mainline Protestantism also brought contention and disagreement among evangelicals. Illustrative are responses to the feminist movement rooted in the 1960s and 1970s, the cultural debates over homosexuality, ties between religion and politics, and the increasing concern for ecology.

Evangelical denominations were among the most reluctant to ordain women or grant them positions of leadership within congregations. Some found in the creation narrative in the first chapter of Genesis, in which woman is fashioned from the rib of the first man, an indication that divine intention subordinated female to male. Additional support came from New Testament passages that urged women to be subject to their husbands (e.g. Ephesians 5:22), to refrain from speaking in church, and not to instruct men in matters of faith. Those taking this position opposed the Equal Rights Amendment to the US Constitution, proposed in 1972 but never ratified.

Yet feminist issues gave birth to organizations that revealed how divided evangelicals were over gender issues and the role of women in the church. Christians for Biblical Equality (CBE), for example, emerged in 1969. Drawing support primarily from biblical inerrantists, CBE sought to rethink gender roles to allow full equality to women while adhering to a literal reading of the biblical text. In 1973, some evangelical feminists crossed denominational lines to form the Evangelical Women's Caucus (renamed the Evangelical and Ecumenical Women's Caucus in 1990). This group, which sponsored the journal *Christian Feminism Today*, called not only for the ordination of women, but for discussion of issues as diverse as inclusive language and homosexuality, It became known for advocating full inclusion, regardless of gender or sexual orientation, in evangelical churches.

More traditional approaches received a voice when the *Christianity Today* publishing empire launched *Today's Christian Woman* in the late 1970s. Although the journal ceased publication in 2009, it promoted traditional gender roles for women, despite surveys indicating that its readers no longer fit the image of the ideal Christian woman the magazine promoted; many had entered the paid labor force, experienced divorce, and looked for greater equality for women in both church and society. Efforts to craft another alternative came from the Council on Biblical Manhood and Womanhood, organized in 1987 in part as a response to the CBE, whose position was seen as undermining biblical authority. For this group, the biblical mandate required distinct and separate gender roles, but ones that were complementary and equally necessary for human happiness.

Women's issues reflected the disproportionate gender ratio within all Protestant groups, whether evangelical or mainline. Since the eighteenth century, if not earlier, women outnumbered men as church members by at least a two-to-one ratio. Some evangelicals, even if hesitant to recognize women in leadership roles, launched efforts to draw men into the ranks of the faithful. One early effort was the Christian Men's Network, founded by Edwin Louis Cole (1922–2002) in 1977. Reaching its peak influence in the 1980s, Cole's group promoted "maximized manhood," promoting male spirituality and leadership within both church and family. The most well-known ministry targeting men is Promise Keepers, started in 1991 by former University of Colorado football coach Bill McCartney (1940–). For a time in the 1990s, Promise Keepers drew thousands of men to religious rallies held in football stadiums, places regarded as typically "male" spaces, where speakers urged them not only to be faithful husbands and fathers, but to accept their God-given role as spiritual leaders within families and as agents to end racial division. By the early twenty-first century, however, such large-scale endeavors faded.

Issues regarding homosexuality and same-gender marriage plagued evangelicals as much as mainline Protestants. For many evangelicals, homosexuality is a sin, condemned in the Hebrew Bible's Levitical code and in the Christian New Testament writings attributed to St. Paul. For them, marriage is limited to a covenant between one man and one woman, although some wrestled with the implications of the rising divorce rate. Gay-supportive groups within some evangelical denominations and congregations remained more beneath the surface than in the mainline. Some became more affirming, acknowledging the cultural influences on biblical texts relating to same-gender matters as they had with passages making women subordinate to men.

The Evangelical and Ecumenical Women's Caucus pleaded for rethinking religious hostility to lesbians. Brian McLaren insisted that homosexual persons as children of God deserved respect and those in committed relationships deserved pastoral care. Complicating conversations among evangelicals was the view that faith could change one's sexual orientation, despite scientific evidence to the contrary. Most "ex-gay" ministries such as Exodus, International had evangelical roots. Nevertheless, some congregations welcomed gay, lesbian, and transgender persons into membership and positions of leadership. Like mainline Protestants, most evangelicals found hatred of homosexuals and violence against them inconsistent with Christian faith. A well-known exception is independent Baptist pastor Fred Phelps (1929–), whose Kansas-based followers organize anti-gay demonstrations at events ranging from funerals of military personnel to gay pride celebrations. Many of the debates among evangelicals over gender roles and sexuality will again come under examination from a different perspective in Chapter 10.

On matters of feminism and sexuality, evangelicals increasingly split on generational lines. Older evangelicals held more conservative positions; younger evangelicals were more accepting, seeing poverty, social justice, peace, and the environment as more pressing. Some seasoned evangelicals took a broader view. Theologian Ron Sider (1939–), for example, helped organize Evangelicals for Social Action in 1978. Although the group initially focused on economic injustice and the unequal distribution of wealth, its vision gradually expanded. Jim Wallis (1948–), founder of the Sojourners community in Washington, DC, has long called for living out one's faith in the world, not through partisan politics but through alleviating human suffering resulting from unemployment, lack of housing, poverty, or blatant injustice.

Wallis and Sider are among those calling for a new respect for the environment as God's creation, not as a commodity to enhance human comfort. This approach also undergirds the Evangelical Environmental Network (EEN), founded in 1993. The EEN supports sustainable living and environmental care through its journal, *Creation Care*. In addition, many evangelicals cooperate with other groups, including non-evangelical ones, through the National Religious Partnership for the Environment. We will return to the "culture wars" over many of these issues that distinguish evangelicals from others in Chapter 9.

What made evangelicalism plausible?

The evangelical approach to scripture presumes belief in the supernatural, just as the understanding of religious experience – being "born again" – presumes the validity of feeling and emotion. Both seemed marginalized in the twentieth century's fascination with science and technology, representing the ascendancy of reason. But the shortcomings of scientism became increasingly apparent. Use of the atomic bomb in World War II showed not only what science could do, but also its destructive power. The Vietnam War added to that awareness, bringing the horrors of war into American homes through television. Experimentation with illicit drugs, symbolized by claims that LSD generated authentic religious experience, added to the perception that science and sheer rationality might not bring utopia. Evangelicalism's emphasis on feeling suggested that human life shorn of an affective dimension was flawed. Evangelicalism offered a counterpoint to rationalism and scientism taken to extremes.

Evangelicalism's affirmation of biblical authority and "traditional" values also seemed a welcome alternative to the ambiguity generated by an age of social protest and situation ethics that made individuals the final arbiters of right and wrong, truth and falsehood. Such uncertainty led to the apocalyptic horror of *The Late, Great Planet Earth* or the despair of those "left behind" when the rapture whisked believers off to heaven. This secure authority went deeper than that which Dean Kelley had

---

Box 5.3 What gives evangelicalism credibility?

To attract adherents, evangelicalism, like other religious orientations, had to convince people that it was worth believing, that it was plausible, and would provide a framework of meaning for their lives. Giving plausibility to evangelicalism were:

- use of media to promote belief in the supernatural;
- popular recognition that experience or feeling, not just thinking, gives life meaning;
- increasing awareness of the limits of science and technology to create the ideal life.
- a sense that right belief and allegiance to absolute authority alleviate the angst caused by the ambiguities of a postmodern age.

offered as a reason for conservative growth in the 1960s. Now it stood in marked contrast to postmodernism. Difficult to define precisely, postmodernism denotes a way of thinking that rejects any absolute authority outside of individual experience in every arena of life. By using biblical inerrancy to buttress the authority of scripture and advocating traditional gender roles thought to be sanctioned by scripture, evangelicals (and especially fundamentalists) built life on an impregnable foundation.

The rise of Pentecostalism

By the twenty-first century, the forces enriching fundamentalism were also revitalizing Pentecostalism. Many analysts believed that Pentecostalism would soon dominate global Christian life. Henry Pitney VanDusen (1897–1975), president of New York City's liberal Union Theological Seminary, predicted in the late 1950s that a "third force" was about to eclipse other forms of Christianity. That third force was the Pentecostalism that penetrated both Protestant and Roman Catholic branches of Christianity.

The modern Pentecostal movement first caused a stir in the early twentieth century In 1906, revivals in Los Angeles at which glossolalia (speaking in tongues) was prevalent attracted national attention. That year, in the mountains of North Carolina, the Church of God formed, claiming that the charismatic "gifts of the spirit" described in the New Testament – primarily glossolalia and divine healing – were accessible to contemporary believers. Several Pentecostal denominations formed to sustain this vision, but critics remained skeptical of the enthusiasm and emotionalism associated with Pentecostalism, dismissing as "holy rollers" those who said the Spirit empowered them to speak in tongues or to heal. In the late 1940s and 1950s, Pentecostalism benefited from a fresh interest in divine healing and charismatic gifts. One well-known healing evangelist was Oral Roberts (1918–2009), who conducted old-fashioned revivals at which hundreds claimed experiences of healing, and who also pioneered the use of television ministries to promote his message.

In the 1960s other Pentecostal expressions experienced growth beyond the historic Pentecostal denominations such as the Assemblies of God and the Church of God (Cleveland, TN). Charismatic clusters formed within many Protestant denominations. Roman Catholics sponsored conferences and retreats for Catholics who felt the Spirit's power. Pentecostal denominations and congregations experienced accelerated growth as the twentieth century drew to a close. The American Religious Identification Survey (ARIS), for example, indicated that the overall number of Pentecostals in the US grew 73.8 per cent between 1990 and 2008. During that period, the Assemblies of God witnessed a growth of 31.3 per cent and the Church of God (Cleveland, TN), 12.4 per cent. Given mainline Protestant decline, the growth becomes more stunning.

Among non-denominational congregations, the previously mentioned Association of Vineyard Churches blends traditional evangelical and charismatic (Pentecostal) styles. The same holds for a congregation in Texas known globally because of its use of television. The Lakewood Church in Houston, established in 1959 by one-time Southern Baptist John Osteen (1925–99), now claims in excess of 40,000 members with the founder's son, Joel Osteen (1963–) its senior pastor. The congregation purchased a sports arena, transforming it into a place for worship.

Pentecostalism benefited from the same social and cultural factors that buttressed evangelical plausibility generally. In retrospect, the overall evangelical ascendancy had roots in some forces emerging in the 1950s. The baby boom era birth rate boosted all evangelical groups even more than it did mainline Protestantism; more conservative bodies experienced a greater rate of growth proportionately than the mainline. When the mainline birth rate began to decline, the birth rate among evangelical groups dropped slightly if at all. Many evangelicals rejected artificial means of contraception, believing, along with the Roman Catholic Church, that use of such devices interfered with the mandate to "be fruitful and multiply" (Genesis 1:28).

Pentecostal groups have also profited disproportionately from the increase in immigration from Latin America since the 1965 changes in immigration law, whose broader implications will be discussed later. Documented (and undocumented) immigrants from Latin America identified primarily with Christianity, but their style of Christianity tends to be charismatic and Pentecostal, regardless of denomination. More orthodox in belief and traditional in approach to issues such as homosexuality, Latino/a immigrants cemented Pentecostalism's growth.

Evangelical expressions of Protestant Christianity were poised to replace mainline denominations in terms of both numbers and cultural influence in the twenty-first century. The same could not be said for the nation's largest single religious group, the Roman Catholic Church, even though it, too, benefited from the new immigration.

Key points you need to know

- Early fundamentalists retreated from engagement in society, seeing the world as evil.
- Some leaders tried to make evangelicalism more intellectually and culturally respectable.
- Fears that religious and cultural values were eroding prompted evangelicals to become more politically active.
- The civil rights movement and cognate liberation movements convinced evangelicals that respect for authority had vanished.
- Evangelicals wanted to redirect American religious and common life, but had little success.
- Evangelicals ably used communications media.
- Groups like the Moral Majority and Christian Coalition helped direct fundamentalist interest in politics.
- Evangelicals, like mainline Protestants, experimented with forms of congregational life.
- Cultural factors joined with religious ones to make evangelicalism plausible.
- Today, Pentecostalism is eclipsing other evangelical expressions.

Discussion questions

1 What does evangelicalism mean? How are fundamentalism and Pentecostalism related to evangelicalism?
2 Why were fundamentalists once content to stay on the sidelines? What drew them to become active participants in public life?
3 How would you account for the resurgence of evangelicalism in the 1960s?
4 What led some to promote the intellectual respectability of evangelicalism?

5   Why did evangelicals think there was widespread disrespect for authority in American life?
6   How did evangelicals try to reshape American religious and political identity?
7   In what ways did the public schools become the battleground in the culture wars of the later twentieth century?
8   How did evangelicals make use of communications media?
9   What gave credibility to evangelicalism's vision for American life?
10 How and why did Pentecostalism eclipse fundamentalism as the major public face of evangelicalism?

Further reading

Alexander, P. (2009) *Why Pentecostalism Is the World's Fastest Growing Faith*. San Francisco: Jossey-Bass, 2009.
American Religious Identification Survey (2008) www.americanreligionsurvey-aris.org/ (accessed 4 October 2010).
Balmer, R.M. (2006) *Mine Eyes Have Seen the Glory: A Journey into the Evangelical Subculture In America*, 4th edn, New York: Oxford University Press.
Carpenter, J. (1999) *Revive Us Again: The Reawakening of American Fundamentalism*, New York: Oxford University Press.
Cox, H. (1994) *Fire from Heaven: The Rise of Pentecostal Spirituality and the Reshaping of Religion in the Twenty-First Century*, New York: Addison-Wesley.
Hankins, B. (2003) *Uneasy in Babylon: Southern Baptist Conservatives and American Culture*, Tuscaloosa: University of Alabama Press.
Henry, C.F.H. (1947) *The Uneasy Conscience of Modern Fundamentalism*, Grand Rapids, MI: Eerdmans.
Hunter, J.D. (1991) *Culture Wars: The Struggle to Define America*, New York: HarperCollins.
Marsden, G.M. (2006) *Fundamentalism and American Culture: The Shaping of Twentieth-Century Evangelicalism, 1870–1925*, 2nd edn, New York: Oxford University Press.
Pew Forum on Religion and Public Life (2010) www.pewforum.org/Topics/Religious-Affiliation/ (accessed 17 November 2012).

6 American Catholicism
A "ghetto" church no more

In this chapter

This chapter examines the ethos of American Catholicism and forces such as immigration and anti-Catholicism that shaped it. Then it discusses the impact of the Second Vatican Council and shows how social and cultural movements of the 1960s left their own imprint on Catholicism. The next section surveys trends within American Catholicism from the 1970s on, such as its moving from an inward-looking posture to one more involved in society. The chapter looks at the decline in the number of priests and women religious (nuns) over the last half century and at the recent scandals regarding sexual misconduct on the part of priests. Finally, the focus turns to the "new immigration" from Latin America, concluding with some observations about what might lie ahead if trends now in place continue.

Main topics covered

- How earlier immigration patterns made ethnicity vital to the texture of American Catholicism.
- Ways in which Protestant suspicion about Catholicism influenced Catholic identity.
- The increasing social and cultural acceptance of Catholicism by the mid 1950s.
- Catholicism's transformation because of changes launched by the Second Vatican Council.
- American Catholics' response to reaffirmation of traditional church teaching on matters such as birth control and all-male celibate priesthood.
- Why Catholicism experienced a decline in attendance at Mass and in the numbers of men entering the priesthood and women taking religious vows.
- The impact of the civil rights movement, feminism, and war protest.
- Scandals concerning alleged sexual misconduct on the part of priests.
- The importance of immigration from Latin America after 1965.
- Catholicism's future in the US.

American Catholicism in the 1950s: emerging from the "ghetto"

Although colonial Spanish and French explorers and missionaries brought their Catholic faith with them, Catholicism's strength in the US comes from two major waves of immigration. In the three decades or so before the Civil War, millions of Irish came to the US. In the 1840s alone, around two million Irish made their way to America. This Irish presence had an enduring impact; for at least a century Irish priests and prelates dominated the American church. Then in the decades between the Civil War and World War I another surge in immigration brought millions from southern, central, and eastern Europe.

Catholic immigrants often encountered hostility. American Protestants long harbored a suspicion of Catholics and their faith. Many thought Catholicism incompatible with democracy, believing that religious loyalty to church leaders – especially the pope in Rome – superseded loyalty to the state. In addition, the Catholic cycle of ritual activity, celebration of the Mass in Latin (a language none spoke and few understood), and veneration of the saints that struck outsiders as superstition stirred anti-Catholic sentiment. So did the Catholic reliance on a parochial or parish school system to educate children. Catholics sought a learning environment devoid of the Protestant assumptions informing public school curricula; Protestants thought parochial schools would never mold students into good citizens in a democracy.

Immigration patterns unintentionally encouraged folk to settle in neighborhoods, mostly in northern cities, where they surrounded themselves with what was familiar during the transition to a new national identity. So Czechs tended to settle in their own ethnic enclaves, as did Italians, Poles, Ukrainians, and a host of others. Parishes took on ethnic dimensions, keeping alive folk traditions associated with places of origin even as communicants were becoming Americans. The distinctive character of Catholic belief and practice, Protestant hostility to all things Catholic, and tightly knit ethnic neighborhoods and parishes combined with the hierarchical, authoritarian structure of Catholicism as an institution to give immigrant Catholicism what many historians have called a "ghetto" mentality. That is, Catholic enclaves remained isolated from others as if people were living in a ghetto with others of the same heritage, sometimes even frowning on marriage to another Catholic across ethnic lines.

Although Catholics constituted the largest single religious group in the nation by 1850, the millions of immigrants arriving between the Civil War and World War I caused Catholic numbers to mushroom. These immigrants often took low-paying jobs in the nation's burgeoning factories. For roughly two generations, the educational attainment of Catholics lagged considerably behind that of Protestants, especially in terms of the proportion having earned college degrees. For two to three generations Catholics were also under-represented in the ranks of business executives, political leadership, and other high-profile positions. Anti-Catholic sentiment was responsible for some of the challenges that confronted the children and grandchildren of immigrants as they sought to shed their identity as religiously and ethnically "other." For many, it was simply a matter of time and adjusting to the culture.

The era of the First World War marked the first moves away from this "ghetto" mentality. When Catholics largely supported the Allied cause, some suspicion abated.

Immigration restrictions in the 1920s meant that ethnic communities became more thoroughly Americanized; a reduction in immigrants made it harder to sustain distinctive ethnic subcultures. Occasional anti-Catholicism still erupted. The national election of 1928, when a major political party nominated a Catholic for the presidency for the first time, rekindled the embers of anti-Catholicism. But with Depression and another world war, differences faded.

By the 1950s, with "godless communism" threatening a righteous nation, emphasizing what divided Americans into different ethnic or religious communities made little sense. Rather, emphasizing what all Americans held in common became a way to promote shared American identity. In 1955, sociologist Will Herberg, in his highly acclaimed *Protestant, Catholic, Jew*, insisted that the vast majority of Americans saw little difference among Protestantism, Catholicism, and Judaism in terms of their nurturing persons of moral character to be productive, responsible citizens. Herberg regretted the functional equivalency of these three major traditions, for he believed that in the process of becoming like each other, they had all lost their prophetic stance and their ability to critique culture.

Many analysts have demonstrated that by the mid twentieth century, American Catholics had also achieved parity with their white Protestant counterparts in terms of educational attainment, type of employment, and family income. The shift across the twentieth century is astounding. Estimates suggest that in 1900, for example, only about 5 per cent of Irish American Catholics, many of whom had ancestors in the major wave of pre-Civil War immigration, had white-collar jobs. Over two generations, then, only a handful of Irish American Catholics had entered the more elite ranks of the work force. By 1990, however, about two-thirds of the nation's Catholics – regardless of ethnic heritage – held white-collar posts, and 40 per cent of Catholic families had annual incomes in excess of $50,000, well above the national average. Other perspectives on ethnicity inform some of our discussion in Chapter 12.

In addition, marriage between Catholics and non-Catholics steadily increased in the years after Vatican II; in this regard, Catholics, like other Americans, ignored religious boundaries that had once fostered a distinctive religious identity. As Catholics took their place in the cultural mainstream, they not only looked more like their Protestant counterparts in terms of socioeconomic measures, but they also echoed many of the trends evident in mainstream Protestantism when it came to their religious life and having to respond to challenges posed by larger society. They also garnered greater social and cultural acceptance.

A symbol of that acceptance came in 1960 when the Democratic Party nominated the Catholic John F. Kennedy for the presidency. Kennedy dispelled fears that church authorities would dictate political policies when he addressed the Greater Houston (Texas) Ministerial Association in the midst of the campaign. He asserted his commitment to the constitutional separation of church and state, insisting he would draw a firm line between his personal faith and his policies as president. His narrow victory over Richard Nixon in that election became another sign that Catholicism no longer had a "ghetto" identity.

Figure 6.1 The 1960 election of the Roman Catholic John F. Kennedy as president of the US symbolized the ways American Catholics had overcome hostile attitudes and made their way to the center of American life.

Courtesy of AFP/Getty Images

Box 6.1 Kennedy quells anti-Catholic fears

In September 1960, less than two months before he narrowly defeated Richard M. Nixon for the US presidency, John F. Kennedy sought to quash fears that a Catholic president would be beholden to church authorities in formulating political policy and would place personal faith above the common good. Kennedy said:

> I believe in an America where the separation of church and state is absolute; where no Catholic prelate would tell the president – should he be Catholic – how to act and no Protestant minister would tell his parishioners how to vote ... I believe in an America that is officially neither Catholic, Protestant, nor Jewish; where no public official either requests or accepts instructions on public policy from the Pope, the National Council of Churches or any other ecclesiastical source ... Finally, I believe in an America where religious intolerance will someday end, where all men and all churches are treated as equals, where every man has the same right to attend or not to attend the church of his choice.
>
> (J.F. Kennedy, "Address to the Greater Houston Ministerial Association,"
> www.americanrhetoric.com/speeches/jfkhoustonministers.html,
> accessed 14 October 2010)

Vatican II and the transformation of Catholicism

On 9 October 1958, Pope Pius XII (1876–1958) died. Nineteen days later, the College of Cardinals elected Angelo Giuseppe Roncalli (1881–1963), the prefect of Venice, to succeed him. Roncalli took the papal name of John XXIII. Pius XII was the last pope to benefit from an almost unquestioned aura of authority accorded to the papacy by the Catholic faithful. He strengthened that authority by invoking the doctrine of papal infallibility, the idea that the pope cannot err when making certain pronouncements about faith and practice, when in 1950 he proclaimed as dogma (official doctrine) the belief that the Virgin Mary, the mother of Jesus, had been taken up or assumed into the heavenly realm rather than facing mortal death. This view is known as the doctrine of the Blessed Assumption.

Most expected John XXIII, almost 77 years old when he became pope, to have a brief tenure, and church officials thought little of consequence would result from his papacy. However, roughly three months into his papacy, John XXIII called for a council to bring Catholic prelates from around the world to Rome to scrutinize all aspects of church life, making recommendations for change that the pope called *aggiornamento* or updating. The Second Vatican Council, or Vatican II, opened in October 1962 and held its final sessions in 1965.

For the American church, the significance of Vatican II lay as much in the atmosphere of expectation that surrounded it as in the changes it authorized, though many of those had a profound impact. Would the church end its long-standing opposition to use of artificial means of birth control? Would it admit women to the priesthood? Would laity share authority with priests in overseeing the ministry of local parishes? Would the church acknowledge truth in other religions, especially other branches of Christianity? Would strictures against marriage between Catholics and non-Catholics end, and would divorced persons be welcomed at the Eucharist? These questions and more created an aura of excitement. The answers that came sometimes pleased, sometimes bewildered, and sometimes disappointed the faithful.

Some changes prompted by Vatican II altered American Catholicism. When the Mass became celebrated in English rather than Latin, with the priest facing the people, worship lost some of its mystery and luminous sacrality. Yet these shifts stirred a liturgical renewal that influenced many Christian denominations. Hymnody, the songs included in worship, became transformed. Churches experimented with musical genres such as folk and rock. Some incorporated musical traditions from other cultures. The practice of confession, once an austere private baring of one's soul to a priest hidden behind a screen, became a corporate rite of reconciliation, replacing fears of doing penance to atone for shortcomings with the joy of forgiveness. Parish councils drew lay folk into planning and carrying out the ministry of the church. Recognition of marriage across Christian traditions not only reflected what had become a cultural commonplace, but also muted potential conflict within families over religious identity.

Change also came to those engaged in professional ministry. Orders of women religious or nuns rewrote guidelines; many shed the distinctive habit or garb of a bygone era for street clothes. Blending in with others stripped nuns of the aura of stern authority that went with black robes and wimples. Formation of priests took new directions. Seminaries no longer had to give preferential treatment to theological systems reflecting the thought of the medieval giant, Thomas Aquinas. Soon hundreds of nuns and priests had given up their vocations or vows, plunging into secular life.

Some joined ministers and rabbis in protests that were part of the civil rights movement and then the antiwar activities of the Vietnam era. Among the more well known were the brothers and one-time priests Daniel (1921–) and Philip (1923–2002) Berrigan, who shocked the more traditionally religious when they appeared for a time on the US Federal Bureau of Investigation's list of "most wanted fugitives." Some matters unique to the engagement of American Catholics in such social movements receive fuller treatment in Chapter 15.

The Second Vatican Council also gave increased visibility to the bishops of the church. The American bishops met regularly, often commenting on pressing social problems. Their endeavors reflect one way in which the church responded to the panoply of issues confronting all Americans, including mainline Protestants and evangelicals. Early on, the bishops spoke out against the nuclear arms race. In addition, the United States Conference of Catholic Bishops has sent representatives to testify before Congressional committees on issues such as immigration and the controversy surrounding undocumented or illegal immigrants. An official statement from the American bishops in 1999 addressed both the moral and legal issues surrounding labor conditions, calling for laws to extend principles of justice to the workplace. The bishops have also strongly opposed the practice of abortion that had given evangelicals political energy. A pastoral letter in 2000 argued, for example, that legalized abortion in the US advanced a "culture of death." Three years later, the bishops strongly opposed moves to recognize same-gender unions or marriages, reaffirming the traditional view that God designed marriage to embrace only one man and one woman. The conservative stance taken by the bishops on some issues echoed traditional church teaching, but disappointed those hoping for more openness and change. It also allied church leaders with some once seen almost as enemies of Truth, especially conservative evangelical groups.

Box 6.2　Catholic bishops oppose abortion

The following extract, from a resolution adopted unanimously by the United States Conference of Catholic Bishops at their annual meeting on 7 November 1989, is one of many statements urging Catholics to oppose "pro-choice" efforts to sustain and expand abortion rights:

> For us abortion is of overriding concern because it negates two of our most fundamental moral imperatives: respect for innocent life, and preferential concern for the weak and defenseless. As we said three years ago in reaffirming our Pastoral Plan for Pro-Life Activities: "Because victims of abortion are the most vulnerable and defenseless members of the human family, it is imperative that we, as Christians called to serve the least among us, give urgent attention and priority to this issue. Our concern is intensified by the realization that a policy and practice allowing over one and a half million abortions annually cannot but diminish respect for life in other areas." No Catholic can responsibly take a "pro-choice" stand when the "choice" in question involves the taking of innocent human life.
>
> (From "Resolution on Abortion,"
> www.usccb.org/prolife/tdocs/resabort89.shtml, accessed 18 October 2010)

Vatican II spurred leaders to attempt to influence public life. It also left some hopes unfulfilled. For example, the introduction of the "pill" just as plans for the council got underway led many to think the church would jettison the traditional prohibition against use of artificial means of birth control. Hope increased when a Vatican II commission recommended change. But in his encyclical *Humanae Vitae* (1968), Paul VI (1897–1978), who succeeded John XXIII, upheld traditional church teaching. In addition, calls to enhance opportunities for women aroused by second-wave feminism, along with a growing shortage of priests, fueled expectation that the church would soon allow both women priests and married priests. But official policy recognized only a celibate male priesthood as the norm, a position reasserted by Pope John Paul II (1920–2005).

Whither the Catholic faithful?

Despite the updating of Vatican II, Catholicism in the US seemed adrift. Attendance at Mass plummeted steadily. The biggest loss came among younger Catholics who did not see regular attendance as integral to their spirituality. This erosion paralleled trends among mainline Protestants. Another parallel came in a lower birth rate for Catholic families whose roots in the US stretched back to the beginning of the twentieth century or earlier. Although official teaching banned using artificial means of birth control, American Catholic women, according to many polls, used the "pill" in roughly the same proportion as the population at large. Clearly, church mandates did not necessarily determine behavior, even among those who self-identified as "good" Catholics.

Other issues relating to sexuality continued to agitate the faithful. One already noted was the refusal of the church to reconsider the all-male priesthood. Consequently there was an erosion of vocations among women religious. Many chafed at the notion that the ministry of nuns was inferior to that of male priests. In addition, liberation theology, with its claim that faith freed all persons to develop their full potential, took hold in much of American Christianity after its initial stirrings in Latin America. Catholic women theologians began to develop perspectives, some of which will be discussed in Chapter 17, that linked calls for women priests, the feminist impulse sweeping through the larger culture, and liberation thought.

By 2010, more than half of all parish priests served more than one congregation. Roughly one-quarter of them were foreign-born and recruited from abroad in an effort to compensate for the dramatic decline in the number of men entering seminaries. Deacons and lay ministers offered some respite, but so did women religious and some women who worked as lay ministers. Hence a decline in priestly vocations meant that women did take on more pastoral functions, albeit without authority to administer the sacraments.

The cultural divide over homosexuality also left its mark on post-Vatican II American Catholicism. In 1969, a San Diego priest who was also a professional psychologist began a ministry with gay and lesbian Catholics that evolved into a national organization called Dignity. At first, scores of local parishes opened their doors to Dignity for meetings that often included a Eucharistic celebration. However, as church authorities continued to label homosexual behavior of any sort as sin, many bishops began to refuse to allow Dignity chapters to meet on church property. Despite active opposition from the church leadership, Dignity has continued to grow, becoming a Catholic voice for inclusion of gays and lesbians in both church and society with its presence felt most strongly in urban areas. The contentious conversation over homosexuality illuminates some of the discussion in Chapter 10.

Nothing, however, had the force of a wrenching internal scandal, one that erupted in America and then in much of Europe, as the twenty-first century opened. The uproar concerned sexual abuse perpetrated by priests, most often directed at young boys. In many cases, allegations came to light decades after the abuse had occurred, although bishops and other leaders appear often to have known of the improper activity. The church faced stinging criticism for its decades-long efforts to cover up the problem and its failure to discipline priests who had broken not only civil law but the church's moral law. Some high-ranking leaders, such as Boston's Cardinal Bernard Law, were forced to resign. Thousands of men (and women) have reported sexual abuse going back to the 1960s; by 2010, hundreds of priests had been defrocked and some sentenced to prison terms. Organizations such as Voice of the Faithful, founded in Boston in 2002 when the scandal first broke open, have called for significant change in how priestly formation occurs, accountability and discipline when charges of misconduct arise, and support systems for the individuals victimized and their families. Moves to require psychological testing of candidates for the priesthood in an effort to identify potential pedophiles and predators seemed to many only meager first steps.

Scores of court cases forced the church to pay large sums to victims to compensate for the emotional and physical trauma they had suffered. The payments, totaling more than two billion dollars by 2010, threatened the financial stability of the church, which was already, like other religious bodies, watching monetary support from the faithful steadily decline. Consequently, many dioceses watched their financial base disintegrate; by 2010 at least seven dioceses in the US had filed for bankruptcy protection.

Even so, the scandal continued into the second decade of the twenty-first century. By then similar charges had come to light in places such as Ireland and Germany, some suggesting that Pope Benedict XVI (1927–) was complicit in efforts to cover up accusations brought against priests in Germany while he served as archbishop of Munich. As the crisis became global, Vatican leaders set up a symposium in Rome in early 2012 at which bishops and heads of religious orders, in consultation with experts on child abuse, theologians and ethicists, and psychologists, would recommend a church-wide policy designed to prevent abuse in the future and to respond to cases when they occurred.

Skeptics faulted the church for waiting so long to take such action; many doubted that a single policy would work across cultures. Those already disaffected with the church found in the scandal fresh support for their critique. More significantly, though, the millions who remained faithful found their trust in the church and its leaders shattered. Students of the American church suggest that the scandal will infect the church for decades to come.

Perhaps abortion was the only issue relating to sexuality where views of many of those who remained faithful Catholics meshed with church teaching and views of leaders. Grass-roots opposition to abortion retained strength among American Catholic laity, although Catholics were not of a single mind. To many observers, the range of controversies over women, homosexuality, sexual abuse by priests, and even abortion underscored what seemed a chronic problem of dealing with the nature and character of human sexuality. Tradition trumped scientific understanding. As a result, the mystique of the church's teaching authority crumbled.

Nonetheless, millions continued to identify themselves as Catholic, often demonstrating a popular devotion to aspects of Catholic practice that reflected a generations-old intertwining of ethnicity and religion. Robert Orsi, for example, has shown that despite the movement of descendants of Italian immigrants from areas of East Harlem in New York City, thousands still return each year to honor the Madonna, the Virgin Mary, in a street festival and procession that echoes popular devotion of decades earlier. Orsi has also demonstrated how thousands remain devoted to the saints – he looked particularly at women's devotion to St. Jude – in their personal spirituality, even if they do not always adhere to church teaching or attend Mass as frequently as earlier generations did. In other words, a popular Catholicism, one defined by the people themselves, flourishes alongside institutional expressions that may have increasingly less appeal to the faithful.

The new face of Catholicism in the twenty-first century

Unlike mainline Protestant groups, the Catholic Church in the US has continued to grow in the decades after World War II, albeit not at the same rate as the population has grown. In 1990, for example, the nation was home to a population of around 248.7 million people. Around 65 million were Catholics. By 2008, the nation's population had grown by around 20.9 per cent to just over 301.6 million. Although the number of Catholics had increased to around 75 million, the church's growth rate was only around 15.5 per cent, meaning that the proportion of Americans who identified as Catholics had dropped slightly. However, these figures mean that the number of Catholics almost equals the number identified as evangelical Protestants.

Since the birth rate for American Catholics with family roots in earlier waves of immigration is close to that of the overall population, Catholic growth does not come primarily from replenishment. Rather, it results from the "new immigration" that got underway in 1965 with major changes in US immigration laws. Those changes ended a system in effect for more than a generation that placed quotas on both how many immigrants could enter the US each year and how many could come from any particular nation. The resulting immigration surge made the totals from 1990 onwards surpass those of the major wave of immigration preceding World War I. The new immigration included a huge surge in those coming from Mexico, the Caribbean, other areas of Central America, and South America.

The overwhelming majority – perhaps somewhere between three-fifths and two-thirds – of post-1965 Latino or Hispanic immigrants are Christians identified with the Roman Catholic heritage. With a birth rate higher than that of the general population, these immigrants are transforming the character of the American Catholic Church. But their style of Catholicism or their way of being Catholic is quite different from that of Catholics with European ancestry.

Catholicism from Mexico to the southern tip of South America has a rich history of blending traditional Catholic belief and practice with deeply imbedded ways of being religious, reflecting the long history of tribal cultures in the Americas. In some areas, African influences have also become part of the mix. For tribal cultures, American or African, a vibrant sense of the supernatural expressed through exuberant song and dance shapes religiosity. Consequently, Latino Catholicism has long been more emotionally energetic than the comparatively staid forms of European Catholicism that once informed the American church. Latino Catholics have added to traditional

Box 6.3 How Hispanics are transforming American Catholicism

In April 2007, the Pew Hispanic Center and the Pew Forum on Religion and Public Life issued a comprehensive report on how the surge of immigration from Latin America underway since 1965 was altering the US religious landscape, especially the Roman Catholic Church. In that report, researchers noted:

> About a third of all Catholics in the U.S. are now Latinos, and the study projects that the Latino share will continue climbing for decades. This demographic reality, combined with the distinctive characteristics of Latino Catholicism, ensures that Latinos will bring about important changes in the nation's largest religious institution. Most significantly given their numbers, more than half of Hispanic Catholics identify themselves as charismatics, compared with only an eighth of non-Hispanic Catholics. While remaining committed to the church and its traditional teachings, many of these Latino Catholics say they have witnessed or experienced occurrences typical of spirit-filled or renewalist movements, including divine healing and direct revelations from God. Even many Latino Catholics who do not identify themselves as renewalists appear deeply influenced by spirit-filled forms of Christianity.
>
> (From "Changing Faiths: Latinos and the Transformation of American Religion," www.pewhispanic.org/reports/report.php?ReportID=75, accessed 22 October 2010)

church practice an appreciation of personal ecstatic religious experiences akin to that prevalent among Pentecostal or charismatic Protestants. Those filled with the spirit, whether Catholic or Protestant, share an understanding that God moves in individual lives and historical events to effect miraculous healing, to provide a sense of power, and to nurture vitality and joy in people of faith. This more lively approach supplements and enriches the sacramental life of the church and its cycle of rituals.

At the same time, in part because Catholic folk in much of Central and South America see the church there as intertwined with oppressive economic and political powers, Latino religiosity has nurtured a stronger individualism and a disregard for accepting church positions on many social issues as binding. Latino Catholics are more liberal on matters of economic and social justice such as immigration reform than most other Catholics. But on some issues they are more conservative. Latino Catholic immigrants, for example, are more likely to believe that homosexual identity is a deterrent to being a faithful Catholic than even more conservative non-Latino American Catholics.

The Latino presence is reshaping the character of the American Catholic Church. It is bringing a more vibrant and Pentecostal flavor to worship. It is buttressing the most conservative postures on the burning social issues of the day – save for debates over immigration reform and economic justice. By 2010, the Latino style had become the new face of American Catholicism. With immigration showing little sign of abating, the Latino influence will become ever more significant. By the beginning of the second decade of the twenty-first century, the future of American Catholicism had become inextricably wedded to Latino ways of being Catholic.

Figure 6.2 A Latino man prays outside a church in Los Angeles that serves primarily the
Hispanic immigrant community which accounts for most Catholic growth in the
twenty-first century. The mural on the wall of the church shows the Virgin Mary
depicted as the Queen of Mexico

Courtesy of David McNew/Getty Images

A church with roots in European immigration survived with a "ghetto" mentality. At the same time, it became subject to the same interaction with the larger culture that influenced various Protestant denominations. Rocked by sex scandals, the church again sees its destiny tied to immigration. Now, however, the immigration is coming not from Europe, but from the Americas south of the US. We return to the impact of immigration on contemporary American religion, including American Catholicism, in Chapters 18 and 19.

Key points you need to know

- Immigration and hostility to Roman Catholicism shared the character of the Catholic church in the US in the nineteenth and early twentieth centuries.
- At one time, Catholics in the US had a "ghetto" mentality and flourished on the margins of the larger society.
- By the mid twentieth century, Catholics had entered the mainstream of American life.
- The Second Vatican Council updated church teaching and practice, transforming how Catholics understood their identity as Catholics.
- Since Vatican II, fewer persons have entered religious vocations as priests and nuns, but the visibility of bishops as public voices of the church has increased.
- Catholics, like others, have faced division over such matters as feminism, homosexuality, and legalized abortion.
- At the beginning of the twenty-first century, scandals over alleged sexual abuse perpetrated by priests shook the Catholic Church.
- Numerous forces have eroded the teaching authority, or magisterium, of the church.
- Nevertheless, the Catholic Church in the US continues to grow, thanks to a steady increase in Catholic immigrants of Latino background, who bring a charismatic style and also a conservative posture on most social issues.

Discussion questions

1   Why was American culture perceived to be hostile to Catholicism at least until the time of World War I? Why did that hostility begin to evaporate?
2   What does it mean to say that American Catholicism had a "ghetto" mentality before the middle of the twentieth century? What ended that image for Catholicism?
3   What evidence demonstrates that Catholics achieved cultural parity with Protestants by the last half of the twentieth century?
4   What changes mandated by the Second Vatican Council had the greatest impact on the church in the US? Why? Why were some Catholics disappointed with the results of the council?
5   Why do some analysts speak of a "crisis of authority" in US Catholicism since World War II? What brought about that crisis?

6   What changes and challenges have come to the Catholic priesthood in the US since the Second Vatican Council?
7   How are Catholic responses within American Catholicism to controversial issues such as feminism, homosexuality, and abortion similar to and different from the responses of both mainline and evangelical Protestantism? How would you account for the differences?
8   How has the role of women within the Catholic Church in the US changed in the years since World War II?
9   Why do some believe the scandal over sexual abuse by priests is the most significant challenge confronting the Catholic church today?
10 How and why are Latino immigrants changing and transforming American Catholicism?

Further reading

Baggett, J.P. (2009) *Sense of the Faithful: How American Catholics Live Their Faith*, New York: Oxford University Press.
D'Antonio, W.V., Davidson, J.D., Hoge, D.R., and Gautier, M.L. (2007) *American Catholics Today: New Realities of their Faith and their Church*, Lanham, MD: Rowman and Littlefield.
Davidson, J.D. (2005) *Catholicism in Motion: The Church in American Society*, Liguori, MO: Liguori Publications.
Dolan, J.P. (2003) *In Search of an American Catholicism: A History of Religion and Culture in Tension*, New York: Oxford University Press.
Herberg, W. (1955) *Protestant, Catholic, Jew: An Essay in Religious Sociology*, Garden City, NY: Doubleday.
Orsi, R. (1996) *Thank You, St. Jude: Women's Devotion to the Patron Saint of Hopeless Causes*, New Haven, CT: Yale University Press.
—— (1985) *The Madonna of 115th Street: Faith and Community in Italian Harlem. 1880–1950*, New Haven, CT: Yale University Press.
Pew Hispanic Center and Pew Forum on Religion and Public Life (2007) *Changing Faiths: Latinos and the Transformation of American Religion*, www.pewhispanicorg/reports/report.php?ReportID=75 (accessed 22 October 2010).
Podles, L.J. (2007) *Sacrilege: Sexual Abuse in the Catholic Church*, Baltimore: Crossland Foundation.
Steinfels, P. (2004) *A People Adrift: The Crisis of the Roman Catholic Church in America*, New York: Simon and Schuster.

7 Contemporary Judaism
Interweaving religious and cultural identities

In this chapter

Discussion of American Judaism in the 1950s, exploring the significance of Israel for Jewish identity and internal transformation resulting from cultural assimilation, opens the chapter. How American Jews responded to social movements of the 1950s and 1960s forms the basis for the second section. Next the focus turns to the symbolic role of the 1967 Six Day War. The chapter then examines issues of Jewish identity as a cultural or ethnic phenomenon. The final section probes current trends in American Jewish life.

Main topics covered

- America Judaism in the 1950s.
- Jewish identity as both a religious and a cultural/ethnic phenomenon.
- The role of Israel as symbolic and political reality.
- How American Judaism responded to social currents of the 1960s.
- The impact of the Six Day War of 1967 on Jewish consciousness.
- How the US became home to flourishing Hasidic Jewish communities, revitalizing Orthodox expressions of Judaism.
- Determining how many Americans identify with Judaism.
- The impact of immigration on American Judaism.

American Judaism after the war

Judaism in America, well established by the middle of the nineteenth century, had remained small. As with Catholicism, Judaism grew significantly thanks to immigration between the Civil War and World War I. Like Catholics, Jews often encountered discrimination and hostility. But there were differences. In Europe, Jews had frequently suffered persecution and faced legal restrictions on their participation in society. The American environment, despite lingering anti-Semitism, seemed more welcoming and hospitable. The First Amendment assured freedom of religious expression. Jewish citizens became actively engaged in public life, elevating their socioeconomic status by taking advantage of public higher education, working with labor unions to improve the status of workers, and adapting to a new society while maintaining a distinctive culture grounded in the European Jewish experience.

American Jews developed ancillary institutions both as a response to anti-Semitism and social exclusion, and as a way to sustain their identity. Here similarities and differences with other immigrant communities appear. Among Catholic immigrants, such institutions and even Catholic parishes often emerged along national lines, with Italian Catholic immigrants, for example, using those that served Italian American families, Polish Catholic immigrants those that served Polish American families, and so on. Given the restrictions many European nations placed on Jews until well into the nineteenth century and the overt persecution manifested by pogroms in areas of Slavic and Russian Europe, Jews had little affective identity with their nation of origin but more with a complex religious and cultural heritage. Jewish hospitals, summer resorts, and even colleges and universities celebrated this shared identity in ways that cut across national boundaries, solidifying a Jewish cultural and ethnic heritage, if not a religious one.

Adaptation occurred as Jews assimilated into American life. The changing role of home and synagogue provides one illustration. For centuries Jewish practice highlighted what happened in the home, not in the synagogue. Membership in a synagogue or attendance at services therefore has never measured Jewish identity as in much of Christianity. In traditional Jewish life, home-based ritual and practice centered on the dietary regime prescribed in the Torah, from what foods are eaten to how they are prepared and served. In addition, at sundown on Friday, the lighting of candles in the home marked the beginning of the Sabbath, the holy day of rest that punctuated time with a sacred quality.

Surrounded by non-Jews in the US, many relaxed family observance. Sometimes getting kosher products was impractical, if not impossible. Some compromised, adhering to tradition at home, but abandoning it in public when, for example, they dined in non-kosher restaurants. In a Christian-dominated society, strict Sabbath observance faded; many Jews joined Christian neighbors in marking the weekend, not the seventh day of rest.

At the same time, however, synagogues, once places devoted to study of Torah and reflection on Jewish law, became religious institutions akin to Christian churches. There the observant came to worship, not just to study and pray. Rabbis gradually added to their role as teachers of Torah the pastoral functions of a minister or priest.

The greatest adaptation came when German Jewish immigrants in the nineteenth century spearheaded the movement known as Reform Judaism. Influenced by Enlightenment rationalism and the expansion of opportunities in Germany to participate in political and cultural life, they scrutinized the Jewish heritage to find what seemed essential to Jewish spirituality, abandoning what was wedded to ancient Middle Eastern culture. Reform Jews added English prayers to services, jettisoned much of the kosher dietary guidelines, and made other accommodations to a predominantly Christian society. For a time, Reform seemed poised to be the primary form of Judaism in the US.

Immigration just before World War I shattered that expectation. Thousands who came then were more drawn to tradition, to ways of acting and believing that almost had an eternal aura. Some, shocked at Reform's modifications, insisted on following what they had always deemed as right and became known as Orthodox Jews. But the freedom offered by America stirred some who found Orthodoxy stultifying to discard overt religious practice. Many sought a middle ground between Orthodoxy's apparent rigidity and Reform's excessive accommodation to culture. Their effort to keep, but

Box 7.1 Major branches of American Judaism

Although what happens in the home is foundational to Jewish religious practice, Jewish institutional life in the US has taken shape around four approaches:

- Orthodox Judaism refers to the branch or denomination adhering most closely to tradition and to the path set forth in the Torah. For the Orthodox, being Jewish is a matter of religious faith usually based on birth, not merely ethnic identity. Synagogue worship is likely to rely heavily on prayers in Hebrew, gender roles are more clearly defined, and observance of the Law is central for individuals in their pursuit of holiness. Hasidic Jews comprise an ultra-orthodox subset.
- Reform Judaism emerged in Germany and then in the US in the mid nineteenth century. An effort to update Jewish practice, Reform jettisoned much traditional practice (and belief) as wedded to the ancient past. Reform Jews, for example, are the least likely to believe strict adherence to kosher dietary guidelines is basic to being Jewish.
- Conservative Judaism, known as Masorti outside the US and Canada, also has mid-nineteenth-century German roots. Not as strict as the Orthodox, Conservative Jews believed that Reform abandoned too many essentials. With a high regard for scripture, a trait shared with the Orthodox, Conservative Jews are generally open to critical, scholarly analysis of texts, a trait shared with Reform Jews. Conservative Judaism, because of its moderate, centrist position, became the largest branch of American Judaism.
- Reconstructionist Judaism, the most liberal branch, emerged in the US around 1920. It tends to emphasize enduring Jewish ethical principles, but not traditional observance and practice, believing much is out of step with rational, modern understanding. Reconstructionist Judaism is the denomination most open to new ideas and to using knowledge from contemporary culture to understand faith.

Other understandings of Judaism also are part of American life. Some are primarily secular, some predominantly ethnic, and some oriented to a broad scientific interpretation of Jewish teaching.

update, what was foundational gave birth to Conservative Judaism, first in Germany in the mid nineteenth century and then in the US at the beginning of the twentieth. Soon Conservative Judaism, not Reform, became the largest branch of American Judaism. It remained so until the beginning of the twenty-first century. Conservative's openness to adjusting traditional practice joined with the more liberal Reform and a secularized Judaism to remake American Judaism. However, in the early twenty-first century – thanks in part to the movement of some synagogue-affiliated Jews from Conservative congregations to Reform and to concerted efforts of Reform leaders to attract those who shared the values of Reform, but had abandoned practice or affiliation – Reform was again on the ascendancy, probably eclipsing Conservative Judaism in terms of adherents.

One consequence of the openness of both Reform and Conservative Judaism in the American context to some cultural adaptation was the skyrocketing increase in marriages of Jewish Americans to non-Jews. In locales with small Jewish populations, the pool of eligible Jewish marriage partners was also small, creating a greater likelihood of a Jew marrying someone from another faith tradition. As the influx of Jewish Americans into public universities increased, contact with non-Jews and the likelihood of young men and young women meeting marriage partners from different religious orientations accelerated. The sense that Jewish identity was as much a cultural as a religious heritage also eroded the emphasis on endogamy (marriage within the faith); faith was only one component of a cultural identity and not necessarily the most important. Families blending traditions were less likely to adhere to Jewish home practice, such as a kosher diet, and less likely to raise children with a self-conscious Jewish religious identity. The importance of family in transmitting religion from one generation to the next receives additional scrutiny in Chapter 8.

Two events in the middle third of the twentieth century awakened a sense of Jewishness, even among non-observant Jews. One was the Holocaust, the systematic effort of the Nazi regime in Germany to eradicate the Jewish population in lands it conquered. Stories from concentration camp survivors and the horrors of Nazi persecution stirred people everywhere to be more self-conscious about preserving their religio-cultural heritage. The second was the establishment of the nation-state of Israel on 14 May 1948. Efforts to recreate a Jewish state, often grouped together as Zionism, gained ground after World War I. The defeat of the Ottoman Empire in the war meant that several Middle Eastern territories became British protectorates. Pressure to grant them independence mounted after World War II. The new nation of Israel was not identical to the biblical land so designated. Centuries of occupation by Muslims and others complicated political realities in the region. Many neighboring Muslim nations resented the creation of Israel. Consequently military hostilities erupted when Israeli independence was authorized.

For American Jews, whether Zionists or not, the state of Israel carried symbolic significance. It represented not only the biblical land nurturing Judaism, but also a homeland for all Jews, regardless of national citizenship. Even Jews well assimilated into American society felt bonds with Israel. Their immigrant ancestors had few emotional ties to the nations from which they migrated; Israel as place was their true homeland. Urging the US government to support Israel unconditionally in its conflicts with neighboring nations helped assure that another Holocaust would never occur. Israel thus became a symbol of Jewishness even for those American Jews who no longer observed any of the Torah's religious rites. So long as Israel endured, Judaism would not disappear, no matter how much assimilation into American culture transpired.

American Judaism and the social currents of the 1960s

The social transformations of the 1960s affected Judaism just as they did all American religious groups. American Judaism had a long history of social activism when the civil rights movement began. Having endured centuries of exclusion in Europe, Jews refused to accept second-class status in the US. Accordingly, many identified with social reform movements, ones often linked to the Democratic party. Numerous leaders of the early labor union movement, for example, came from Jewish immigrant

Figure 7.1 American Jews and their supporters jubilantly filled New York City's Times Square
on 14 May 1948 to celebrate the creation of Israel as an independent nation

Courtesy of NY Daily News/Getty Images

stock. Many also felt an affinity with African Americans once the civil rights movement
got underway. Both shared a history molded by discrimination, racism, and
marginalization.

Jewish leaders active in the civil rights movement generally came from the
Conservative and Reform branches and from those who saw their Jewishness as a
cultural identity rather than a religious one. Some Southern Jews remained on the
sidelines because they feared an anti-Semitic backlash if they attacked racial
segregation. Nonetheless, prominent Jewish figures became immersed in the movement.
Among the speakers at the 1963 March on Washington, for example, was Reform
rabbi Joachim Prinz (1902–88). German-born Prinz became an outspoken critic of the
Nazi regime, fleeing to the US in 1937. At the time, Prinz was president of the American
Jewish Congress, founded in 1918. Prinz's presence indicated that a premier Jewish
organization advocated social justice and supported the movement.

Abraham Joshua Heschel (1907–72), a well-known Jewish philosopher and
theologian, walked with Martin Luther King, Jr., in the famous voting rights march to
Selma, AL, in March 1965. Heschel understood discrimination. In 1938 the Gestapo
in Germany arrested him and deported him to Poland. He came to the US in 1940.
Heschel, who lost two sisters in the Holocaust, was a tireless advocate for civil rights
for all.

Second-wave feminism also brought challenges. Betty Friedan (1921–2006), whose
1963 book *The Feminine Mystique* helped launch the movement and who served as
first president of the National Organization for Women, had Jewish roots. Historically,
complexity marked women's roles in the Jewish tradition. Menstruation and childbirth,
according to Torah, render women unclean until they complete rites of purification.

Frequently, a woman's standing depended on her father, husband, sons, or brothers, although exceptions were frequent. Traditionally, only men counted when determining if the requisite number for daily prayer had assembled. Synagogues provided separate seating by gender, with women often placed behind a screen. For centuries, the heritage excluded women from the study of Torah and the rabbinate. Yet women also had a place of honor. Women oversaw family rites. At sundown Friday, the Sabbath began when the wife and mother lit ritual candles in the home. Popular lore also identified anyone as Jewish who had a Jewish mother, not a Jewish father. Second-wave feminism encouraged many Jewish women to claim a more central place in Jewish life and to reinterpret many practices once marginalizing them, recasting them to affirm the unique experiences of women.

Women also sought admission to the rabbinate. Reform led the way in ordaining female rabbis when Cincinnati's Hebrew Union College ordained Sally Priesand

---

Box 7.2 Rethinking women's roles in contemporary Judaism

Rabbi Elyse M. Goldstein (1955–), a Pennsylvania native, served Reform temples in Canton, MA, and Toronto before becoming director of Kolel, the Adult Centre for Liberal Jewish Learning in 1991. She has written extensively about rethinking interpretation of the Torah, making a strong case for ways Jewish women can appropriate what was once regarded as a male-oriented tradition, In this excerpt, she looks at the *mikvah*, the ritual bath once required of women after menstruation or childbirth to restore purity, from a feminist perspective:

> As a feminist, I have struggled with the Jewish menstrual taboos for many years ... It is inexorably linked to having a husband, to making oneself ready to return to sexual relations with one's male partner, to being connected to a man ... Why then was I, a Reform rabbi and committed feminist, splashing around in the mikvah? ... The mikvah has been taken from me as a Jewish woman by sexist interpretations ... I was going to take back the water. To take back the water means to see mikvah as a wholly female experience: as Miriam's well gave water to the Israelites so too will the mikvah give strength back to Jewish women ... To take back the water means to open up the mikvah to women not attached to men ... To take back the water means to dip on Rosh Codesh, when the moon and sea and women's cycles become one ... To take back the water means to turn the mikvah into a Jewish women's center: with Torah learning and books available, maybe even feminist shiurim [lectures], not just sheitl [wigs worn by Orthodox women] advertisements and pamphlets on keeping a kosher home ... The water is ours: it is the fluid of our own bodies and a deeply moving experience of connection to Mother Earth ... It is our Jewish history.
>
> (From Elyse Goldstein, "Take Back the Waters: A Feminist Re-appropriation of Mikvah," *Lilith* 15 (1986): 15–16, as found in *In Our Own Voices: Four Centuries of American Women's Religious Writing*, ed. Rosemary Radford Ruether and Rosemary Skinner Keller, San Francisco: HarperSanFrancisco, 1995, pp. 147–50)

Figure 7.2 In 1972, Sally Priesand became the first Jewish woman to be ordained a rabbi in the US. She was part of the Reform tradition

© Bettmann/CORBIS

(1946–) in 1972. The Reconstructionist Rabbinical College ordained its first woman, Sandy Eisenberg Sasso (1947–), two years later. Conservative Judaism debated the issue for another decade. Finally, in 1985, its major institution, the Jewish Theological Seminary of America, authorized the ordination of Amy Eilberg (1954–). As with mainline Protestant denominations, the branches of Judaism admitting women to the rabbinate have seen a steady increase in the number of women preparing for ordination.

Jewish groups have also confronted contention in dealing with issues surrounding homosexuality. Like many Christian denominations, Jewish bodies proved reluctant to move beyond the apparent condemnation of homosexuality in Leviticus, chapter 18, lest the result lead to abandoning all behavior and belief grounded in the Torah. Orthodox Jews insist that the Levitical Code is binding. For them homosexuality remains an abomination. Reconstructionism and Reform have proved the most willing to adapt. In 1990, the Reform Central Conference of American Rabbis sanctioned ordination of homosexuals to the rabbinate. A decade later, it approved a resolution affirming same-gender relationships, but allowed individual rabbis to decide whether to officiate at same-gender unions. Reconstructionists have likewise accepted homosexual rabbis and cantors, and called for recognition of same-gender marriages.

In 1992, Conservative Judaism's Committee on Jewish Law and Standards called for acceptance of gays and lesbians in congregational life, but bans on ordination of gays and lesbians and on same-gender commitment ceremonies remained. In 2005, the committee, aware that some Conservative synagogues held same-gender commitment services and that some homosexuals served as rabbis, called for more study and reflection, while deploring anti-gay violence. Consensus eluded American Judaism as it did all religious bodies. The many ways various movements for equality impact American religious life come under scrutiny from a different perspective in Chapters 10 and 15.

The Six Day War and continuing issues of Jewish identity

Some events in the 1960s had more impact on the religious consciousness of American Jews than others. For example, non-Jews could relegate the continuing turmoil in the Middle East, especially the Six Day War of June 1967, to the realm of politics and international affairs. For Jews, such events carried religious import.

Israel's victory over Egypt and other Arab states in the Six Day War, fought between 5 June and 10 June 1967, was a symbolic phenomenon, although Israel seized control of critical areas such as the West Bank. Two decades of hostility preceded the war; several armed conflicts have followed. The war signaled that Israel could defend itself against outside attack while extending influence over territories also claimed by Palestinians and, in some cases, neighboring Arab states. The war vindicated the efforts of American Jews to press the US government to offer unquestioned support for Israel. In time, however, Israel's harsh treatment of Muslim Palestinians in conquered territories came to appall even some American Jewish leaders, hindering efforts to craft an enduring peace.

The war had great impact on American Jewish identity The non-observant and those on the margins of organized Jewish life found the war stimulated a renewed awareness of what it meant to be Jewish. Fresh pride in affirming a Jewish consciousness followed, even for those for whom Jewishness was an ethnic identity rather than one of faith. Such endeavors paralleled to a rise in ethnic awareness and pride throughout American culture.

The dual role of Israel as a mythic place or fulcrum for Jewish life, and as a nation-state, again came into play As noted above, many earlier Jewish immigrants did not think of themselves as coming from the nation they left behind in the way, for example, that Italian immigrants might think of themselves as Italian Americans. Now they linked themselves to Israel – even if they had never visited Israel or lived there – for Israel's existence as a place seemed secure.

The interest in declaring one's self as Jewish went deeper than standard guidelines accepted by historians suggested for descendants of immigrants. That axiom held that among immigrant groups, the first generation born in the US tried to assimilate as quickly as possible, abandoning whatever was distinctive about the ethnic and national character of the migrating generation. But the next generation searched for roots by reclaiming what had been lost in acculturation. For large numbers of Jews, Israel now symbolized a cultural heritage and a way of life informing who they were.

For religious Jews, Israel's new stature stirred interest in Jewish practice and in reconciling Jewish law with a modern, if not postmodern, world. Although precise numbers remain elusive, by the 1970s, for example, college and university Jewish groups were noting greater commitment to following old traditions. Jewish writers, many affiliated with Reform and Conservative branches, produced books exploring how to adhere to Torah in daily life, especially how to maintain an observant home in a world where technology had transformed everything from food production to the design of kitchens. Some addressed intermarriage, probing how to maintain a Jewish identity within a family blending multiple religious traditions.

The growth of ultra-Orthodox Hasidic Jewish communities in the US added to this renewed sense of Jewish identity. Many had come to escape Nazi persecution during World War II. The Chabad-Lubavitch, one of the largest Hasidic groups, settled in the Crown Heights section of Brooklyn, NY. Under the leadership of Rabbi Menachem Mendel Schneerson (1902–94), the community flourished. It grew in numbers and in influence.

Box 7.3 Ushering in the messianic age

Noted historian of American Judaism Jonathan Sarna has described how Rabbi Menachem Mendel Schneerson, as leader of the Chabad-Lubavitch, saw the Hasidic community's role in ushering in the long-expected messianic age. Many, Sarna noted, expected the catastrophe of World War II and the Holocaust to be history's last epoch before the messiah came. Sarna writes:

> When that prophecy failed, they experienced grave disappointment. The Rebbe [Schneerson] through his lectures and outreach efforts to Jews around the world, his widely publicized pronouncements, and his interpretations of Israel's role in the divine plan, rekindled messianic hopes ... Many of those efforts focused on the observance by Jews of a single commandment and returning "lost" Jews to the fold. Personal emissaries ... established Chabad centers in communities large and small and modeled a fervently Orthodox lifestyle, often at personal sacrifice, so as to strengthen Jewish religious consciousness and hasten the messiah's coming.
>
> (J.D. Sarna, "Chabad-Lubavitch," in *Encyclopedia of Religion in America*, ed. C.H. Lippy and P.W. Williams, Washington: CQ Press, 2010, vol. 1, p. 423).

Schneerson, open to modernizing the Hasidic style without abandoning strict adherence to Torah, became an icon of Jewish commitment and identity for many outside the movement. Some regarded him almost in messianic terms. Various Chabad-Lubavitch communities have started synagogues, expanded work with Jewish college students through Chabad Houses, and strengthened their financial base. What sets Chabad-Lubavitch apart from other Orthodox is the conviction that adhering strictly to Torah and inviting fellow Jews to become observant pave the way for the promised messianic age.

American Judaism in the early twenty-first century

Estimates of how many Jews there are in America vary widely, with the highest claiming that in 2010 around 6.5 million Americans were Jewish, a number slightly larger than the number of Jews in Israel. Others put the 2010 American Jewish population in 2010 closer to 5.2 million, down from 5.5 million in 1990. Most analysts believe the lower number more accurate. As with mainline Protestants, Jews have a birth rate that has dropped steadily since the 1960s, although Hasidic Jews, the least likely to use artificial contraception, have a much higher internal birth rate than others.

Several factors account for the difficulty in pinpointing precisely how many Jews there are in the US. Intermarriage means that many persons of Jewish heritage are found in families blending multiple religious traditions. Scores identify themselves as "secular" Jews and "ethnic" Jews, but not "religious" Jews. Many who are otherwise unobservant nevertheless attend services on Yom Kippur, the Day of Atonement, regarded as the most sacred day in the Jewish religious calendar. Many also mark Passover and celebrate Chanukah or Hanukkah, the festival of lights when gifts are exchanged, and which occurs around the same time as Christmas. Yet the number of Jews in the US, however one counts, has remained much smaller than the influence of the heritage on American life and culture, thanks to extraordinary upward mobility, educational achievement, and stunning success in professions ranging from business to politics, popular entertainment to literature.

Immigration has solidified some sectors of the American Jewish community. Around 1970, western nations began to pressure the Soviet Union to allow a higher rate of Jewish emigration. Success was modest until the Gorbachev regime launched many policy changes in the late 1980s. Emigration continued after the Russian Federation came into existence following the collapse of the Soviet Union in 1991. The story is complicated, since many had first to migrate to secure proper documents to enter the US. In the first four decades after 1970, somewhere between one-third and two-fifths of Jews leaving Russian areas eventually wound up in the US.

Immigration to and from Israel has also been complicated. After Israel gained its independence in 1948, a few thousand American Jews started to relocate there each year. The constant military turmoil in the region made this out-migration short-lived. For most of Israel's history, Israeli immigration to the US, mostly Jewish, has surpassed American immigration to Israel. By 2010, this pattern was slowly changing. Americans moving to Israel tend to be Orthodox, drawn to Israel in part because of the Orthodox influence on Israeli culture and popular style, not its impact on politics and policies. We will return to the larger story of links between American religion and both ethnicity and immigration in Chapters 18 and 19.

Although Israel remains a potent symbol for the identity of American Jews, they have exhibited an increasing ambivalence towards Israeli policies in the Middle East. More secure in their place in American life, they are now somewhat less likely to affiliate with the Democratic party than previously. A broad commitment to social justice, however, remains vital. Present trends suggest a slow increase in the numbers of Jews who observe traditional practices, slightly adapted for a postmodern world. Some commentators believe that Muslims now outnumber Jews in the US. If so, Judaism in another generation may no longer be part of the triad of faiths – Protestant Christianity, Catholic Christianity, and Judaism – long thought to reflect the religious pulse of the nation. Nonetheless, Judaism's place in America remains secure.

Key points you need to know

- How an atmosphere combining freedom with an undercurrent of hostility shaped American Judaism.
- The interplay between a Jewish religious identity and an ethnic/cultural one.
- Differences among the main branches or denominations of Judaism (Orthodox, Reform, Conservative, Reconstructionist).
- Ways in which intermarriage affected American Judaism.
- The impact of the Holocaust on Jewish consciousness.
- How Israel is a symbol as well as a place for American Jews.
- The impact of social currents of the 1960s on Judaism.
- Why and how the Six Day War influenced American Jews.
- A slow, but steady increase in observance of tradition by American Jews.
- The role of Hasidism, especially the Chabad-Lubavitch, in prompting this interest.
- Why it is difficult to determine how many Jews there are in the US.
- The impact of recent immigration, especially from the former Soviet Union, is changing American Judaism.

Discussion questions

1 How did the American environment affect the development of Judaism in the US?
2 How did Jewish immigrants adapt and assimilate? In what ways is the story of American Judaism similar to and different from the story of Roman Catholic immigrants?
3 Why did Jewish religious identity for some become instead a cultural and ethnic identity? What forces sustain that distinction?
4 What distinguishes the various branches of Judaism in the US from each other?
5 Discuss the impact of intermarriage on American Jewish life.
6 How did the Holocaust leave its imprint on contemporary Judaism in America?
7 Explain the role of Israel as both symbol and place in American Jewish life.
8 In what ways did the response(s) of American Judaism to social currents of the 1960s such as the civil rights movement, second-wave feminism, and debates about homosexuality echo those of other groups? In what ways were they distinctive?
9 How is the role of women in American Judaism evolving?
10 Why did the Six Day War have religious significance? What did it mean to those for whom Judaism represents a cultural, not a religious, heritage?
11 What prompted a renewed interest in traditional Jewish observance in recent years? What role did a group such as the Chabad-Lubavich play in stimulating that interest?
12 What makes it difficult to ascertain with precision just how many Jews there are in the US?

Further reading

Alpert, R.T. and Staub, J.J. (2000) *Exploring Judaism: A Reconstructionist Approach*, Elkins Park, PA: Reconstructionist Press.

Cohen, S.M. and Eisen, A.M. (2000). *The Jew Within: Self, Family, and Community in America*, Bloomington: Indiana University Press.

Eisen, A.M. (1997) *Taking Hold of Torah: Jewish Commitment and Community in America*, Bloomington: Indiana University Press.

Fishkoff, S. (2003) *The Rebbe's Army: Inside the World of Chabad-Lubavitch*, New York: Schocken Books.

Goldman, K. (2000) *Beyond the Synagogue Gallery: Finding a Place for Women in American Judaism*, Cambridge, MA: Harvard University Press.

Goldstein, E.I. (2006) *The Price of Whiteness: Jews, Race, and American Identity*, Princeton, NJ: Princeton University Press.

Gurock, J.S. (1996) *American Jewish Orthodoxy in Historical Perspective*, Hoboken, NJ: KTAV Publishing House.

Kaplan, D.E. (2003) *American Reform Judaism: An Introduction*, New Brunswick, NJ: Rutgers University Press.

Sarna, J. (2004) *American Judaism: A History*, New Haven, CT: Yale University Press.

Weinberg, D. (1996) *Between Tradition and Modernity*, New York: Holmes and Meier.

Wertheimer, J. (2002) *Jews in the Center: Conservative Synagogues and their Members*, New Brunswick, NJ: Rutgers University Press.

8 Transmitting religion

In this chapter

In this chapter, we explore how religions are transmitted, communicated, and conveyed to individuals in American society. The most important social institution for transferring religion is the family. We describe how the family transmits religious affiliation or not and how religion conveys ideas about proper family norms and structures. Next, we describe how religious congregations convey religion, with special attention to megachurches. We then turn to the role of the mass media in transmitting religion, focusing on the role of the Internet in promoting or challenging religious beliefs and on how the media communicate a general religious culture. Finally, we explore what happens when individuals change religious beliefs, emphasizing definitions and causes.

Main topics covered

- Religious belief is individually held but socially transmitted and embedded.
- Religion is primarily passed on through the family, although the relationship between the family and religion is weakening.
- Local congregations instill religion through religious education and worship.
- Very large and "megachurches" have a growing impact on American religious life.
- Changing media forms have long influenced the way that religion is transmitted and have forced religious institutions to adapt.
- The Internet has greatly expanded the opportunity for individuals to learn about religion, but also represents a threat to religious authority.
- Religious switching and conversion occur for a variety of reasons.

Religion as socially transmitted

In previous chapters, we explored large-scale religious changes among the mainline religious expressions in contemporary America. But how does one "get" religion? In this chapter, we answer that question by looking at various ways in which religion is transmitted and communicated in American society.

This chapter assumes that religion is socially embedded, just as, for example, our ideas of culture, language, gender roles, and race are imparted by various social institutions. At the same time, religious beliefs are individually held, and people "live" religion in their own ways, as the discussion of individual theories of religion in Chapter 2 pointed out. In particular, individuals shape the meanings of religious experiences in their personal lives and worldview in ways that are tied to, but distinct from, societally and institutionally defined beliefs and practices. That said, religion – including beliefs, practices, and cultures – is transmitted through various agents, such as the family, congregations, and the media.

The family

Religion and family are vitally intertwined in contemporary American society. The primary avenue of religious transmission is through the family. By that we mean that most people get their first ideas about religious belief and practice from their families. Research on the religious views of adolescents demonstrates that teenagers most often model their own religious beliefs and practices after those of their parents.

Table 8.1 reports information from the 2007 Pew Religion Landscape Survey about the percentage of people in various religious groups who were raised in that group and who were affiliated with that group at the time of the survey. In most religious groups, including the major Protestant traditions, Catholicism, Mormonism, Judaism,

Figure 8.1 Most people get their first ideas about religious belief and practice from their families. Having family prayer before meals, a common practice for many Christians, is one way a religious practice is transmitted to children

Courtesy of Joel Sartore/Getty Images

Islam, and Hinduism, the majority of people currently affiliated with that tradition were raised in that tradition. On the other hand, the majority of Buddhists, as well as those affiliated with faiths or with Christian denominations that are small in size, were raised in a different religious group. In addition, most of those who have no current religious affiliation were raised in a religious group. We explore the process of changing religious traditions, especially conversion, later in the chapter. Researchers usually pay particular attention to the various Protestant traditions in Table 8.1 because the majority of Americans are Protestant.

The family's power to transmit religion varies across an individual's life cycle and among different generations of Americans. In Chapter 4, we described the typically understood religious life cycle, in which religious affiliation and engagement is high for children (usually in their parent's religion), falls during late adolescence and young adulthood (ages 18 to 29), and generally increases as people age and become parents. Recent research demonstrates that religious affiliation is lower for more recent generations at the same point in their religious life cycle.

Figure 8.2 presents trend information from the 1972 to 2002 General Social Survey data, a survey of a random sample of Americans that occurs every two years, on the proportion of the population unaffiliated with a religion over time. The figure separates these trends by generation, tracking the percentage of those unaffiliated with religion in the millennial generation (those born in 1981 or later), generation X (those born

Table 8.1 Percentage of people changing affiliation within major religious groups

Panel A: Protestant traditions

Current Protestant tradition:	Outside Protestantism	% who switched from …	
		Another Protestant family	Raised as a member
Evangelical churches	18	31	51
Mainline churches	16	30	54
African American churches	10	21	69

Panel B: Other religious groups

Current religion:	% switched affiliation	% raised as a member
Catholic	11	89
Jewish	15	85
Hindu	10	90
Buddhist	73	27
Muslim	40	60
Mormons	26	74
Other Christian	90	10
Other faiths	91	9
Unaffiliated	79	21

Source: 2007 US Religious Landscape Survey, Pew Research Center Forum on Religion & Public Life, http://religions.pewforum.org/

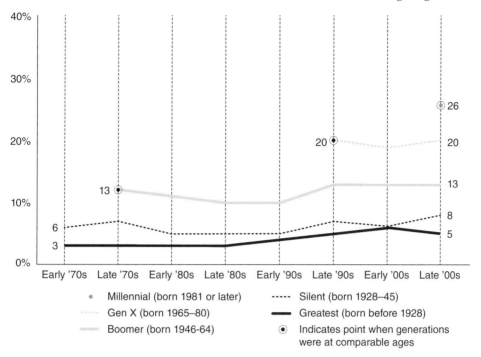

Figure 8.2 Percent unaffiliated with a religion, by generation

Source: Pew Research Center's Forum on Religion & Public Life, "Religion Among the Millennials," © 2010, Pew Research Center, http://pewforum.org/docs/?DocID=510

between 1965 and 1980), baby boomers (born between 1946 and 1964), the silent generation (born between 1928 and 1945), and the greatest generation (born before 1928). This figure reveals that when the generations were at comparable ages (all between ages 18 and 29), 26 per cent of the millennial generation were religiously unaffiliated, 20 per cent of generation X were unaffiliated, and 13 per cent of baby boomers were unaffiliated. This same research demonstrates that the millennial generation is less likely than the generation X or baby boomer generations to attend religious services and more likely to report that religion is not important in their lives. On the other hand, this most recent generation continues to report religious belief, including the belief in God and the afterlife, and religious behaviors, such as engaging in prayer and meditation, at rates similar to previous generations.

These trends raise important questions about the family's role in transmitting religion in contemporary American society. Why do adolescents and young adults have low levels of religious affiliation? Why do people tend to return to religion as they get older? Why do some people stay affiliated with the religion in which they were raised while others do not? And why is religious affiliation lower among more recent generations? Sociologists have explored all of these questions. Smith and Denton as well as Pearce and Denton describe religion among adolescents and young adults. They find that the majority of American youth are affiliated with a religious group or tradition. During middle adolescence (between the ages of 13 and 17), teenagers view religion to be an important part of their lives; however, they often have difficulty articulating what they believe and how these beliefs impact their everyday lives. During late adolescence (between the ages of 18 and 22) attendance at religious services, belief in God, and frequency of prayer all decline, reflecting the growing autonomy people achieve as they move out of their parents' home. This period of life is often associated with an increased seeking behavior, as described in Chapter 4, and a strong sense of spirituality as distinct from religion but important to life, a phenomenon described in Chapter 16.

Many people return to the religious beliefs and practices in which they were raised as they get older, especially as they get married and have children (although this is happening less in recent generations as described above). Scholars, including Robert Wuthnow, have argued that people return to religion as they get older because they increasingly have to deal with concerns about family, illness, and death. In particular, as people have children, they frequently desire to raise those children in the same faith that they were raised in or to instill a moral education in them. Moreover, most religious institutions emphasize the needs of adults with families more than the needs of young adults, making religious participation more attractive as people enter adulthood. Finally, as people age, they are more likely to emphasize the relationships and social networks that religion provides, due to the social function of religion described in Chapter 1.

Of course, some people never disaffiliate from religion and others never return to their parents' religion as they get older. Researchers have explored the reasons for these differences. They find that people who are close to their parents and have many friends in the religion are less likely to disaffiliate because they do not want to alienate or lose their relationships with close friends or family. Additionally, those who attended church frequently as a child or come from a family where all members of the immediate family share the same religion are less likely to disaffiliate in late adolescence and early adulthood. On the other hand, children who attend church less often or who come from a family where there is no shared religion are more likely to disaffiliate during late adolescence and early adulthood, and are less likely to return as they age.

Finally, researchers have developed a number of explanations for why religious affiliation is lower among more recent generations. Much of Chapters 2 and 16 are devoted to describing the decline in traditional religious authority in contemporary American society. Another explanation is generational reinforcement, in which the earlier generations influence the succeeding generation, so what started with the baby boomers has been magnified in subsequent generations. The expansion of attendance at institutions of higher education may play a role, given that those with higher educational attainment are less likely to be religiously affiliated. Finally, the rise in religious seeking behaviors, religious consumerism, individualized faith, and hybrid forms of spirituality, described in Chapters 2 and 16, contributes to a decline in religious affiliation among the young. This trend may be magnified by the Internet as a form of information gathering and social interaction, as we shall see below.

Religions also transmit norms and attitudes about the family. The majority of research in the sociology of religion on this topic explores how the Christian faith, particularly among evangelicals, influences family decisions and how those relationships are changing. Robert Wuthnow, for example, found that the more frequently young adults go to church, the more likely they are to value marriage and desire children. In addition, young adults who attend evangelical Protestant churches are more likely than others to believe that sex outside of marriage is wrong. Other researchers have examined the complex way in which evangelical men and women define their family roles. For example, evangelical men often define themselves as both servants to their wife and children and as spiritual leaders of their wife and children, an understanding that requires them always to balance the two roles. In the same way, evangelical women are both powerful and powerless. That is, they are powerful because they run the household and raise children, but they are powerless because they are taught to be submissive to their husbands as well as to God. Ideas about the family are also intimately tied to issues of gender and sexuality, which are covered in the next two chapters.

Box 8.1 Men as leaders and servants

John Bartowski (2007: 160) uses in-depth interviews with evangelical men who were active in the Promise Keepers movement to show how these men define themselves both as servant and spiritual leader to their wife and children, as illustrated in the quotes below:

> The man is to be the leader of the home and to make the final decisions. Now, if we love our wives as Christ loved the Church and was willing to die for it, what does it tell you about what decision you ought to be making? ... Put it into practice terms, and it's this. In the decision-making process, somebody always has to be able to break the tie ... Now if we enter into that situation, both of us with servant's hearts, then I'm here to please you and bless you. Then my decision, though it's my decision to make, my decision is going to be in favor of you, rather than in favor of me.
>
> (Hal, a married man with no children)

> What I really do is I pray more. I pray more for my kids and pray more for my wife. I am the spiritual leader of the house. So anything that goes on in the house has to follow what the Bible tells us is true. I lead prayer sessions in the house. What we're doing is just doing the things that Jesus tells us to do. You know, love your neighbor as much as you love yourself ... I have a responsibility to be the church leader of the house. Whether I accept it or not, the Bible says it's there. I'm supposed to be the one who is in charge of the spiritual well-being of the household and by that [I understand that] I need to be leading the family Bible studies, praying for my wife and children.
>
> (Phil, a married man with three children)

Religious congregations and institutions

Local religious congregations and institutions play a primary role in transmitting religion because they are at the center of people's religious experience. All religious congregations and institutions communicate religious beliefs and rituals through worship and religious education. Worship consists of religious rituals and beliefs carried out as an act of devotion. Recall the discussion in Chapter 1 of Durkheim's definition of religion. For Durkheim, religious rituals, beliefs, and worship build a moral community for all those who hold those beliefs. Thus, worship transmits religion by promoting a sense of solidarity and cohesion within the congregation. As described in Chapter 2, congregations are constantly refining worship styles, rituals, and belief emphases in order to attract and retain members. Recall here the changes that mainline congregations have made in response to the decline in participation, as described in Chapter 4, the changes that evangelical congregations have made in order to grow, as described in Chapter 5, and the changes that Catholic parishes have made due to Latino immigration and influence, as described in Chapter 6.

Education, when performed by congregations, involves the teaching of the beliefs, doctrines, rituals, and behaviors expected of members of the congregation and religion. In contemporary America, religious education often takes the form of supplementary classes such as "Sunday school," "Hebrew school," Bible studies, or catechism classes. In many Christian traditions, some congregations have parochial schools affiliated with them that also engage in religious education. Many faiths also offer private college and graduate-level religious schools. As described in Chapter 5, these schools have flourished in the evangelical and fundamentalist Christian traditions.

Just as all congregations engage in worship and education, there is a common organizational form that most congregations, regardless of religion, take in the US. This form includes voluntary membership, lay leadership, offering a variety of services to members, and large organizational networks. Other common organizational features include services occurring during the weekend and on week nights and physical locations that resemble churches. This organizational form began in the Protestant and Catholic traditions, but has become the dominant organizational form for all major religious traditions in the contemporary US. Sociological research demonstrates that immigrant religions adopt this organizational form within a generation of entering the US (see Chapter 19). This common organizational form transfers a common understanding across religions of what participation in a congregation entails.

The majority of religious congregations in the US have about a hundred members. However, a growing trend among Protestant congregations has been the rise of the "megachurch." Megachurches are those that average over two thousand attendees in a given week. Examples of these megachurches are given in Chapters 5 and 11. Mark Chaves documents trends in megachurch growth in twelve large Protestant denominations, evenly split between mainline and evangelical traditions, from 1900 to 2004. The number of megachurches has grown steadily over the period of study, but accelerated rapidly in the 1970s. In addition, megachurches are getting larger, with more people and resources concentrated in the very largest churches in all denominations. For example, in 1970, 5 per cent of Protestants in the twelve largest denominations were members of the largest 1 per cent of churches; in 2002, 12 per cent were members of the largest 1 per cent of churches.

Megachurches conduct worship and religious education in different ways than other congregations, due to their larger size and additional resources. All megachurches use a variety of contemporary media forms to transmit their message. For example, megachurch worship services are often televised and/or streamed live on the Internet, the songs and music at services can use full bands and choirs with extensive training and practice, and many megachurches have an extensive presence on the web, including using blogs, podcasts, videos, and online advertising to spread their message. To further education and solidarity, all megachurches use small groups designed to reflect particular interests or needs of members and to develop a sense of family and community among participants. These small groups are reinforced by large paid and volunteer staffs that seek to connect people to the church and each other. In some cases, informal networks of family and friends often attend the same megachurch, adding to the sense of community.

Box 8.2 Characteristics of megachurches

The growth and spread of megachurches have changed how many Americans experience religious worship and education. Megachurches are very different from the typical church:

- weekly attendance of 3,585;
- seating for 1,709;
- four weekly services;
- twenty pastors;
- thirty administrative staff;
- heavy reliance on volunteers;
- emphasis on small groups and evangelism;
- diverse church membership in terms of age, race/ethnicity, education levels, occupations, and income.

(Source: Thumma and Travis 2007; Chaves 2006)

Five types of megachurch communicate religion in different ways. Seeker-focused megachurches seek to attract members from other religious backgrounds and traditions by using messages or worship innovations to attract members. Other megachurches emphasize evangelizing among the unchurched, both in the local community and abroad, through missionary work. Teaching megachurches focus on religious education. Some megachurches, as described in Chapter 11, emphasize the prosperity gospel, which promises wellbeing and wealth. Finally, some megachurches work to attract young worshipers, often by using examples and structures from popular culture.

The media

We live in a world saturated by media, including magazines, books, television, radio, the Internet, online social networks, video games, and text messages. The evolution of media forms and the mass media profoundly influence how religion is transmitted and communicated to people. They also continually force religious institutions and leaders to adapt to new ways of communicating and controlling their message. Each advance in communications technology changes the context of daily life. Religion must adapt to these new media forms to remain relevant. The changes brought about by advances in media technology have always resulted in the increased personalization of religion.

Perhaps the most radical change for religion came with the development of the printing press in the fifteenth century because it made possible the mass distribution of written material for the first time in human history. Among the first books printed for mass distribution was the Bible; soon other religious texts in the language of the people became widely available. The availability of core religious texts stimulated a rapid rise in literacy and meant that the masses, for the first time, did not have to rely on priests or other religious leaders to tell them what was in the religious texts. This expansion of religious knowledge allowed the ideas of the Protestant Reformation to spread quickly, and forever changed the shape of Christianity. Even today, the Christian Bible, particularly the versions that dominate in Protestantism, is among the most widely read and distributed books.

A more recent media revolution came with the rise of the radio and then of television in the twentieth century. Evangelical preachers and churches quickly used these new media to reach larger and larger audiences and get more resources, as described in Chapters 4 and 5. Both orthodox and progressive religious leaders have used these media to spread their messages about appropriate cultural values and actions. As James Hunter demonstrates, these messages are often heavily polarized, with only the most extreme leaders and messages shown on television because debate draws more viewers and more ad money than consensus and compromise. These debates, while contentious, emphasize the role of religion in daily life to American audiences.

Television and radio are not only tools to be used by religious leaders to present their views, they also provide a cultural resource for understanding religion and spirituality by helping define what religion is and is not. There are numerous examples of popular media that explore these questions and transmit both positive and negative

Figure 8.3 Christian broadcaster Pat Robertson has built an extensive media empire to transmit his religious perspective to others. It includes the Christian Broadcasting Network, now seen in 180 countries and broadcast in 71 languages

Courtesy of National Geographic/Getty Images

messages about a range of religious practices. Examples include television shows such as *Touched by an Angel*, *Seventh Heaven*, *Charmed*, *X-Files*, or *Supernatural*, movies such as *Ghost*, *What Dreams May Come*, or *The Sixth Sense*, and video games such as *Diablo* or *God of War*. The television program, *Seventh Heaven*, for example, depicts the family life of a Protestant minister, his wife, and their seven children. Each episode or story arc deals with a moral lesson or controversial theme, such as drug abuse, pre-marital sex, teenage pregnancy, sexual harassment, or racism. The topics are typically approached from an evangelical Protestant point of view, but rarely discussed in explicitly religious terms. While most media forms do not transmit religious morality in such direct ways, they all help people construct notions of what is religious and what is secular, and define themselves in relation to those notions.

Box 8.3 Popular media as a religious resource

Lynn Schofield Clark (2007: 69) used in-depth interviews with seventy-one teenagers to explore how the popular media influences how they understand religion and spirituality. The following quotes demonstrate how these teenagers used the spiritual content of the media they consumed to inform their ideas about religion and spirituality.

> Judgment Day, you don't go straight to heaven or straight to hell ... It's when Jesus is going to come out of the sky and then he's going to take everybody up there who qualifies. I don't know. [The film] *What Dreams May Come*, I think that is what I want my heaven to be like: whatever it is you enjoy will be there and you can see all the people you know that died.
> (Nina, a 15-year-old who regularly attended a Baptist church)

> My view on Catholicism ... but it just kind of always freaked me out. I had nightmares for years about Jesus on the crucifix because you know, you think the Garden of Eden is supposed to be beautiful but then you look at these horrible images, like [the film] *Stigmata* ... and Jesus went through tons of torture. That is just really scary. So, watching *Stigmata* and *Passion of the Christ* reminds me of religion.
> (Maria, a 15-year-old who had limited experiences with formal religion)

The rise of the Internet as a dominant form of communication, information gathering, and media consumption in the late twentieth and early twenty-first centuries has been the latest development in the media that has altered how religion is disseminated and transmitted. The Internet has many functions in people's lives. One is the ability to instantly and constantly connect with religion. In the year 2000, it was estimated that more people were using the Internet for religious purposes than for online dating or banking services. Moreover, the 2003 Pew Internet and American Life Project found that 64 per cent of Americans who accessed the Internet used it for religious and spiritual purposes, such as seeking out information about their religion or interacting with other believers through forums or social sites. Religious groups and institutions are also using the Internet in a variety of ways, including as a means for individuals to participate in rituals, attend services, and interact with other believers. Finally, the Internet also provides a place for believers of small religions to commune with each other online, perhaps making it easier for the new religious movements described in Chapter 7 to survive and flourish. In short, religious worship, education, and socialization are increasingly taking place online in American society.

For religious leaders, the Internet poses a substantial challenge to their authority. Although it gives them a great deal of control over their message, it does not give them any control over messages that oppose or disagree with their stance on religious, political, or social issues. The Internet does not allow the privileging of some religious groups over others. Nor does it give religious leaders means of ensuring that only certain approaches or ideas within a religious group are publicly available.

At the same time that the Internet reduces the power of religious leaders to transmit the religious messages they desire, it increases the power of individual believers to create and define a religious experience that is meaningful for them. Mia Lövheim observed eight web communities focused on Christianity or new religious phenomena such as modern witchcraft, magic, and Satanism. She found that the communities centered on Christian belief, although presented as a way for Christians to share their beliefs with other Christians and seekers, became places for fierce debates between believers and non-believers. On the other hand, discussions in communities focusing on new religious phenomena were based on providing information, such as how to become a witch or magician, as well as answering questions about which practices are more valid than others. Importantly, without the presence of traditional religious authorities and a shared core of beliefs, individuals are able to shape their religious identities in their own ways and create hybrid spiritualities, a phenomenon discussed in Chapter 16.

Online religious experiences are different than face-to-face or traditional religious experiences. Internet posts are generally short, giving limited room to explain beliefs and ideas. Internet communications mask the physical identity of the person, freeing people to present as broad or as narrow an online "self" as desired or even to create many different religious "selves." This kind of freedom allows the formation of multiple or hybrid spiritualities, but can also raise the question of which one, if any, of these online identities is authentic. Although online communities allow people to foster ongoing relationships with others, the constant entry of new members into the communities makes discussions fragmented so that the same debates keep reappearing. The lack of privileged religious authority in online interactions creates a more level playing field, but can cause people to enter into a struggle for control over online spaces. Finally, online religious experiences can either reinforce or challenge people's existing views on religion, depending on how frequently they participant in the online setting and how much power and control they have in that setting. Because religion is increasingly transmitted online, these differences between online and traditional religious experiences will increasingly influence how individuals respond to and understand religion in American society.

Changing religions

Most of the previous discussion about the transmission of religion has concentrated on the reinforcement of beliefs and practices that people already hold. At the same time, however, people sometimes shed beliefs and practices, adopting new ones or even abandoning belief altogether. How they do that is also part of the story of the transmission of religion. Sociologists have defined a number of ways in which people keep, change, drop, or modify their religious beliefs. Religious development is the gradual process of exploring and questioning religious beliefs that individuals go through as they grow from a child to an adult. As discussed above, relationships with family members play a primary role in religious development.

As adults, individuals can change religious beliefs in a number of different ways. Most frequently, the majority of people do not abandon the religious beliefs and affiliation they were raised in, even if they exhibit the development described above. This is called religious retention. People can also combine the religion they were raised in with new beliefs and practices to form hybrid spiritualities. As described in Chapter 16 and above, hybrid spiritualities are increasingly common as people have access to a wider array of religious beliefs and practices due to the Internet and greater religious diversity. Switching is also fairly common and occurs when individuals change to a different denomination within the same religion. A Baptist becoming a Methodist, or an Orthodox Jew becoming a Reform Jew are examples of switching. Switching happens for a variety of reasons, ranging from convenience based on access to a nearby religious institution to a process similar to religious conversion.

Religious conversion is usually defined by sociologists as a radical personal change in religious beliefs. In other words, conversion is more than just a shift of values and belief; instead it is a complete change in an individual's overall thoughts about their own religious lives. A Christian who becomes a Buddhist converts to a new religion and a Muslim who abandons that faith also goes through a religious conversion. Conversion is often thought to be a sudden process, often described as an epiphany or, in the evangelical tradition, being "born again." However, it can also be a gradual process as a result of a period of questioning and reflection.

Sociologists have been particularly interested in the causes of religious conversion. In the popular media, religious conversion is frequently portrayed as a forced act or as the "brainwashing" of the person. However, most research finds that conversion is generally voluntary and occurs without force. Instead, conversion often occurs out of a desire for self-transformation, a desire to fill a need in life, or to seek out new religious experiences and beliefs. This seeking behavior among the baby boomer generation is described in Chapter 4. In addition, younger people are more likely to convert due to dissatisfaction with the religion they were raised in. Those with higher educational attainment are also more likely to convert than persons with lesser educational attainment, because education emphasizes the critical thinking of all areas of life, including religious beliefs. In addition, those with weak social networks within their religion are more likely to convert, as described above. Finally, conversion is most likely to occur due to traumatic life events, such as a death in the family, divorce, unemployment, or health troubles. These life events often cause high levels of stress and feelings of personal inadequacy and limitation. Religion, especially a fresh approach to religion, is attractive during times of stress or trauma because it provides comfort to people and provides a brace against chaos, as described in Chapter 1.

Table 8.2 reports retention, switching (in the Protestant traditions), and conversion into another religion or no religion for major religious groups in the US, based on the 2007 Pew Religious Landscape Survey. Among those who were raised in a Protestant tradition, 52 per cent remained in that tradition at the time of the survey, 28 per cent had switched to a new Protestant tradition, 7 per cent had converted to another

Table 8.2 Retention of childhood members among groups

Panel A: Protestant traditions

Among those raised:	Non-converts	Switched to a new Protestant family	Converted to a non-Protestant religion	Converted to religiously unaffiliated
Protestant	52%	28%	7%	13%

Panel B: Other religious groups

Among those raised:	Non-converts	Converted to another religion	Converted to religiously unaffiliated
Catholic	68%	18%	14%
Jewish	76%	9%	14%
Hindu	84%	8%	8%
Buddhist	50%	22%	28%
Mormon	70%	15%	14%
Unaffiliated	46%	54%	N/A

Source: 2007 US Religious Landscape Survey, Pew Research Center Forum on Religion & Public Life, http://religions.pewforum.org/

religion, and 13 per cent had become religiously unaffiliated. Switching is particularly high among Protestants because there is a wide variety of Protestant denominations and congregations to choose from in the US. Among those raised in Catholicism, Judaism, Hinduism, and Mormonism, over two-thirds stayed affiliated with the religion by the time of the survey, and roughly equal percentages in each religion converted to another religion or became religiously unaffiliated in each religion. These religions have high rates of retention because they have no "nearest neighbor" one can easily switch to and have strong traditions of being passed down within a family and/ or ethnicity. The majority of those raised without a particular religious affiliation had converted to a religion at the time of the survey. This finding is supported by research that suggests that those with no religion are particularly likely to convert during traumatic life events or high stress events.

The process of religious change illuminates many of the ways in which religion is transmitted in our society. Most broadly, it illustrates the ways in which people live and change religions in their own ways. However, the decision to keep or change religious beliefs or affiliation is affected by social institutions, such as the family, religious congregations, and the media. The power of the family and congregations in influencing religious retention, as well as variations in that power, are displayed when we explore the rates retention, switching (in the Protestant traditions), and conversion in the population. Finally, changing media forms, and the Internet in particular, have made it far easier for those who want to change their religious beliefs to explore alternatives, as evidenced by the rise in hybrid spiritualities and the increasing numbers of people unaffiliated with any particular religion or tradition.

Key points you need to know

- Religion is socially transmitted by the family, religious congregations, and the media. Yet, individuals shape the meanings of religious experiences in their personal lives in ways that are distinct from institutionally defined religion.
- The primary avenue of religious transmission is through the family.
- The family's power to transmit religion varies across an individual's life cycle and between different generations of Americans.
- Religion transmits norms and attitudes about the family.
- Religious education and worship are the primary ways in which religion is transmitted in religious congregations.
- Megachurches, or those with over two thousand weekly attendees, have grown. Megachurches communicate religion in distinctive ways, including small groups and across multiple media formats.
- Religions adapt to each new form of media technology in ways that change the religious experience of believers and challenge the power of religious authorities.
- Religious change takes many forms and has many causes.

Discussion questions

1 Why do most people stay in the religion in which their parents raised them? Why do some people change religions?
2 Why are more recent generations less religiously affiliated than previous generations?
3 How do religions transmit notions of family roles among evangelical men and women?
4 Why are worship and religious education features of all congregations in the US?
5 What is the dominant organization form of American congregations?
6 How do megachurches provide a sense of community when they are so large?
7 What are some ways in which changing media forms have altered how religion is communicated in the US?
8 How are online religious experiences different from face-to-face religious experiences?
9 What are the five types of religious change?
10 What are the causes of religious conversion?

Further reading

Bartkowski, J.P. (2007) "Connections and Contradictions: Exploring the Complex Linkages between Faith and Family," in N. Ammerman (ed.), *Everyday Religion: Observing Modern Religious Lives*, Oxford: Oxford University Press.

Becker, P.E. (1999) *Congregations in Conflict: Cultural Models of Local Religious Life*, Cambridge: Cambridge University Press.

Bobkowski, P.S. and Pearce, L.D. (2011) "Baring their Souls in Online Profiles or Not? Religious Self Disclosure in Social Media," *Journal for the Scientific Study of Religion*, 50(4): 744–62.

Brasher, B. (2004) *Give Me That Online Religion*, Camden, New Brunswick, NJ: Rutgers University Press.

Chaves, M. (2006) "2005 H. Paul Douglass Lecture: All Creatures Great and Small: Megachurches in Context," *Review of Religious Research*, 47(4): 329–46.

Clark, L.S. (2007) "Religion, Twice Removed: Exploring the Role of Media in Religious Understandings among 'Secular' Young People," in N. Ammerman (ed.), *Everyday Religion: Observing Modern Religious Lives*, Oxford: Oxford University Press.

Edgell, P. (2006) *Religion and Family in a Changing Society*, Princeton, NJ: Princeton University Press.

Hall, D. (1998) "Managing to Recruit: Religious Conversion in the Workplace," *Sociology of Religion*, 59(4): 393–410.

Hunter, J.D. (1991) *Culture Wars: The Struggle to Define America*, New York: Basic Books.

Nelson, T.J. (2005) *Every Time I Feel the Spirit: Religious Experience and Ritual in an African American Church*, New York: New York University Press.

Pearce, L. and Denton, M.L. (2011) *A Faith of their Own: Stability and Change in the Religiosity of America's Adolescents*, Oxford: Oxford University Press.

Sherkat, D.E. and Wilson, J. (1995) "Preferences, Constraints, and Choices in Religious Markets: An Examination of Religious Switching and Apostasy," *Social Forces*, 73(3): 993–1026.

Snow, D.A. and Machalek, R. (1984) "The Sociology of Conversion," *Annual Review of Sociology*, 10: 167–90.

Thumma, S. and Travis, D. (2007) *Beyond Megachurch Myths*, San Francisco: Jossey-Bass.

Wuthnow, R. (2010) *After the Baby Boomers: How Twenty- and Thirty-Somethings are Shaping the Future of American Religion*, Princeton, NJ: Princeton University Press.

Zinnbauer, B.J. and Pargament, K.I. (1998) "Spiritual Conversion: A Study of Religious Change Among College Students," *Journal for the Scientific Study of Religion*, 37(1): 161–80.

9 Religion, politics, and government

In this chapter

This chapter explores the relationship among religion, politics, and government in the contemporary US. It begins by describing possible relationships between religions and civil governments. It next turns to the two elements of the First Amendment to the Constitution of the US that apply to religion. The third section probes why religions want to influence politics and research on the extent to which they try to do so. The chapter then discusses some of the sociological research on religion and political behavior, looking at the "culture war" thesis and more recent research on religion and political behavior that focuses on religion in the political culture, religion's effect on shaping social policy preferences, and religion and partisan voting.

Main topics covered

- The three primary relationships between religion and civil governments: state-dominated religions, religious theocracies, and separate spheres.
- The First Amendment to the US Constitution with its guarantees that the US government will not establish a state religion and ensures individuals' rights to believe and practice what they want; continuing debates about the limits and meaning of religious freedom in the US.
- How and why religions attempt to influence the political process and governments for a variety of reasons.
- The culture wars to instill visions of society into American life.
- Religion shapes people's attitudes towards political, social, and policy options and stances.
- Religious voting patterns since 1960 and why they have not changed significantly, even as politicians have become more religiously polarized.

Religion, politics, and government

Religion, politics, and government have a long, intertwined, and complicated history around the world and in the US. For example, the history of the US begins with British citizens settling in America in order to ensure religious freedom for themselves, but it is also true that the colonies started by these immigrants excluded, sometimes violently, those of other religious faiths. Additionally, as described by Diana Eck, the protection of religious freedom enshrined in the Bill of Rights is an idea rooted in a Protestant theological point regarding the granting of free will. Moreover, as described in Chapter 18, the explosion of diverse religious expressions and practices in the contemporary US is a direct result of changes to immigration law, a government policy. Finally, many divisive political issues in the US in the early twenty-first century are tied to issues of religious belief and practice. These include debates about abortion, gay marriage, the appropriate role of science, and redistribution of resources, and are tied to issues of religious belief and practices.

Although there are many ways in which religion and civil governments can be related, the three most prevalent possibilities are state-dominated religions, religious theocracies, and separate spheres for religion and government. State-dominated religions are those in which the state or rulers use religion to strengthen or legitimate their power. This was Marx's idea of what religion is when he said "religion is the opiate of the people." As described in Chapter 15, religions will go along with this relationship because, like any other institution, religious institutions are dependent upon the favor of those in power. State-dominated religions are usually used to reinforce existing social arrangements and impede social change. The most famous historical example of a state-dominated religion (popularized in the television series *The Tudors*) was the establishment of the Church of England and rejection of the Roman Catholic Church and the Pope's authority over King Henry VIII's right to a marital annulment in the sixteenth century. The creation of a church headed by the king consolidated all political and religious power and claims to legitimate rule into the civil government. In the American context, the colony of Maryland was predominantly Catholic, although officially neutral in religious affairs. In 1701, the Church of England was proclaimed the official church of the colony. Over the course of the eighteenth century, Maryland Catholics were barred from public office and then disenfranchised, and laws were passed restricting their property rights.

Religious theocracies are those in which the legal system of the country is dominated by explicitly religious law and governed by religious elites. For example, the government of Iran in the early twenty-first century is a religious theocracy, as is the very small city-state of the Vatican. A historical example is ancient Egypt, in which the Pharaoh was seen as a God on earth. Religious theocracies are different from state-dominated religions because religious belief provides the basis for political rule as opposed to religions serving the needs of the state. Theocracies were very common in early societies and, as political systems, are not particularly problematic if religious beliefs and practices are shared by all members of the society. Modern, globalized societies and increasing religious diversity in many countries make theocracies hard to sustain because of the high potential for social instability as minority religious groups resist the imposition of religious law and as global concerns about human and civil rights come to the fore. The Mormon experience described in Chapter 14 highlights the tensions associated with religious minorities and the difficulties associated with maintaining a religious theocracy in a pluralistic society.

Finally, religion and government can be separate spheres. In the US, this is more commonly referred to as the separation of church and state or religious freedom. The assumption that a separate spheres relationship is endemic to modern societies underlies the revised secularization theory reviewed in Chapter 2. This arrangement prevails in the US and most other democracies. In this relationship, the balance between religion and politics is constantly in flux and is the result of the ability of religious groups to have, or not, their religious groups and practices inform policy and laws. As we shall see in the rest of the chapter, having religion and government "separate" means, in fact, that religions will actively engage in the political process and there is likely to be perpetual tension around the proper workings of the relationship.

Religious freedom in the US

Box 9.1 First Amendment to the United State Constitution

Here is the wording of the First Amendment to the US Constitution, providing for freedom of religion and what has long been called "separation of church and state":

> Congress shall make no law respecting an establishment of religion, or prohibiting the free exercise thereof; or abridging the freedom of speech, or of the press; or the right of the people peaceably to assemble, and to petition the Government for a redress of grievances.

The First Amendment to the US Constitution states that "Congress shall make no law respecting an establishment of religion, or prohibiting the free exercise thereof ..." These clauses enshrine religious freedom as an unalienable right of all Americans, although precisely what that freedom entails has frequently caused contention. The first clause of the amendment is called the disestablishment clause and prohibits Congress from creating a state religion. The framers of the US Constitution were strongly opposed to an official or state religion in the form of a theocracy or even a state-sponsored church and thought this clause important enough to put it first in the Bill of Rights. This clause laid the groundwork for the distinct separation of church and state and, in particular, the segregation of religion into a separate sphere of social life. In practice, this separation has evolved in historical phases through social and cultural shifts. For example, the split between mainline and evangelical Protestants and the disconnection between religion and public schools and universities documented in Chapters 4 and 5 is evidence of the weakening Protestant hegemony in the US, while the rise in religious diversity described in Chapter 18 is evidence of the weakening Christian hegemony in public life. For religious groups, this separation has costs, such as the reduced ability of religious groups to regulate social life in a variety of areas. However, it also has benefits, such as the increased religious vitality that may be caused by religious diversity, described in detail in Chapter 2, and the ability of religious institutions to call for radical or permanent social change because they are independent from the government (Chapter 15).

The second clause ensures that individuals have the right to believe and practice religious beliefs without undue interference from the state – in other words, the free exercise of religion. It is important to note that this clause does not regulate an individual's behavior towards those of other religions. Although religious freedom is guaranteed for all religious believers, in practice there are distinct advantages to being a member of a majority religion. A majority religion is taken for granted as "normal" by law and social policies and existing legal, political, and social structures have a difficult time accommodating minority religions. For example, many public and private institutions are closed on major Christian holidays, but those of other religious backgrounds have to seek special permission to be excused from work on days sacred to their traditions.

The meaning of the separation of church and state and the free exercise of religion is the subject of intense debate and of numerous legal battles and court decisions. Since World War II, many of these battles center on the distinction between freedom *of* religion and freedom *from* religion. To some people, separation of church and state refers to a wall that protects government and politics from religious influence. To others, the separation of church and state is to protect religion from interference from the state and to preserve religion's independence as a source of belief and conscience for its followers. Court decisions on first amendment issues support parts of both positions. For example, mandated prayer, devotional Bible reading, and the teaching of both creationism and intelligent design in the public schools have all been ruled unconstitutional. However, courts have has also ruled that citizens can't challenge a state law that public funding, through school vouchers, can be used to fund attendance at religious schools. The impact of these rulings on religion weaves through most of the chapters in this part of the book, but especially Chapter 4.

Box 9.2 Major Supreme Court decisions related to religious freedom

In the past century, there have been over 100 Supreme Court decisions that shaped the scope of the First Amendment as it relates to religious freedom in the US. For a complete listing of these cases, see http://religiousfreedom.lib.virginia.edu/court/. Some major cases are:

West Virginia State Board of Education v. Barnette (1943)

As part of instituting a required curriculum teaching American values, the state of West Virginia mandated that students and teachers salute the flag. A group of Jehovah's Witnesses refused to salute the flag because it represented a graven image that was not to be recognized. In an 8–1 decision, the Court ruled that the school district violated the rights of students by forcing them to salute the American flag.

Engel v. Vitale (1962)

In New Hyde Park, New York, the school day opened with a required prayer approved by the Board of Regents. In a 6–1 decision, the Court ruled that prayers could not be required to be recited in public schools.

Abington Township School District v. Schempp (1963) and
Murray v. Curlett (1963)

These two cases involved a Pennsylvania law that required children to hear and read portions of the Bible as part of their public school education. The Court ruled 8–1 that school-sponsored Bible reading in public schools is unconstitutional.

Lemon v. Kurtzman (1971), Earley v. DiCenso (1971), and
Robinson v. DiCenso (1971)

These three cases from Pennsylvania and Rhode Island involved public assistance to private schools, some of which were religious. The Court unanimously ruled that the assistance was unconstitutional and instituted the "Lemon Test" for analyzing legislation that did not violate the First Amendment. The Lemon Test includes three criteria:

1   The law must have a secular purpose.
2   The primary effect of the law must neither advance nor inhibit religion.
3   The law must not foster an excessive government entanglement with religion.

Larson v. Valente (1982)

A Minnesota law required charitable groups to register with the state's Department of Commerce. Religious groups who solicited more than 50 per cent of its contributions from members or affiliated organizations were exempt from registering. The Court ruled 5–4 that the Minnesota law was unconstitutional because it placed a burden on certain religions. This decision prevents states from passing laws that might favor certain types of religion. To pass the Lemon Test, the state would have to exempt all religions from complying with the law.

Edwards v. Aguillard (1987)

Louisiana had a "Creationism Act" that prevented the teaching of evolution unless it was accompanied by the teaching of biblical creationism. Neither was required to be taught, but the former could not be taught without being grouped with the latter. In a 7–2 decision, the Court invalidated Louisiana's "Creationism Act" because it did not have a secular purpose and, therefore, violated the Disestablishment Clause.

Religious influence on politics and the government

Modern governments have many important functions. They define who is entitled to citizenship and what the benefits of citizenship are. Property ownership, race, and gender have all been the basis for the rights of citizenship in the US. Governments set national policies and priorities; for example, the state decides whether building up the military will take precedence over ensuring health care for citizens or funding education.

Governments set tax policies and redistribute money through the tax system, including how taxes are collected, whether tax is progressive or regressive, who pays taxes, and what kinds of behavior are rewarded via the tax collection process (for example, deductions for dependents, tax credits for green energy programs or charitable contributions, and making religious organizations tax-exempt). Governments redistribute money through government programs, such as Social Security, Medicare, Medicaid, defense spending, and others. As described in Chapter 12, faith-based organizations secured better access to US government funding for their social service activities that help them serve the poor and needy because of the development of various faith-based initiatives.

Finally, governments make rules and laws for citizens and increasingly regulate everyday behaviors. For centuries, governments have had basic laws protecting human life and private property. However, the rise of the modern "welfare state" has increased the regulation of everyday behaviors such as restrictions on what we eat and drink, how we can advertise goods and services, what safety equipment we must use, what teachers say and teach to kids, what doctors say, zoning laws, child-protection laws, drug laws, etc.

In any political system, religious groups are likely to have preferences about all of these functions. In democracies, religious groups try to influence the political process by working to elect politicians who will work to set national priorities, policies, and laws and rules that reflect their wishes. This is particularly true when there is a clash between what the government allows its citizens and what religious groups require of their members. In a contemporary example, the 2010 Affordable Care Act required that religious employers pay for birth control as part of health care plans provided to employees. This raised considerable controversy among Catholics, even though the majority of Catholic women use birth control. The controversy resulted in a compromise in which the insurer would be required to pay for birth control for women and religious employers could not prevent their employees from receiving birth control.

Given this array of functions, it should be no surprise that religious groups and people aim to influence politics and the government (politics can be defined as the struggle for control over government and its functions). One way in which they can do so is through social movement protest, including the civil rights movement described through Part II, or sometimes violent acts, as described in Chapter 15. However, in the contemporary US, most religious groups choose to influence the political process through electoral politics, including political organizing, petitioning political leaders, voter registrations, and voting, instead of using protest movements or violence. Kraig Beyerlein and Mark Chaves, in a 2003 study quantifying the political activities of religious congregations in the US, found that more than 40 per cent of congregations engage in some form of political activity, a very high level of engagement when compared to other non-political and non-religious organizations. They also found that there is significant variation in the type of political activity across congregations; for example, evangelical/conservative Protestant congregations engage in politics by distributing Christian Right voter guides. Black Protestant congregations register voters, open their doors to candidates, and distribute voter

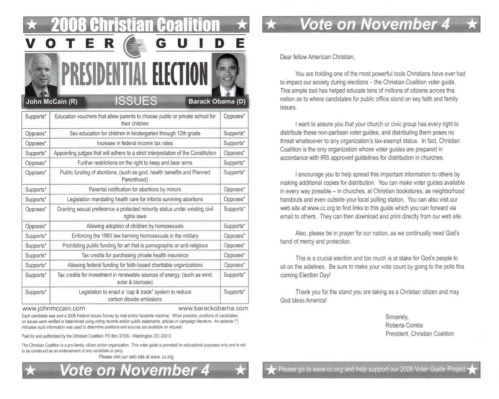

Figure 9.1 Some religious groups try to influence the way people vote by distributing guides about issues or candidates. This is a voter guide for the 2008 presidential election distributed by the Christian Coalition

© Editorial Image, LLC/Alamy

guides from sources other than the Christian Right. Some congregations also take an active role in the delivery of social services, which we explore in Chapter 12.

The "culture wars" thesis

There has been a substantial amount of sociological research concerning the relationship between religion and politics, particularly around the political and policy preferences of various religious groups. One of the better known sociological analyses concerning the relationship between religion and politics emphasizing the political and policy preferences of various religious groups is James Davison Hunter's *Culture Wars* (1991). He argued that by the end of the twentieth century, there were two camps in American culture. One consisted of the Orthodox, or those who believe that there should be clearly defined rules or limits on human behavior. This camp includes religious conservatives. The other camp takes in the Progressives, or those who believe that their own thinking and experience should define their actions. Progressives draw on rationalism and sometimes on relativism, or the notion that no cultural expression is better than others. They tend to be found in mainline and liberal groups if they have any religious affiliation. Both Orthodox and Progressive groups attempt to instill their vision of society into the public sector by influencing four social institutions: the law and politics, the media, the family, and education.

Hunter's book has influenced public debates about the role of religion in politics and government. However, most recent sociological research finds that Americans are not split into two religious camps around all issues. Instead, research by Davis and Robison, done in 1996, finds that a vast array of economic and social policies, including tax policy, the role of the government in redistribution, spending priorities, and preferred foreign policy stances, are not closely linked to religion. For example, across religious traditions and commitment, people are evenly split between a preference for a smaller government or a larger government. Strong majorities of every religious group believe that the government should do more to help the poor and that the US should concentrate more on domestic problems than world affairs. Finally, the majority of Americans are concerned with environmental protection and many want stricter laws to that effect. Instead of religion, attitudes towards these policies are driven by political party affiliation and social class.

However, Davis and Robison, along with more recent researchers, find that religious differences are the primary predictor, and source of division, of attitudes toward gender and family related issues. For example, as described above, the role of religion in public schools has been, and continues to be, a contentious issue in American society. While courts have played a significant role in determining how religion is represented in public schools, inconsistent and contradictory rulings have left school officials and families confused about what religious practices are allowed and have resulted in significant variation across localities in these issues. This matter takes on particular importance as 85 per cent of school-aged children in America are educated in public schools. As noted in Chapter 5, some evangelicals have taken to starting their own schools or home schooling children in order to avoid these battles.

One of the more controversial and divisive social policy issues is the issue of abortion. Most people in religious traditions have firm views toward one side of the debate. As shown in Table 9.1, Evangelical Protestants and Mormons are likely to believe that abortion should be illegal in most or all cases, while mainline Protestants, Muslims, Hindus, and those with no religious affiliation believe it should be legal in most or all cases. The 2007 Pew Religious Landscape Survey, some of the results of which are shown in Table 9.1, also finds that views on abortion differ within religious groups, with those that exhibit high levels of religious commitment or church attendance being much more likely to believe that abortion should be illegal than those less committed. An issue that is often related to abortion concerns stem cell research. Research finds that those who attend church more frequently and report strong religious beliefs are more likely to be opposed to stem cell research. The reasons for this division are connected to the rise of American evangelism as a political force, as described in Chapter 5.

Another controversial and divisive social issue is that of homosexuality and the rights of same-sex couples to marry. As shown in Table 9.2, Pew Research polling has found significant differences across religious traditions in the proportion of those in favor of allowing same-sex couples to legally marry. Those who attend church less than weekly, mainline Protestants, Jews, and the religiously unaffiliated are more likely to favor it than others. However, and importantly, there have been consistent increases in support over time across religious traditions. The long and contentious battle about the acceptance of homosexuality within American religious groups is a

Table 9.1 Attitudes toward abortion

	Abortion should be legal in most/ all cases	Illegal in most or all cases
Total population	51%	43%
Evangelical Protestants	33%	61%
Mainline Protestants	62%	32%
Black Protestants	47%	46%
Catholics	48%	45%
Mormons	27%	70%
Jews	84%	14%
Muslims	48%	48%
Buddhists	81%	13%
Hindus	69%	27%
No religious affiliation	70%	27%

Source: 2007 US Religious Landscape Survey, Pew Research Center Forum on Religion & Public Life, http://religions.pewforum.org/

Table 9.2 Favor allowing gays and lesbians to marry legally

	1996	2008	2010
Total population	27%	38%	42%
Evangelical Protestants	13%	17%	20%
Attend church weekly	8%	10%	14%
Attend church less	25%	28%	31%
Mainline Protestants	27%	40%	49%
Attend church weekly	15%	34%	35%
Attend church less	30%	42%	53%
Black Protestants	23%	27%	28%
Attend church weekly	–	19%	22%
Attend church less	–	37%	37%
Catholics	32%	42%	46%
Attend church weekly	21%	34%	34%
Attend church less	37%	51%	59%
Jews	–	75%	76%
No religious affiliation	45%	63%	62%

Source: Religion and Attitudes Towards Same-Sex Marriage, Pew Research Center Forum on Religion & Public Life, Feb. 2012, http://pewforum.org/uploadedFiles/Topics/Issues/Gay_Marriage_and_Homosexuality /same-sex-marriage–10-detailed-tables.pdf

central focus of Part I. We also discuss more of the sociological evidence about this issue in Chapter 16.

Issues of appropriate gender roles and family structures also are affected by religious belief. For example, evangelical Protestants and the more religiously orthodox favor stricter divorce laws. In addition, sociological research has found gender and religious differences in regard to proper gender roles, with evangelical Protestant and more orthodox women having more traditional ideas about gender roles, while other women have more liberal views of gender roles, and men tend to be somewhere in the middle. This issue is also explored in Chapter 10.

Religion and political behavior

Sociological theory and research find that religion affects political behavior in both subtle and obvious ways. Most broadly, Rhys Williams and Richard Wood argue that the US has a common political culture centered on ideas of a good, moral society in which justice and rights ordained by a higher power are foundations of society. This political culture has its roots in mainline Protestant theology and values. In order to be successful, politicians must appeal to this common political culture.

Although there is substantial agreement around this common political culture, there is substantial disagreement about the role government should play in protecting or enforcing morality in society. For example, data from the 2007 Pew Religious Landscape Survey shown in Table 9.3 finds that evangelical Protestants, Mormons, and Muslims are more likely to say that the government should protect morality while other religious minorities and the unaffiliated are more wary of government roles in legislating morality. Additionally, the 2003 American Mosaic Project Survey finds that evangelical Protestants and black Protestants are more likely to believe that society's standards of right and wrong should be based on God's laws, while Catholics, religious minorities, and those with no religious affiliation are particularly unlikely to believe this to be true. Moreover, Americans of all religious faiths are evenly divided about whether churches should express views on politics, according to the Religious Landscape Survey. These disagreements are rooted, in part, in the divide between mainline and evangelical Protestants that is the focus of Chapters 4 and 5.

Table 9.3 Government's role in protecting or enforcing morality

	The government should do more to protect morality	I worry the government is getting too involved in the issue of morality	Society's standards of right and wrong should be based on God's laws
Total population	40%	52%	44%
Evangelical Protestants	50%	41%	65%
Mainline Protestants	33%	58%	40%
Black Protestants	48%	42%	66%
Catholics	43%	49%	35%
Mormons	54%	39%	N/A
Jews	22%	71%	21%
Muslims	59%	29%	40%
Buddhists	26%	67%	7%
Hindus	44%	45%	20%
No religious affiliation	27%	66%	13%

Sources: Columns 1 and 2 are from the 2007 US Religious Landscape Survey, Pew Research Center Forum on Religion & Public Life, http://religions.pewforum.org/. Column 3 is from the 2003 American Mosiac Project Survey

Table 9.4 Political ideology

	Conservative	Moderate	Liberal
Total population	37%	36%	20%
Evangelical Protestants	52%	30%	11%
Mainline Protestants	36%	41%	18%
Black Protestants	35%	36%	21%
Catholics	36%	38%	18%
Mormons	60%	27%	10%
Jews	21%	39%	38%
Muslims	19%	38%	24%
Buddhists	12%	32%	50%
Hindus	12%	44%	35%
No religious affiliation	21%	39%	34%

Source: 2007 US Religious Landscape Survey, Pew Research Center Forum on Religion & Public Life, http://religions.pewforum.org/

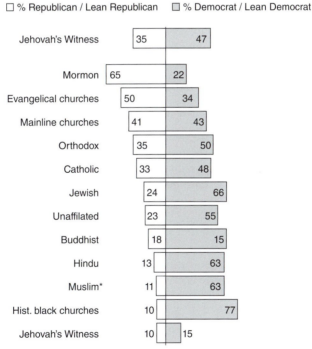

*From "Muslim Americans: Middle Class and Mostly Mainstream." Pew Research Center, 2007.

Question: In politics TODAY, do you consider yourself a Republican, Democrat, or Independent? [IF INDEPENDENT, NO PREFERENCE. OTHER. ASK]: As of today do you lean more to the Republican Party or more to the Democratic Party?

Figure 9.2 Party affiliation of religious tradition

Source: Pew Research Center's Forum on Religion & Public Life, "U.S. Religious Landscape Survey," © 2008, Pew Research Center, http://religions.pewforum.org/pdf/report2religious-landscape-study-chapter–2.pdf

The sharp differences in social and cultural views mean that there are often political differences among major religious groups. For example, most evangelical Protestants and Mormons have a conservative ideology and identity as Republicans. Mainline Protestants are more likely to be politically moderate and are evenly split between Republicans and Democrats, while Catholics, Jews, Muslims, Hindus, Buddhists, and the religiously unaffiliated are more likely to be moderate or liberal in political ideology and are more likely to be Democrats.

Conservative religious groups, such as the Moral Majority and the Christian Coalition, and, more recently, the Republican Party, have worked to mobilize voters, especially evangelical Protestant voters, around social and cultural issues, as discussed in Chapter 5. Research has found that politicians have become more polarized in their voting patterns over time, due to the effectiveness of these groups at reaching the political elite. However, Clem Brooks and Jeff Manza, in a study of differences in voting patterns from 1960 to 1992, find that individual voting patterns based on religion have not changed significantly since 1960. In other words, evangelical Protestants have consistently voted for Republicans, while most mainline Protestants and Catholics have consistently voted for Democrats. The relative size of the religious groups then becomes magnified in importance in the political process, with the largest religious groups having the most political traction. Michael Hout and Claude Fischer suggest also that the political organization of evangelical Protestantism is partially responsible for the rising number of religious unaffiliated because many people don't like the tight connection of these conservative politics and evangelical Protestants.

Key points you need to know

- Religion, politics, and government have a long, intertwined, and complicated history around the world and in the US.
- The three primary possible relationships between religion and civil governments include state-dominated religions, religious theocracies, and separate spheres.
- The First Amendment to the US Constitution guarantees that Congress shall not establish a state religion and ensures an individual's right to believe and practice what they want.
- There continue to be contentious debates about the limits and meaning of religious freedom in the US. These battles center on the distinction between freedom *of* religion and freedom *from* religion.
- In the contemporary US, most religious groups choose to influence the political process through electoral politics, including political organizing, petitioning political leaders, voter registrations, and voting.
- The "culture wars" thesis, as advanced by James Hunter, argues that the orthodox and progressives are at "war" to instill their vision of society into American life.
- Most recent sociological research finds that Americans are not split into two religious camps around all issues.

- Religion shapes individuals' attitudes towards social and cultural issues, including the role of religion in public schools, abortion, same-sex marriage, gender roles, and family structures.
- There are major political differences between religious groups.

Discussion questions

1   What are some advantages in legal matters and social policy that come to those who are members of a majority religion?
2   What are the disestablishment clause and the free exercise clause?
3   Do you believe that The First Amendment guarantees freedom *of* religion or freedom *from* religion?
4   What do you think is the proper relationship between religion and the government? Why?
5   Do you believe that there is a culture war between the orthodox/conservatives and liberals/progressives in the US?
6   Why is it that religious differences seem to have little impact on economic and fiscal policy?
7   Why do you think people of all religious affiliations have become more accepting of same-same sex marriage over the past fifteen years?
8   Why do you think the mapping of religious and political affiliation has stayed so stable since 1960?

Further reading

Beyerlein, K. and Chaves, M. (2003) "The Political Activities of Religious Congregations in the United States," *Journal for the Scientific Study of Religion*, 42: 229–46.

Brooks, C. and Manza, J. (1997) "Social Cleavages and Political Alignments: US Presidential Elections, 1960–1992," *American Sociological Review*, 62: 937–46.

Cooper, D.E. and Palmer, J. (1998) *Spirit of the Environment: Religion, Value, and Environmental Concern*, London: Routledge.

Davis, N. and Robinson, R. (1996) "Are the Rumors of War Exaggerated? Religious Orthodoxy and Moral Progressivism in America," *American Journal of Sociology*, 102: 756–87.

Eck, D. (2001) *A New Religious America: How a "Christian Country" Has Become the World's Most Religiously Diverse Nation*, San Francisco: Harper.

Hout, M. and Fischer, C.S. (2002) "Why More Americans Have No Religious Preference: Politics and Generations," *American Sociological Review*, 67: 165–90.

Hunter, J.D. (1991) *Culture Wars: The Struggle to Define America*, New York: Basic Books.

Lindsay. D.M. (2008) "Evangelicals in the Power Elite: Elite Cohesion Advancing a Movement," *American Sociological Review*, 73: 63–82.

Smith, C. (2000) *Christian America? What Evangelicals Really Want*, Berkeley: University of California Press.

Thomas, R.M. (2007) *God in the Classroom: Religion and America's Public Schools*, Westport, CT: Praeger.

Williams, R.H. and Demerath III, N.J. (1991) "Religion and Political Process in an American City," *American Sociological Review*, 56: 417–31.

—— (1999) "Visions of the Good Society and the Religious Roots of American Political Culture," *Sociology of Religion*, 60: 1–34.

Wood, R.L. (1999) "Religious Culture and Political Action," *Sociological Theory*, 17: 307–32.

10 Gender, sexuality, and religion
with Samantha E. Zulkowski

In this chapter

This chapter highlights the intersections of gender, sexuality, and religion. It first defines sex, gender, and sexuality. Then it turns to gender and religion by looking at differences in religion by gender, how gender norms are understood by different religions, and the increase in women clergy, especially in mainline Protestantism. Links between sexuality and religion are explored later in the chapter, starting with a brief overview of how different groups within Christianity, Judaism, and Islam talk about homosexuality. The section concludes with a discussion on how clergy and congregations shape their own perceptions of homosexuality and how homosexual communities create their own religious identities.

Main topics covered

- The terms "sex," "gender," and "sexuality" cannot be used interchangeably.
- Women are more likely than men to affiliate themselves with a religion, to believe in God or a spirit, and to attend religious services.
- Traditional and orthodox religious traditions place emphasis on distinct gender roles for men and women while more liberal religions stress gender equality.
- Female clergy are more likely to be engaged with broader social issues and use collaborations than are male clergy.
- More orthodox religious traditions view homosexuality as a behavior whereas more liberal traditions view it as an inborn trait.
- By not discussing issues of homosexuality, congregations tend to reproduce the same subordination and marginalization of lesbians and gays as found in the surrounding culture.
- Gays and lesbians have constructed identities to reflect both their sexuality and religiosity despite the fact that conservative religions do not embrace their lifestyles.

Sex, gender, and sexuality

Before discussing the connections among gender, sexuality, and religion, we must distinguish the categories of sex, gender, and sexuality from each other. Sex is a biological and scientific concept that is based upon the characteristics of sexual reproduction. Sex is usually divided into the binary categories of male and female. The category of gender is most often confused with sex. However, gender is socially constructed and refers to the behaviors, norms, actions, and roles that define what it is to be female or male in a given time and place. For example, many patriarchal societies separate male and female roles in the family: women are caretakers of children and men are expected to work and provide money for the family's survival. Since gender is socially constructed, it is always dichotomous, or separated into two distinct categories, and often tied to unequal gender roles that set boundaries for both women and men. The last concept, sexuality, refers to a set of sexual feelings, desires, fantasies, behaviors, and emotions attributed to women and men. Like gender, sexuality is also socially constructed so that it varies in time and place, meaning that different cultures during different eras may describe sexuality or gender in various ways.

Sociologists have shown connections between religion and many issues of gender, gender roles, sexuality, and sexual orientation found in contemporary society. Researchers have been concerned with how religious beliefs vary by gender, the impact of religious beliefs on ideas of proper gender roles and sexual behaviors, debates about women as religious leaders, and the connection between sexuality and religious identity.

Gender and religion

Scholars have found that women are more religious overall, compared to men, according to measurable criteria such as religious affiliation, belief in God or a spirit, and attendance at religious services. Data taken from the Pew Forum's 2007 US Religious Landscape Survey, presented in Table 10.1, illustrate some of the ways in which women are more likely than men to appear to be religious.

Many religious traditions reinforce patriarchal notions of women's inferiority. For example, traditional Christian groups establish clear guidelines for women and men to follow. The Roman Catholic Church forbids women from entering the priesthood, a religious community. This allows men access to higher positions while maintaining women's subordination. In addition, many present-day Orthodox Jews believe that a

Table 10.1 Gender and religious difference

	Women	Men
Affiliated with a religion	86%	79%
Believe in God or a spirit	77%	65%
Pray (at least daily)	66%	49%
Religion is important to their lives	63%	49%
Believe they have a personal relationship with God or a universal spirit	58%	45%
Attend services at least weekly	44%	34%

Source: 2007 US Religious Landscape Survey, Pew Research Center Forum on Religion & Public Life, http://religions.pewforum.org/

position that signifies a high degree of spirituality along with the opportunity to lead woman's role is to maintain the household and family, discouraging her from the study of traditional Jewish texts such as the Talmud. Finally, Islam places many restrictions on what women are allowed to do in the mosque and public life.

Why then are women more likely to participate in religious traditions that hold women to be inferior? Many sociologists have speculated that women are more religious than men since they are vulnerable in male-dominated societies. Some argue that women tend to seek comfort from their suffering through religious avenues. This is especially a factor in cultures where women are seen to be the property of their fathers, brothers, or husbands, depriving them of material possessions and limiting their social outlets. Others maintain that women are more physically vulnerable than men due to the dangers associated with childbirth and their roles as carers of the sick. Women are often reminded of their own mortality, perhaps making them more likely to find solace within religious traditions that speak of comfort and a life after death in the spiritual realm.

Some researchers have focused on gender norms such as the male worker and the female caretaker in order to explain religious differences between women and men. Compared to men, women are more likely to appear "naturally" more emotional and nurturing, more willing to satisfy the needs of others before their own, and more inclined to build and maintain close ties with others. Many traditional religions emphasize these roles as important, placing a high value on taking care of the needy, engaging in self-sacrifice, and creating strong relationships within a community. However, there has been some debate over causal ordering since it is understood that gender roles are socially constructed within a given society. These critics ask whether religious traditions create gendered roles that then are carried outside religious beliefs or whether women and men are socialized into gendered roles that are then "mapped" onto religious belief and participation. For example, some may argue that the perception of women as caretakers in the Roman Catholic tradition stems from their emulating the Virgin Mary as the mother of Jesus. However, it could also be that in a culture where women are expected to be mothers and caretakers, women may look to religion and female figures represented within traditions for inspiration. Men tend to have other available avenues for inspiration such as the workplace where they can excel as the male provider, maintaining the surrounding culture's gender norms. Furthermore, in other work, Charles H. Lippy contends that white Protestant men in America have a long history of constructing strong spiritual identities, focusing on traditional masculine roles such as patriarch, entrepreneur, and businessman.

Religious belief and gender roles

Many sociologists have concluded that religion plays a large part in understanding gender roles of femininity and masculinity. For instance, Linda Woodhead framed the interaction between gender roles and religion in four distinct ways. First, more conservative religious groups tend to support existing structures of gender inequality and legitimize traditional gender roles. Clear-cut gender roles are then established in these groups as a way to counter contemporary society's mixed gender roles approach. Second, in more mainline religious groups, women and men create parallel religious associations in which gender-specific groups dominate religious life. This most often occurs for women as a way to combat the patriarchal structure. Third, more marginal religious groups like neo-pagans form organizations that search for benefits in order to improve the wellbeing of their members as well as provide a way of coping with the dominant gender order. Fourth, other marginal religious groups, including goddess movements, tend to reconstruct gender roles more evenly to distribute power between the sexes or even to emphasize women's power, worshipping females for their ability to give life for example.

Others have focused on the impact of particular religious groups on gender roles. For example, as discussed in Chapter 5, many evangelical and fundamentalist Christian groups place particular emphasis on passages of the Bible talking about traditional and distinct gender roles for women and men. Interestingly, the adherence to traditional roles makes women both powerful as well as powerless. In one study focusing on fundamentalists, Nancy Ammerman found that although women are constrained to the home and appear subordinate to their husbands, they do in fact have the ability to persuade their husbands in household matters. Most women often invest more emotions in the household and may exemplify a better understanding of finances compared to their husbands. However, these distinct gender roles can cause a significant amount of strain for both women and men within marriage and family life. Some evangelical and fundamentalist groups push to maintain traditional gender roles even when it is not economically feasible to practice them. For instance, a husband who cannot meet the financial needs of his family may then see himself as not satisfying the expectations of the worker and provider. On the other hand, a wife who is expected to be the sole caretaker of the household and children may become overwhelmed with her duties as wife and mother. Without help from the other spouse, stress can lead to frustration or even anger that can impact the marital and familial relationships negatively.

Figure 10.1 Women often create groups to help them cope with issues and problems. Here, Muslim women pray during the Women's Islamic Initiative in Spirituality and Equality in 2006

Courtesy of Christian Science Monitor/Getty Images

Box 10.1 Feminist interpretations of sacred texts

Rita M. Gross's book *Feminism & Religion: An Introduction* discusses how feminists have sought to change the patriarchal hierarchies of Judaism, Christianity, and Islam over the years. She states that adherents of these faiths rely primarily on clerical interpretations of sacred texts in order to establish traditional roles for both men and women. Feminists have argued that a distinction must be made between text and interpretation, and that the context of when the scriptures were written should be taken into account with these interpretations. Gross contends that feminists reinterpret scriptures in order to highlight the tradition of protest against injustice and to emphasize the importance of translations in textual study. Gross mentions Phyllis Trible's work on the creation stories at the beginning of the Hebrew and Christian scriptures, which have been seen to make women seem morally weak and evil. The original texts of the origin stories state that man and woman were created in the likeness of God together, not that God created woman from man. Trible claims that the curse of Eve to be ruled over by her husband was in the original passages described as cultural constraints that limit both genders. Although there has been much debate over context and translations, feminist interpretations of the Qur'an are less frequent than interpretations of Hebrew and Christian texts. According to Gross, feminists who question male domination in Islam refer to Sura 4: *An-Nisa'*34, which claims that Allah made men superior to women and virtuous women should remain obedient. Riffat Hassan, a feminist scholar of Islam, argues that this passage does not give men power over women, but rather makes them responsible to care for their wives who are often involved in managing the household. Gross asserts that these ongoing debates among scholars have emphasized the need to reinterpret sacred texts as well as to revisit traditions that may appear discriminatory towards women.

Women in the clergy

During the past few decades, women have become increasingly influential in many Christian denominations by becoming clergy or lay leaders. Chapters 4, 5, and 6 describe some of the controversies caused by these changing roles. According to Mark Chaves, in 1993, 14.3 per cent of theological seminary students in the US were female; by 2006, that figure was up to 34 per cent, and the percentage has been steadily increasing. This mirrors the increase in women becoming doctors and lawyers, jobs that are also traditionally masculine. Then why do some Christian denominations allow women to enter into traditionally male roles within the church? Is there a difference between those churches that ordain women and those that do not yet do so?

Chaves identifies four main influences on whether or not a congregation or denomination will allow women to be ordained. First, there may be pressures coming from within the denomination in which there is a shortage of male clergy. These internal pressures could lead to policy changes to allow women to enter into the clergy to satisfy the needs and wishes of the congregation. Second, there may be external pressures pushing for equal rights for both women and men. This would include pressures from the women's movement as well as pressures from other denominations and the broader culture. Third, a denomination's stance on female clergy typically centers on whether or not the representation of a masculine clergy is key to a religious organization's identity. In this case, both sacramental and biblically inerrant Christian denominations are least likely to ordain women. Going back to the discussion in Chapter 5, evangelical denominations were very reluctant to ordain women due to passages from Genesis and Ephesians claiming women's subordination to men. Fourth, the choice to ordain women depends on internal organization, with denominations that are more de-centralized having more leeway for the congregation to ordain female clergy.

Research also suggests that women exercise different professional styles as leaders than men. Ruth Wallace, along with other researchers, argues that women are more likely to form close relationships with congregants and to use collaborations to meet specific goals. Female clergy are also more likely to be engaged with broader social justice issues and are often more liberal when confronted with issues such as abortion and gay rights than male clergy. However, female clergy often face challenges from traditional beliefs and patriarchal practices. Issues pertaining to appropriate gender roles often create obstacles for female clergy when laypeople question their abilities to represent the church and to lead the congregation. Again, as stated in Chapter 5, biblical inerrantists often refer to the creation story to illustrate women's subordination to their husbands, referencing Eve's creation from Adam's rib as well as her acceptance of the forbidden fruit. In this tradition, females are not regarded to be adequate leaders. In order to combat traditional female subordination, women often attempt to replace patriarchal beliefs with more positive beliefs of gender equality and feminism. For instance, Wallace finds that such parishes replace exclusive language such as the saying "Father, Son, and Holy Spirit" with more inclusive language, "Creator, Redeemer, and Holy Spirit." Wallace remarks that a vast majority of congregants attribute their support for gender equality to female clergy.

Although women's roles continue to change within religious traditions, there are still ongoing struggles for gender equality, especially within conservative and orthodox faiths. Religion not only provides norms for both male and female roles, but also sets boundaries on sexuality and sexual behavior.

Sexuality and religion

The tensions about sexuality that have roiled mainline religions in contemporary America have been described throughout Part II. Such questions as "can homosexuals be ordained?" and "is homosexuality a sin?" have sparked major divisions within religions such as Christianity and Judaism as well as motivated individuals to push for more progressive thinking in other strict religious traditions such as Islam.

Christian denominations throughout the US have presented varying degrees of acceptance of homosexuality. This may be due to a lack of consensus about just what homosexuality entails, policies about gay and lesbian members, and interpretations of the few biblical passages that refer to same-sex sexual behavior. Positions on these issues are strongly affected by the belief of whether or not the Bible is inerrant, members' personal experiences, and new scientific research on homosexuality.

Some strands of the Christian tradition such as Roman Catholicism and Eastern Orthodoxy refer to past policies on homosexuality that discourage same-sex relationships and marriage. Passages from the Bible such as Leviticus 18:22's "Thou shalt not lie with mankind, as with womankind: it is abomination" provide a foundation for conservative religious belief. Conservatives tend to look at homosexuality as a behavior that can be changed or subdued rather than something biological. Such behavior is viewed as sinful, against the traditional norms of marriage and procreation.

However, there has been much debate over passages referring to homosexuality from the Bible. Derrick S. Bailey and George Edwards argue that the few biblical passages that mention homosexuality may have been misinterpreted and are wrongfully used to condemn homosexuals as sinners. The sin of Sodom, for example, may not refer to homosexuality but rather to masculine sexual aggression, gang rape, or inhospitality. Others have come to the conclusion that some passages may even refer to pederasty, or the act of an older man lying with a younger boy, which was common in ancient Greece. More liberal denominations like the United Church of Christ consider these other interpretations, as well as the members' personal experiences with homosexual communities and new scientific discoveries, in order to look at issues of sexual orientation. These denominations consider homosexuality to be an inherent trait that is fixed and not chosen by individuals, one that cannot be changed.

Much like Christian denominations, Jewish groups also fall along a continuum. Stemming from sacred texts such as the Torah and the Talmud, sexual intimacy is regarded as an essential bond between wife and husband in order to procreate. Rabbis of the Talmud state that sexual relations between men go against the natural order since homosexual intercourse would not result in procreation. Traditional Jewish law prohibits the waste of semen and generally forbids the act of male masturbation, restricting many forms of sexual intimacy between male partners. Conservative and Orthodox Judaism often refer to homosexuality as a behavior, consulting the Talmud, which prohibits male homosexual relations among other sexual activities such as incest, adultery, and bestiality. Issues pertaining to homosexual relations among women in sacred texts are only in reference to whether or not women who have had sexual relations with other women are able to marry priests. Jewish women who engage in sex with other women are seen as immoral and can be punished for rebelliousness.

More liberal views on homosexuality in Judaism have created environments that are more open to accepting gays and lesbians, providing more institutional support. Reconstructionist traditions and Reform Judaism generally view homosexuality as part of the individual, a natural alternative to heterosexual orientation. Contemporary scientific studies on homosexuality, then, are integrated with the understanding of sacred scriptures. Still, gays and lesbians struggle for equality in non-Orthodox Jewish organizations since bonds between homosexual couples are not uniformly recognized, nor has there been an influx of gay and lesbian leadership in Jewish communities.

Orthodox Islamic scholars have concluded that humans are naturally heterosexual. For them, homosexuality is a transgression against the natural order set in place by God. They contend that the sacred Islamic text, the Qur'an, explicitly condemns homosexual behavior by referencing Lot's story of breaking away from his people due to their same-sex relationships. Early Islamic law known as the *shari'a* reflects this story, which made homosexuality a punishable offense left to the hands of authorities. Researchers estimate that at least 4,000 homosexuals in Iran have been executed since 1979 under such authority. From a sociological standpoint, much of the negativity towards homosexuality within Islamic countries stems from the perception of the brutal aggressor, a man who uses sexual acts as a tool of power. According to Khalid Duran, homosexual rape among traditional Islamic societies is regarded as an instrument of humiliation, most often used by police in repressive regimes to reinforce submission from subjects. Very few have come forward publicly to announce their homosexual orientation in the Muslim world.

Although conservatives take these teachings as explicit and undeniable, more liberal Muslims believe that the Qur'an can be interpreted in many ways. They assert that passages discussing homosexuality do not condemn this behavior as most dangerous above all other crimes, but rather treat homosexuality in a similar manner as transgressions within heterosexual relationships. This doubt in traditional teachings pertaining to homosexual behavior has helped motivate liberals in Western cultures to think of Islam as an evolving rather than a stagnant religious tradition. The Al-Fatiha Foundation, for instance, was founded in the US in 1997 as a non-profit organization to provide support as well as a safe place for lesbian, gay, bisexual, and transgender Muslims to share their experiences. Having grown steadily over the years, the foundation has turned its attention to promoting Progressive Islam as well as justice, peace, and tolerance for all Muslims.

Box 10.2 Contemporary views on homosexuality in the US

As we discussed in relation to James Hunter's book *Culture Wars*, the topics of gay marriage and homosexual lifestyle have sparked a fierce debate between these two sides. Apologists for gay and lesbian interests call for "marriage" and "family" to be redefined, contending that conservative ideology behind these terms defends the patriarchal family. This in turn creates hierarchies of power through class, race, gender, and sexuality. However, opponents claim that homosexuality represents an assault on biblical truths and an attack on the traditional institution of marriage and family.

Table 10.2 Should homosexuality be accepted or discouraged by society?

	Accepted (%)	Discouraged (%)
Gender		
Men	52	39
Women	64	28
Race		
White	58	35
Black	49	38
Hispanic	64	26
Political affiliation		
Conservative Republican	35	58
Moderate/Liberal Republican	52	41
Independent	63	28
Conservative/Moderate Democrat	61	32
Liberal Democrat	81	14
Religious affiliation		
Protestant	48	44
Catholic	64	26
Unaffiliated	79	15

Source: 2011 Political Typology Survey, Pew Research Center Forum on Religion & Public Life, http://people-press.org/2011/05/04/beyond-red-vs-blue-the-political-typology/

Everyday attitudes towards homosexuality

Although various religious traditions have instituted strict guidelines on sexuality and sexual behavior, members' beliefs and values are often shaped by individual experiences. Over the years, many scholars have been interested in the clergy's role in the ongoing conflict over homosexuality within Christian congregations. Church leaders have played a pivotal part in setting the terms for the debate, influencing the perceptions of followers each week through their sermons. Mainline Protestantism, as described in Chapter 4, illustrates the debate over homosexuality at both the denominational and congregational levels. Laura Olson and Wendy Cadge examine the different approaches of mainline Protestant clergy and how they shape discussions of homosexuality. They found that most clergy focus on the impact of homosexuality on the church rather than society as a whole. Along with this, the majority place priority on denominational issues such as membership loss over individual congregational concerns, limiting the discussion of homosexuality among congregants. However, clergy who did speak about homosexuality in the context of their congregations were more likely to be supportive of gay and lesbian rights than those who spoke primarily about denominational concerns. As discussed in Chapter 4, congregations find themselves torn over the inclusion of gays and lesbians in churches. Many clergy express concern that accepting homosexual identities may undermine biblical authority and create more tension within their church.

Figure 10.2 Some Christian denominations welcome homosexuals as church members and leaders. Here, members of the United Church of Christ, one such denomination, march in the thirtieth annual LGBT parade in Northhampton, MA

© Custom Life Science Images/Alamy

Dawne Moon asserts that discussions in congregations about homosexuality often use emotional language. The most frequently used emotion is pain: homosexuals within congregations express the pain of being marginalized and rejected in order to receive compassion while those who oppose homosexuality use pain to argue that homosexuals go against God's will and thus hinder the religious community. Emotionally charged subjects like the debate on homosexuality create stalemates, polarizing congregations so that unity may be threatened. Discussions of homosexuality then become categorized as "politics" and, as Moon argues, are quickly demonized as agents of conflict that distract from a congregation's obligation to serve God and create a safe haven for all members. Discussion on issues such as ordination and marriage of gays and lesbians are then limited, with very little progress being made. By skirting these issues, some churches may create barriers for homosexuals to attain the same status as heterosexuals, reproducing the subordination and marginalization reflected in the surrounding culture.

A new Christian identity

Despite the fact that many traditional and orthodox faiths do not accept homosexuality, many gays and lesbians do not shed their religious beliefs in order to find faiths more suitable to their lifestyles. Instead, researchers are exploring the idea of identity synthesis, where gays and lesbians construct identities both as homosexuals as well as religious persons.

In a recent study, Krista McQueeny observed how lesbian, gay, and straight-but-affirming church members constructed and performed "good" Christian identities. She contends that the church members she studied – black, white, lesbian, gay, and straight – all faced conflict between homosexuality and Christianity differently because they drew on various resources and personal meanings. McQueeny identifies three group-specific strategies employed by these members pertaining to the construction of a "good" Christian identity: minimizing sexuality, normalizing sexuality, and moralizing sexuality. Minimizing sexuality was most prevalent among black, working-class members who were aware of the sinful and abnormal image of homosexuality. In order to construct a "good" Christian identity, black lesbians in particular privileged race over gender and sexuality, allowing them to claim dignity and worth as Christians by playing on the assumption of heteronormativity, or the assumption that heterosexuality is the normal sexual orientation. Next, McQueeny argues that most lesbian and gay members of predominantly straight congregations normalize their sexual identities by evoking traditionally heteronormative discourses such as manhood, motherhood, and monogamy. The last strategy of moralizing homosexuality was only present in a few black lesbians, gay men, and white straight-but-affirming members. They moralized their sexuality by stating that their sexuality gave them a special calling as Christians to fight stigma and homophobia.

Not only have homosexuals constructed an identity within traditional church settings, but they have also created other outlets to express their identities as lesbians and gays as well as religious. In the book *Gay Religion*, Leonard Norman Primiano discusses Dignity, a group that provides counseling services as well as broad spiritual, educational, and social goals for lesbian and gays who wish to practice the Roman Catholic faith. As stated before, the Roman Catholic Church teaches that homosexuality is morally neutral, but that homosexual acts are morally wrong. The only

Box 10.3 Minimizing, normalizing, and moralizing sexuality

Krista McQueeney (2009) did three years of ethnographic fieldwork and conducted twenty-five in-depth interviews in two lesbian and gay-affirming churches in the Southeast. She presents numerous quotes that illustrated how the pastors and members of these churches attempted to minimize, normalize, and moralize sexuality. Some examples are given here.

Minimizing

> Only once a month will the word "gay" come out of my mouth ... When people come to church and hear something other than sex, sex, sex, they realize this is a real church, and gay people aren't all about sex. Especially in our community, the black community, sex is not something you talk about in church.
>
> (Interview with a pastor)

Normalizing

> We have a great family, our family is kind of different than everybody else's, but we have the same struggles, the same trials, and the same joys any other family with a four-year-old has. And I think that's how we're seen in the church, as just another family with a young child. It doesn't matter that we have two moms, which I think is great.
>
> (Interview with a 42-year-old white lesbian church member)

Moralizing

> It's so wonderful to be in a church where I don't have to leave my sexuality at the door. That's what this church is all about ... Because society has oppressed us ... for so long, we finally had enough and started a place of our own ... where nobody can tell us we're not God's children ... we are God's children, y'all, and I venture to say that we might even be God's chosen ones.
>
> (Field notes from a sermon by a black gay Baptist minister)

solution to the issue of homosexuality, then, is to suppress these urges and live a life of celibacy. On the other hand, Dignity builds a sense of community among lesbians and gays with a foundation in both the Roman Catholic faith and sexual familiarity. The organization gives homosexuals a sense of belonging and support that is not provided in their own parishes and has become a last resort for some to remain practicing Catholics. By forming an organization apart from other Catholic parishes, lesbians and gays are able to embrace and share their identities as both Catholic and homosexual with a diverse set of people without condemnation. However, many authorities prevent gay and lesbian members of Dignity from holding their meetings on church property.

Researchers continue to analyze how religion impacts individual perceptions of gender norms as well as the effects of feminist ideas on various religious organizations. Along with this, scholars contend that sexuality plays a particularly interesting role for gays and lesbians in the construction of their religious identities in the face of opposition. Given the shifting politics of American society, the intersection of gender, sexuality, and religion will continue to be a topic of interest within the field of sociology.

Key points you need to know

- Sex is a biological and scientific concept that is based on the biological characteristics of sexual reproduction whereas both gender and sexuality are socially constructed. Gender refers to the behaviors and norms that define what it is to be female or male while sexuality refers to a set of feelings and desires attributed to women and men.
- Women tend to affiliate themselves with a religion, to believe in God or a spirit, and to attend religious services more often than men.
- Many researchers attribute this difference between genders to women's vulnerability in male-dominated societies.
- Religious groups have impacted individual views on "appropriate" gender roles for both men and women.
- There has been an increase in female clergy over the past few decades, leading to changes in how congregations view women's roles within the church. Researchers suggest that female clergy tend to be more engaged with broader social issues and to use collaborations in comparison with male clergy.
- Conservative religious traditions tend to view homosexuality as a behavior that is sinful and can be changed whereas more liberal traditions look towards homosexuality as an inherent trait.
- Congregations that do not discuss issues pertaining to homosexuality may reproduce the same marginalization homosexuals experience in the surrounding culture.
- Gays and lesbians as well as straight-but-affirming congregants construct identities as "good Christians" despite the fact that conservative religions do not embrace homosexuality as an acceptable lifestyle.

Discussion questions

1 Explain the differences between sex, gender, and sexuality.
2 What are some of the speculations researchers have as to why women tend to be more religious than men?
3 According to Woodhead, what are the four distinct ways in which gender roles and religion interact?
4 How can adhering to strict gender roles impact marriage and family life both positively and negatively?
5 List some of the reasons why some denominations are more open to ordaining female clergy over others.

6 Explain how both conservative and liberal religious organizations view homosexuality.
7 In what ways do clergy and their congregations address homosexuality? How does this affect homosexuals' position within the religious community?
8 How do lesbians and gays construct religious identities that reflect both their beliefs and sexuality?

Further reading

Ammerman, N. (1987) *Bible Believers: Fundamentalists in the Modern World*, New Brunswick, NJ: Rutgers University Press.

Chaves, M. (1996) "Ordaining Women: The Diffusion of an Organizational Innovation," *American Journal of Sociology*, 101(4): 840–73.

Davidman, L. (1991) *Traditional in a Rootless World: Women Turn to Orthodox Judaism*, Los Angles, CA: University of California Press.

Edgell, P. and Docka, D. (2007) "Beyond the Nuclear Family? Familism and Gender Ideology in Diverse Religious Communities," *Sociological Forum*, 22(1): 26–51.

Gross, R.M. (1996) *Feminism & Religion*, Boston, MA: Beacon Press.

Hunter, J.D. (1991) *Culture Wars: The Struggle to Define America*, New York: Basic Books.

Lippy, C.H. (2005) *Do Real Men Pray?: Images of the Christian Man and Male Spirituality in White Protestant America*, Knoxville, TN: University of Tennessee Press.

McQueeny, K. (2009) "'We are God's Children, Y'all': Race, Gender, and Sexuality in Lesbian- and Gay-Affirming Congregations," *Social Problems*, 56(1): 151–73.

Minwalla, O., Rosser, B.R.S., Feldman, J., and Varga, C. (2005) "Identity Experience among Progressive Gay Muslims in North America: A Qualitative Study within Al-Fatiha," *Culture, Health, & Sexuality*, 7(2): 113–28.

Moon, D. (2004) *God, Sex, and Politics*, Chicago, IL: University of Chicago Press.

Olson, L.R. and Cadge, W. (2002) "Talking about Homosexuality: The Views of Mainline Protestant Clergy," *Journal for the Scientific Study of Religion*, 41(1): 153–67.

Pew Report Forum. (2007) "Pew Forum's US Religious Landscape Survey," http://pewforum.org/Datasets/Dataset-Download.aspx (accessed 1 Feburary 2012).

Pew Research Center. (2011) "Pew Research Center's Political Typology Survey," http://people-press.org/2011/05/04/beyond-red-vs-blue-the-political-typology/ (accessed 1 February 2012).

Primiano, L.N. (2005) "The Gay God of the City," in S. Thummas and E.R. Gray (eds.), *Gay Religion*, Los Angeles, CA: Altamira.

Swidler, A. (1993) *Homosexuality and World Religions*, Valley Forge, PA: Trinity Press International.

Wallace, R.A. (1993) "The Social Construction of a New Leadership Role: Catholic Women Pastors," *Sociology of Religion*, 54(1): 34–42.

Walter, T. and Davie, G. (1998) "The Religiosity of Women in the Modern West," *British Journal of Sociology*, 49(4): 640–60.

Woodhead, L. (2007) "Gender Difference in Religious Practices and Significance," in J. Beckford and N.J. Demerath III (eds.), *Handbook of the Sociology of Religion*, London: Sage.

Part III

Moving beyond the mainstream

11 African American religion
Community, conflict, and change

In this chapter

This chapter opens with a discussion of how religion and religious institutions created a sense of community for African Americans, who endured generations of slavery, segregation, and racism. The pivotal role of the church and its leaders in the civil rights movement receives attention in the second section. The third section examines how that era led to the emergence of a distinctive black theology, new directions for religious institutions and their leadership, changes in the role of women, and the need to respond to other social currents of the age. The discussion then turns to the impact of charismatic preachers in developing contemporary African American megachurches and also to the attractiveness of non-Christian options for African Americans, particularly Islam in its manifold expressions.

Main topics covered

- The historic role of the black churches in fostering a sense of community.
- How denominations emphasizing religious experience came to dominate African American religious life.
- The significance of African American churches and religious leaders in guiding the civil rights movement.
- The impact of Martin Luther King, Jr., on African American religion.
- The consequences of the civil rights movement for religious life.
- The changing role of women within African American religious groups.
- The emergence of black theology and Womanist theology.
- How African American religious groups support social justice in some areas but remain conservative in others.
- The influence of charismatic preachers and megachurches.
- Why some found in forms of Islam viable alternatives to Christianity in meeting the religious and spiritual needs of African Americans.

Religion creates community and continuity

The inhumane practice of slavery, legal in much of the US until the Civil War, had an enduring impact on African American religion. As slaves became Christians, they frequently combined elements of their new religious identity with those drawn from the African tribal past. Finding in the Christian message of salvation a call for freedom, African Americans transformed this hybrid spirituality into a force that built strong bonds of community. The "invisible institution," gatherings at night in forest areas on plantations, flourished. A rich spirituality emerged apart from the oppression of slave owners and overseers, even as slave owners also turned to Christian scripture to justify their holding other humans as property.

Central to this unique expression of religion was religious experience. In many cases forbidden by law to learn to read, African Americans found the presence and power of God in inner experience. Religion was something that one felt, not something that one reasoned out through sustained reflection on doctrine and creed. As independent African American denominations emerged in the antebellum period, they generally had an evangelical quality. Most identified with the Methodist and Baptist traditions because of their call for an inner experience of grace as a sign of conversion. Around the turn of the twentieth century, when Pentecostal currents gained ground and African Americans migrated from the rural south to the northeast and north central urban areas and to the west coast, many storefront churches and newer denominations took on a distinctive Pentecostal style. The Azusa Street revival in Los Angeles in 1906, a harbinger of modern American Pentecostalism, owed its success to the dynamic preaching of an African American, William J. Seymour (1870–1922).

In the postbellum south, African American denominations, along with a few other groups, quickly established educational opportunities for former slaves. Many focused on preparing young men for the ministry. In many areas of the south, especially more rural ones, until well into the twentieth century, pastors were frequently the only African Americans with advanced education, and their churches often the only property owned by African Americans. Consequently, the church and the pastor took on a critical role. Pastors became the public voices for African Americans, and churches became bastions of community life that offered social service, recreational, and other activities along with worship and religious work. The church became the center of corporate life for a people denied access to many of the social institutions of the larger culture, thanks to racism and segregation. The church forged a sense of community among all African Americans in its orbit, not just its members.

As a result, churches often became the primary venues where laymen and laywomen honed leadership skills; a segregated society rarely acknowledged their abilities or gave them opportunities to serve. One who struggled as a sharecropper or worked for absurdly low wages as a domestic and therefore lacked power and influence in the larger society, within the church might gain authority and garner great respect. Religious institutions were crucibles to mold leaders, with the clergy the most prominent.

The multifaceted character of the church proved vital when change swept the nation after World War II. One early sign of change came in 1948 when President Harry Truman issued an executive order effectively ending segregation within the US armed forces. Even then, none expected that a cultural revolution would begin less than a decade later when a Montgomery, AL, woman named Rosa Parks (1913–2005) violated local ordinance by refusing to give up her seat on a bus to someone white.

Box 11.1 The church's many roles

Anthony Pinn notes that African American churches have historically emphasized not only matters of faith, but also the social implications of faith, especially those working to end poverty and social injustice. He writes:

> To accomplish this, many black churches developed a variety of social services including libraries, job training, basic education programs, and health-care programs. And these activities on the part of black churches speak to an appreciation for a social form of Christianity that is sensitive to changing cultural and social realities encountered by black Americans and is willing to break the boundaries of "tradition" in order to accomplish this larger objective.
>
> (From A.B. Pinn, *The Black Church in the Post-Civil Rights Era*, Maryknoll, NY: Orbis Books, 2002, p. 12)

Civil rights and African American churches

That December day in 1955 when Rosa Parks broke local law sparked turmoil across the nation. In Montgomery, African Americans gathered at the Holt Street Baptist Church and then also at the Dexter Avenue Baptist Church to coordinate a response. By meeting in religious space, those protesting injustice acknowledged the church as a place to nurture social action. The meetings at Dexter Avenue thrust the church's young pastor, Martin Luther King, Jr. (1939–68), into the spotlight. King quickly became the public voice of the Montgomery bus boycott, which lasted until November 1956, when the US Supreme Court struck down Alabama's bus segregation laws.

The following February, several African American clergy joined other leaders to form the Southern Christian Leadership Conference (SCLC). King became its president. The goal of the organization, building on the success in Montgomery, was to use peaceful, non-violent protest to end legalized segregation throughout the nation. The word "Christian" in the group's name affirmed the centrality of religion to the African American struggle for equality and justice.

Many who supported the activities of the SCLC or who advocated the method of non-violence found the courage in their religious faith to endure abuse and arrest and then to return to protest; we will consider the role of religion in the movement further in Chapters 12 and 15. In the political sector, Fannie Lou Hamer (1917–77) drew on her religious convictions when she vigorously pursued not only gaining voting rights for African Americans in Mississippi, but also challenging the leadership of the Democratic Party to recognize African American delegates at the 1964 Democratic National Convention in Atlantic City, NJ. Hamer worked for several years as a field secretary for the Student Non-Violent Coordinating Committee (SNCC), dedicated to registering African American voters, even if it meant defying state and local laws designed to keep African Americans from exercising the franchise.

King, a compelling orator, understood how religious language stirred African Americans to action and how dynamic language both inspired commitment to civil

Box 11.2 Civil rights and the promised land

On 3 April 1968 in Memphis, TN, Martin Luther King, Jr. delivered what would be his last speech. He spoke at a church, Mason Temple, which was celebrating the ministry of Charles H. Mason, founder of the Church of God in Christ, one of the largest African American Pentecostal denominations. King's rhetoric drew heavily on religious imagery. His address was as much a sermon as a call to support striking sanitation workers. Titled "I See the Promised Land," based on the biblical Moses' gazing from the mountaintop into ancient Israel, it ended with these words:

> Well, I don't know what will happen now. We've got some difficult days ahead. But it doesn't matter with me now. Because I've been to the mountaintop. And I don't mind. Like anybody, I would like to live a long life. Longevity has its place. But I'm not concerned about that now. I just want to do God's will. And he's allowed me to go up to the mountain. And I've looked over. And I've seen the Promised Land. But I want you to know tonight that we, as a people, will get to the Promised Land. And I'm happy tonight. I'm not worried about anything. I'm not fearing any man. Mine eyes have seen the glory of the coming of the Lord.
>
> (From M.L. King, Jr., "I See the Promised Land,"
> www.famousquotes.me.uk/speeches/Martin_Luther_King/4.htm,
> accessed 13 November 2012)

rights work and threatened a white racist society. That society also trumpeted religious rhetoric, having added "under God" to the pledge of allegiance the year before the Montgomery bus boycott. In essence, King masterfully used the technique and style of black preaching, laden with biblical allusions, to rouse his audiences and to expose the hypocrisy of those who refused to use their political power to dismantle legal segregation.

For King, non-violent protest and social justice had deep religious roots. Mahatma Gandhi, venerated in India for crafting a decades-long movement protesting British colonial rule that resulted in India's independence in 1947, found in the Hindu tradition a basis for non-violent civil disobedience. King readily acknowledged his indebtedness to Gandhi. King found another model for joining faith and social justice as a graduate student at Boston University. He absorbed the thought of late nineteenth and early twentieth century Social Gospel thinkers such as Walter Rauschenbusch. The Social Gospel insisted that individual salvation made little sense unless the social structures that dehumanized persons changed. The nascent labor movement's demands for higher wages and better working conditions provided the backdrop for the Social Gospel. For King, the goal was the transformation of every social, political, and economic institution that separated people by race or relegated some to second-class status because of race.

Much of what King advocated resonated with the biblical tradition. In July 1963, he orchestrated a March on Washington that bore all the marks of a religious revival and effectively used the rhetoric of civil religion, but with a new twist. In a powerful

Figure 11.1 The Rev. Martin Luther King, Jr., the voice of the civil rights movement, showed
how African American churches put their commitment to social justice into
practice

Courtesy of the Library of Congress Prints and Photographs Division

speech, King used biblical references to envision a nation actually embracing the
liberty and equality enshrined in documents such as the Declaration of Independence.
In 1965, the SCLC and SNCC spearheaded a march from Selma, AL, to Montgomery,
the state capital, which took on the character of the triumphal entry of Christ
depicted in the gospels, especially when it resulted in bloodshed on a Sunday in
March, the sacred day of the week for Christians. King journeyed to Memphis, TN,
in April 1968 in support of striking sanitation workers. Here, the Thursday before
Christians celebrated Holy Week and the crucifixion of Jesus, King died at the hands
of an assassin. Already a renowned religious and political figure, King became a
martyr, shedding his blood for the core values of the nation – liberty, justice, and
equality for all.

Not all found religious expression an appropriate or even viable springboard for
action. After all, the Christian tradition informing the black churches had also
provided religious support for slavery. Proponents of slavery used Christianity and
its scriptures to sustain racial inequality and to insist that African Americans were
inferior to whites. If some found in the Christian message of ultimate salvation a call
for freedom from oppression, others believed it to be the source of racism and
segregation.

Some who rejected Christianity drew on alternative religious visions. They affiliated
with a hybrid form of Islam, the Nation of Islam or the Black Muslims. Although it
was led by Elijah Muhammad (1897–1975), the Nation of Islam found its most
prominent voice in Malcolm X (1925–65), minister at a Black Muslim temple in New

York City. Preaching a message of racial separation and labeling the racist whites the devil personified, the Black Muslims appeared more radical than King and the SCLC, and more open to condoning violence to achieve desired ends. Three years before King, Malcolm X had died at the hands of an assassin when, returning from the traditional Muslim pilgrimage to Mecca, he advocated racial inclusivity, repudiating the Black Muslim insistence on racial separation and the inferiority of whites.

After civil rights: the new faces of African American religion

The civil rights movement, although it had an impact on all American religious culture, dramatically transformed African American religious life. One unanticipated result was a change in the role of the church and its clergy within the African American community. The civil rights movement opened fresh opportunities for many African Americans to pursue academic training and enter professions where they had once been marginalized. Consequently, the ministry ceased to be the only vocation of prestige and influence within the black community. Gifted persons who once would have gravitated to pastoral ministry turned to other professions – medicine, law, business, industry, and so on.

The end of legalized segregation also gave African Americans greater access to social and cultural institutions. The church itself began to lose its prominence as the most vital organizational structure serving African Americans. Many non-religious roles the churches had once assumed became transferred to other groups. Just as mainline white churches showed decline and an inability to retain a younger generation, so, too, many African American congregations, especially those associated with Baptist and Methodist denominations, began to lose numbers and see their influence dwindle. African Americans of the post-civil rights generations were less likely to remain engaged with organized religions as they moved into adolescence and young adulthood. Some analysts predicted that a crisis for the church would come by the middle third of the twenty-first century if the patterns in place continued.

As other religious groups, African American churches have had to address the role of women in religious life. For generations, African American churches saw auxiliary work, from keeping records to raising funds for missions, as the domain of women within congregations and even denominations. Some women served as stewardesses and deaconesses, assisting male pastors in preparing the church for worship and tending to persons in need. More familiar and perhaps more powerful were those who, through maturity and reputation for piety, became known as "church mothers." In countless congregations, the church mothers wielded great influence and authority, even if they lacked formal positions of leadership.

With the civil rights era and the rise of second-wave feminism, African American women began to press for ordination to professional ministry. They found precedent in many urban storefront congregations, usually Pentecostal in style, that looked to dynamic women preachers for spiritual leadership. They also looked to a handful of women ordained as deacons in the later nineteenth century in groups like the AME and AME Zion denominations. Not until the 1980s, however, were significant numbers of women recognized as pastors in most of the African American Methodist bodies. Some Baptist and Pentecostal groups gradually followed, although many, such as the Church of God in Christ, remained reluctant to welcome women into the ministry. Regardless, all African American churches rely heavily on the spiritual leadership women provide in local congregations. The struggle for equality for women in the black churches is far from over.

The response of African American religious groups to social issues has sometimes differed from that of predominantly white groups. Much of that difference emerges from the history of dealing with slavery and racism. For example, African American religious groups have been in the forefront of the struggle to alleviate poverty, largely because a disproportionate number of their adherents are in the lower economic clusters of American society. Churches have also vigorously addressed issues such as teen pregnancy and households headed by single women in response to the higher rate of both within the African American population. American military engagement in Southeast Asia in the 1960s and 1970s produced a mixed response from African American religious leaders. Martin Luther King, Jr., stunned many when he opposed the Vietnam War; he believed that sustaining the war in Vietnam drained government resources that could combat injustice caused by racism, poverty, unemployment, and lower levels of education among African Americans. Others disagreed, insisting that support for government policy demonstrated that African Americans were responsible loyal citizens.

On other issues, African American churches have exhibited a traditional, sometimes conservative stance. For example, although theologian James Cone has called for inclusion of gays and lesbians in both church and society, African American churches have been more inclined than mainline white groups to label homosexuality as a sin, to oppose same-gender marriage, and to refrain from welcoming homosexuals into positions of leadership, especially the ranks of the clergy. Even when HIV and AIDS disproportionately affected the black population, churches were slow to address matters of sexuality in ways that might reduce the risk of black Americans contracting the virus. The complicated ways African American religion has dealt with issues relating to gender and sexuality receives more discussion in Chapter 10.

Moving in new directions: televangelists, megachurches, and Islam

Before the twentieth century ended, new dimensions were reshaping African American religious life. The civil rights movement spurred extraordinarily creative developments in African American religious thought, bringing first the emergence of what has been called black theology, religious thought grounded in the experience of racism and tied to liberation from oppression. Later, female thinkers spawned a Womanist theology based on African American women's encounters with both racism and sexism. Each will be discussed in Chapter 17. In addition, the expressive worship and energetic preaching associated with African American religion took new forms in the age of mass communication. Just as white evangelicals made deft use of television and formed megachurches, a matter we examined from another vantage point in Chapter 8, so too did African American preachers. But distinctive characteristics mark the African American experience.

Thomas Dexter (T.D.) Jakes (1957–) remains a prominent African American televangelist and megachurch pastor. His non-denominational Potter's House church in Dallas, TX, claims a membership of more than 30,000. Early in his career, Jakes launched numerous television ministries. By the second decade of the twenty-first century, his programs were airing on several networks, including Black Entertainment

Television, the Trinity Broadcasting Network, and Daystar Television Network. More attention came when Jakes led a prayer service in Washington, DC, the morning of President Barack Obama's inauguration in 2009. Creflo A. Dollar, Jr. (1967–) has also built a successful megachurch empire. His World Changes Church International in Georgia's Fulton County reports a membership of more than 30,000. Like the Potter's House, it has no denominational affiliation. Such megachurches generate considerable income, and Dollar's ministries came under US Senate investigation after critics suggested that Dollar used donations to the church ministries to support a lavish lifestyle.

What sets Dollar and Jakes apart from many pastors is their emphasis on the "Prosperity Gospel." This phenomenon also undergirds the ministry of white Pentecostal preacher Joel Osteen and others like him. Echoing ideas associated with the Gospel of Wealth of later-nineteenth-century American white Protestantism, the Prosperity Gospel argues that God intends for the faithful to reap great material benefits; in other words, they are to prosper financially. Wealth signals divine blessing. Critics, however, challenge the core of Prosperity Gospel teaching, claiming that it ignores the historic commitment of African American religion to social justice, especially to mitigating the poverty and unemployment that persist within the African American population. To critics, the Prosperity Gospel offers a motivational message coming from secular inspirational discourse rather than from the teaching of Jesus found in the Christian New Testament.

Some prominent African American megachurch pastors retain denominational ties. Eddie Long (1953–), for example, heads the New Birth Missionary Baptist Church in DeKalb County, Georgia. Unlike some others, Long received a traditional theological education. His ministry builds on standard, conservative evangelical ideas of obedience and submission. For Long, the man of faith should submit totally to God; the woman of faith in turn should submit totally first to her father and then to her husband. Long insists that only such submissiveness will maintain order in human life and society because it reflects the divine will in creation. Womanist thinkers reject Long's approach, finding it demeaning to African American women who face discrimination because of both gender and race. In Long's teaching, sexual purity is also paramount. Hence in the fall of 2010, Long's ministry faced severe challenges when several young men claimed that Long had forced them to perform homosexual acts with him. The scandal reached closure in 2011 in a private settlement.

The increasing appeal of non-Christian religions has also changed African American religious culture. That appeal built on the Nation of Islam (Black Muslims) prominent in the 1960s. Before his death, Malcolm X crafted an expression of Islam based on what he observed on his pilgrimage to Mecca. Then, following the 1975 death of the Nation of Islam's primary architect, Elijah Muhammad, the movement experienced division. One branch looked to Elijah Muhammad's son, Warith Deen Muhammad (1933–2008), for leadership and moved closer to traditional Sunni Islam. Another major group, intent on retaining the teachings of Elijah Muhammad while downplaying the demonization of whites (and even accepting whites as members), had Louis Farrakhan (1933–) at the helm. Farrakhan organized the "Million Man March" in 1995 to urge African American males to assume more responsibility for their families and to embrace ethical integrity in all aspects of life. Held in Washington, the march recalled the one Martin Luther King engineered in 1963 at the peak of the civil rights movement.

Figure 11.2 American Nation of Islam leader Louis Farrakhan in 1995 rallied African Americans in the "Million Man March" in Washington, DC, to encourage black men to affirm their responsibilities to their families and to the African American community

© James Leynse/Corbis

Both these Nation of Islam sects offer African Americans a sense of order, commitment, and purpose. Devoid of associations with slavery and discrimination plaguing black denominations that emerged from white counterparts, these forms of Islam provide an alternative to Christianity in finding meaning and purpose in life. A small, but not insignificant immigration from Africa since immigration law changed in 1965 has brought to the US Africans who were already Muslim. Some identified with the Nation of Islam and its offshoots, while others have – where possible – joined with other Muslims to form mosques and community centers.

Other features of the new pluralism have left their mark. From the Caribbean area came immigrants who brought a hybrid expression of religion, Santeria, which joined traditional African, Roman Catholic, and indigenous practices. Other immigrants from Africa have stirred a renewed interest in traditional African tribal religious expression, long thought snuffed out in America as Christianity took hold among slaves in the antebellum period. Some African Americans have aligned with strands of Buddhism, although the numbers remain very small. Analysts estimate, however, that somewhere between 10 per cent and 20 per cent of Americans affiliated with Soka Gakkai, a Buddhist sect with roots in Japan, are of African descent, but given the difficulty in determining the total number of Soka Gakkai practitioners in the US, that range could mean that as few as 4,000 and as many as 60,000 African Americans claim Soka Gakkai as their religion.

Box 11.3 The challenges of the twenty-first century

Writing in 1990, C. Eric Lincoln and Lawrence H. Mamiya end their study of African American Christianity with a concluding chapter titled "The Black Church and the Twenty-First Century: Challenges to the Black Church." They anticipated that the following would be the most vital challenges:

- the divide between secularized and religious African Americans, with those who were secularized increasing in number;
- inroads of neo-Pentecostal expression throughout African American denominations;
- the rising influence of Islam with the African American population;
- efforts at ecumenical cooperation among African American groups and between African American groups and predominantly white groups;
- decline in prestige and authority among clergy within African American communities.

For a full discussion, see C.E. Lincoln and L.H. Mamiya, *The Black Church in the African American Experience*, Durham, NC: Duke University Press, 1990, pp. 382–404.

As more African Americans have entered professions to which they were once denied access and more have moved upwards in terms of economic standing, more have likewise followed a path similar to what mainline Protestants first confronted with the baby boom generation. That is, they have looked to an idiosyncratic, highly personalized spirituality to provide a religious base for their lives, abandoning formal affiliation with organized religion.

By the second decade of the twenty-first century, African American religious life was becoming increasingly diverse. At the same time, African American denominations continued their historic witness for social justice, tempered with a traditionalist approach when it came to controversial issues such as homosexuality. As others, African Americans expanded their horizons, with megachurches led by charismatic preachers attracting thousands, and with alternative religions such as Islam and even Buddhism providing a religious home for some.

Key points you need to know

- African American churches became centers of community life as much as religious institutions and clergy the spokespersons for the black community.
- Personal experience has long characterized African American style.
- Religious institutions often provided the only places where African Americans could cultivate and exercise leadership skills.
- Religion nurtured and sustained the civil rights movement and its leadership.

- Civil rights advocate Martin Luther King, Jr., joined religious faith with social protest to set an example for all African Americans.
- Some, wary of Christian support for civil rights activity, turned to alternative religions such as the Nation of Islam.
- African American women have struggled with discrimination based on racism and on sexism.
- African American religious groups illustrate a mix of conservative and liberal positions on contemporary social issues.
- Megachurches and charismatic preachers advocating a Prosperity Gospel have developed among African Americans.
- A growing number of African Americans continue to find non-Christian religions, especially forms of Islam, attractive.

Discussion questions

1   How and why did the churches take on the role of being the central social institution within African American communities? How has the role of the churches changed in the decades since the end of World War II?
2   How has the role of African American clergy shifted since the civil rights movement?
3   In what ways is the civil rights movement a religious phenomenon within African American life? How did the churches prepare African Americans for participation and leadership in the civil rights movement?
4   How did Martin Luther King fuse together religion and social protest?
5   Why were some African Americans drawn to the Nation of Islam during the civil rights era and later? Compare and contrast Malcolm X and Martin Luther King as persons who drew on their faith to call for social change.
6   How have women's roles changed in African American religious culture in the decades since the close of World War II?
7   Compare and contrast the response of African American churches and white religious institutions to social issues such as the Vietnam War and homosexuality.
8   Why does the Prosperity Gospel of some megachurches appeal to African Americans?
9   Why do non-Christian religions continue to attract African Americans?

Further reading

Billingsley, A. (1999) *Mighty Like a River: The Black Church and Social Reform*, New York: Oxford University Press.
Gilkey, C.T. (2000) *If It Wasn't for the Women … : Black Women's Experience and Womanist Culture in Church and Community*, Maryknoll, NY: Orbis Books.
Lincoln, C.E. and Mamiya, L.H. (1990) *The Black Church in the African American Experience*, Durham, NC: Duke University Press.
Morris, A. (1984) *The Origins of the Civil Rights Movement: Black Communities Organizing for Change*, New York: Free Press.

Pinn, A.B. (2002) *The Black Church in the Post-Civil Rights Era*, Maryknoll, NY: Orbis Books.
Smith, D.B. (2004) *Long March Ahead: African American Churches and Public Policy in Post-Civil Rights America*, Durham, NC: Duke University Press.
Washington, J.M. (ed.) (1986) *A Testament of Hope: The Essential Writings of Martin Luther King, Jr.*, San Francisco: Harper and Row.
Wilson, J. (2009) *Watch This! The Ethics and Aesthetics of Black Televangelism*, New York: New York University Press.

12 Religion, race, and poverty

In this chapter

Racial inequality and separation are pervasive issues in American life, extending even to American religious life. In this chapter, we explore the causes and consequences of the racial segregation of congregations in American life. In particular, we show how racial segregation leads to increased stereotyping of others, creates distinct religious subcultures, and shapes attitudes about other races in ways that perpetuate racial inequality. We next discuss the literature on racially integrated congregations, including their promise and the difficulties associated with creating them. We then describe the sociological research on issues raised in the previous chapter, focusing on the African American church. Finally, we explore the role of religion in providing services to the poor or needy.

Main topics covered

- Racial segregation
    - is a persistent feature of American religious life, with roots in the racial split of Protestant churches caused by slavery.
    - shapes perceptions of racial and religious "others" in predictable ways.
    - of religion shapes attitudes towards other racial groups and explanations for racial inequality in ways that perpetuate racial inequality.
- Racially integrated congregations may help reduce racial inequality by bringing people of different races into close contact with each other. There are significant barriers to creating racially integrated congregations.
- The contemporary role of the African American church is influenced by both racial inequality and racial segregation.
- Some religious groups are engaged in providing services for the poor and needy, but many are not.

Racial inequality in American religious life

Racial inequality is a fact of American life. On average, African Americans and (to a lesser extent) Latinos in America, as shown in Table 12.1, have less wealth and less income than white Americans and are thus more likely to live in poverty. They also have higher unemployment rates and are more likely to be uninsured. Moreover, whites and Asian Americans are 20 per cent more likely to complete high school and twice as likely to receive a college degree as are African Americans and Latinos. In addition, African Americans are more likely than whites to die of heart disease, stroke, liver disease, diabetes, AIDS, accidental injury, homicide, and all kinds of cancers. These inequalities have numerous causes, but are not related to biological differences in intelligence, physical ability, or economic behavior between racial groups. Instead, racial inequality in the American experience can be traced to the needs of colonial economic structures and the development of racist explanations to justify ongoing economic and political inequality.

Racial groups are also separated and segregated from each other in American life. This divide reinforces patterns of racial inequality. If you randomly selected two people from the same neighborhood or school, they would be of the same race 80 per cent and 60 per cent of the time, respectively. Seven out of ten Americans have same-race social circles (defined as the five people they talk to most often). Ninety-five per cent of married Americans are married to someone of the same race, although interracial relationships and marriages are increasing.

Does this racial segregation persist in American religious life? Martin Luther King, Jr., repeatedly said that "eleven o'clock Sunday morning is the most segregated hour and Sunday school is still the most segregated school of the week." This is still true today. Research from the ongoing National Congregations Study found that if you randomly selected two people from the same congregation, they would be of the same race 98 per cent of the time. Ninety-three per cent of American congregations can be considered racially homogeneous (meaning that more than 80 per cent of the members of that congregation are of the same race). This segregation is most prominent among Protestant denominations, with 95 per cent of Protestant congregations being racially homogeneous. Other denominations and families are more integrated, with 14 per cent of Catholic congregations being racially mixed and 27.5 per cent of mosques, temples, and synagogues being racially mixed. Thus, the larger the religious tradition, the more segregated it is. In addition, the more choices people have of places to worship, the more they choose to be with people who are racially similar.

Table 12.1 Racial inequality in American life

Race	Median household net worth (2008)	Median household income (2008)	Poverty rate (2010)	Unemployment rate (2010)	Medical un-insurance rate (2009)	Incarceration rates (2006, men)
White Americans	$90,000	$65,000	13.0%	8.2%	12.0%	0.07%
Asian Americans	$92,000	$73,578	12.1%	7.0%	17.2%	0.04%
Latino Americans	$8,000	$40,466	26.6%	10.8%	32.4%	1.9%
African Americans	$6,000	$39,879	27.4%	15.5%	21.0%	4.8%

Source: Current Population Survey 2010, US Census Bureau 2009, Federal Bureau of Investigation 2007

Causes of the racial segregation in religion

There are two major sources of the racial segregation of religion: the historical division of American Protestant congregations into African American and white churches and the development of immigrant churches and religions. Chapter 11 described the history of the African American church, particularly how the split between African American and white churches is rooted in the American heritage of slavery and racism. Although there have been extensive efforts on the part of some churches to foster racial integration and unity and although racially based organizational structures within white denominations have largely broken down, there has been remarkably little progress towards racial integration between African American and white churches at the congregational level. For example, white churches, on average, have only 2 to 3 per cent African American membership. This historical division of religion is self-reinforcing, with white and African American churches developing distinct cultures and concerns (described below and in Chapter 11) that make it difficult to integrate the two religious expressions.

As described in Chapter 18, immigrants bring their religions with them when they come to the US. Although these churches quickly adapt to US congregational forms, as described in Chapter 19, those who practice non-Christian religions or Christian congregations that hold services in a foreign language are likely to be highly racially segregated. In fact, ethnic ties and consciousness of national origins are pervasive in such congregations, with little overlap between worshippers of different ethnic backgrounds.

Consequences of the racial segregation in religion

Sociologists have focused extensive research on the consequences of racial segregation for how Americans understand racial inequality, particularly unequal outcomes for African Americans. They have found that racial isolation shapes our perceptions of racial others, creates distinct religious cultures, and shapes racial attitudes in ways that perpetuate racial inequality.

Classic research in social cognition demonstrates that the isolation of groups from each other in everyday life has predictable consequences for our understanding of others. This research distinguishes "in-groups" or those who are in an individual's group and with whom one interacts frequently and "out-groups" or those who are not in the group and therefore with whom one does not regularly interact. Racial isolation creates biased perceptions of racial in-groups and out-groups. In isolated environments, similarities among in-group members are exaggerated and differences with out-group members are exaggerated. This results in a minimizing of differences among out-group members so they are more easily stereotyped. Further, exaggerated similarity and difference result in differential attribution of positive and negative behaviors, such that people are more likely to evaluate in-group members positively and believe that positive actions are attributed to an individual's "goodness" or "moral character," while negative actions are attributed to structural forces outside the person's control. On the other hand, out-group members are evaluated more negatively and those negative actions are attributed to failure of the individual, while positive actions are attributed to structural forces such as government hand-outs or reverse racism. Moreover, we are more likely to remember positive experiences with in-group members and negative experiences with out-group members, dismissing contradictory experiences as exceptions to the "rules" we cognitively develop about in-groups and out-groups.

Social cognition research suggests that these biases result from any form of racial segregation. Racial isolation in religious life, however, magnifies these biases because, as discussed in Chapters 1 and 11, religion strengthens the social bonds within the religious group by, in part, heightening the group's distinctions from other groups. In other words, due to racial segregation, religious in-groups and out-groups are nearly identical to racial in-groups and out-groups.

Religion also creates separation between the races by developing distinct explanatory cultures. Research demonstrates that religion provides individuals with what Ann Swidler calls a cultural "toolkit" that helps people organize experiences and evaluate reality. For believers, these tools are often explicitly based in faith and are central to the ways in which they interpret and organize other situations and experiences, including how they make sense of issues of racial inequality. The white evangelical Protestant toolkit has been the subject of the most scholarly attention. Michael Emerson and Christian Smith argue that it consists of accountable freewill individualism, relationalism, and antistructuralism. Accountable freewill individualism is the theological understanding that one is accountable to other people, but most importantly to God, for their freely made choices. Relationalism is a strong emphasis on interpersonal relationships, rooted in the theological understanding that salvation can come only from a personal relationship with Christ. Antistructuralism is the inability or unwillingness to accept explanations based on social structural influences, such as prejudice, discrimination, or high levels of unemployment.

In contrast, the African American Protestant toolkit is built on community action to change systems of inequality, collective responsibility for social inequality, and structuralist explanations for racial inequality in American society. The African American church, then, uses these tools in order to establish places for promoting collective social action. The Catholic toolkit is built on communalism, or a rejection of individualistic explanations for, and responsibility toward, social inequality, which favors structural and institutional approaches to social problems. This toolkit is connected with the Catholic history, described in Chapter 6, of helping poor immigrant groups, and with the labor movement and its critique of capitalist structures and the government that supports them.

Sociological research demonstrates that the social cognition biases and the distinct explanatory cultures and toolkits that result from the racial segregation of churches combine to shape attitudes towards other racial groups and to provide explanations for racial inequality. Emerson and Smith, along with others, using data from 1996, find that white evangelical Protestants are more likely to favor individualistic explanations for African American inequality, such as a lack of motivation and ability, and less likely to favor structural explanations, like discrimination or a lack of access to education. These racial attitudes, combined with social isolation from African Americans, lead white evangelicals to resist structural and group-based understandings of inequality.

Eric Tranby and Penny Edgell have also done research that focuses on these issues. An overview of their findings is reported in Table 12.2. In addition to confirming Emerson and Smith's findings, Tranby and Edgell found that regardless of religious tradition, whites who are highly involved in religious activities are less sympathetic to explanations for racial inequality that point to white privilege and domination, such as discrimination or bias in laws and institutions, and are also less likely to favor structuralist accounts, such as a lack of access to good schools and jobs. On the other hand, they found that white Catholics are more sympathetic to explanations for African American inequality that place the responsibility on whites, such as prejudice and discrimination, and are less likely to blame poor upbringing for inequality. These results are mediated in part by education and gender, with less educated, but religiously involved, whites and non-religious women being more sympathetic to the structural explanation of African American disadvantage, while the more educated religiously involved and evangelical women are less likely to believe that racial inequality stems from biased laws and institutions and are more likely to blame African American inequality on poor upbringing in African American families.

Tranby and Edgell also investigated how religion shaped explanations for racial inequality among African Americans and Hispanics. African Americans who hold orthodox religious beliefs are more sympathetic to explanations for racial inequality focused on bias in laws and social institutions, and to structural causes, such as a lack of access to good schools and social connections. This finding represents a toolkit built on discourse about the lack of access to good schools, good jobs, and good education, and a discourse about the crisis in the African American family. Hispanic Catholics are especially likely to think that biased laws and social institutions are important explanations for explaining African American inequality. This finding reflects that Catholicism provides a set of religious cultural tools that favor structural and communal understandings of racial inequality and foster institutional solutions.

Sociological research demonstrates that the social cognition biases, distinct explanatory cultures and toolkits, and fully separate explanations for racial inequality that result from the racial segregation of churches combine to perpetuate racial

Table 12.2 Attitudes towards African American inequality among religious groups

	Which of the following are important explanations for African American inequality?				
	Prejudice and discrimination	*Discriminatory laws and institutions*	*Lack of access to good schools and social connections*	*Lack of effort and hard work*	*Poor family upbringing*
Population	80.7%	53.8%	54.2%	70.9%	86.2%
White Evangelical Protestants	72.1%	34.1%	32.8%	71.5%	85.9%
White Mainline Protestants	76.6%	34.7%	41.0%	60.8%	81.3%
White Catholics	78.8%	39.2%	50.8%	63.8%	85.8%
African American Protestants	91.7%	87.7%	78.4%	83.3%	88.1%
Hispanic Catholics	85.2%	60.2%	62.3%	80.3%	84.4%
Attends church monthly or more frequently	78.7%	53.2%	52.5%	74.0%	86.7%
Attends church less than monthly	82.9%	54.5%	56.0%	67.4%	85.7%

Source: 2003 American Mosaic Survey

Table 12.3 Preferred solutions for African American inequality

	African Americans should not receive special help with jobs and schools	African Americans should not get more economic help from the government	Charities should do more to help African Americans
Population	43.5%	45.8%	44.7%
White Evangelical Protestants	59.7%	65.1%	29.4%
White Mainline Protestants	49.7%	49.4%	43.1%
White Catholics	48.9%	50.9%	50.1%
African American Protestants	19.0%	20.7%	59.4%
Hispanic Catholics	41.5%	40.1%	42.9%
Attends church monthly or more frequently	44.5%	46.8%	47.0%
Attends church less than monthly	43.7%	45.7%	45.4%

Source: 2003 American Mosaic Survey

inequality in the US. First, people place in-group needs and priorities above those outside of the group. Because of this and because of racial segregation, resources and social networks are more likely to be shared within, rather than across, racial groups.

Second, distinct toolkits and racial attitudes combine to favor different solutions to racial inequality. As shown in Table 12.3, white evangelical Protestants and whites who are more religiously involved tend to oppose both government and private charitable solutions for inequality, such as affirmative action programs or economic help. Instead, reflecting their emphasis on relationalism, white evangelical Protestants emphasize interpersonal and faith-based solutions to racial inequality; in particular, they seek to convert people to Christianity as a way to develop strong cross-racial relationships. White Catholics favor private charitable solutions over government ones, while African American Protestants and Hispanic Catholics favor both government and private charitable solutions for racial inequality. These preferences are more than symbolically important. A long line of sociological research demonstrates that government programs, such as affirmative actions, poverty alleviation, and anti-discrimination laws are the most effective in reducing societal levels of racial inequality. Neither private charities nor cross-racial relationships strongly affect societal levels of racial inequality, although they can make a difference in the lives of individuals. Thus, the racial segregation of churches has a profound impact on perpetuating ongoing racial inequality in the US.

Racially integrated congregations

If the segregation of American religious life is partially responsible for racial inequality, might more racially integrated congregations help alleviate or reduce racial inequality? Recent research by Brad Christerson, Korie L. Edwards, and Michael Emerson suggests that this may be the case. They find that racially integrated congregations promote social ties across groups, with 83 per cent of individuals who attend a racially

---

Box 12.1 Evangelical Protestant solutions to racial inequality

Michael Emerson and Christian Smith (2000) argue that the evangelical toolkit helps explain white evangelical approaches to solving the race problem as well. Evangelical solutions emphasize the need to get to know people of other races, to "love thy neighbor," and for everybody to become a Christian. Evangelicals are, in turn, extremely mistrustful of, and often vehemently opposed to, structural and state-based solutions to racial problems because they do not address what they believe to be the true roots of the problem. Second, evangelical solutions to race problems do not "advocate for or support changes that might cause extensive discomfort or change their economic and cultural lives" (2000:130). Thus, Emerson and Smith argue that while many evangelicals may want to see an end to race problems, they are constrained by their "toolkit" to call only for voluntaristic, faith-based solutions that would achieve the desired effects gradually and incrementally, such as converting people to Christianity and forming strong cross-racial relationships.

---

mixed congregation reporting having one or more opposite race friends in their social circles. These social ties serve to reduce the social cognition biases and stereotypes about race described in the previous section because members of racially integrated congregations have more positive attitudes about people of different races. These congregations also appear to reduce racial inequalities between members, such that members of these churches are, on average and regardless of race, economically better off than members of non-racially mixed congregations. This effect appears to be caused by membership in the church, but the causal effect is particularly hard to unravel. Additional research finds that members of racially integrated congregations develop racial attitudes that reflect structural understandings of racial inequality. Members also emphasize interpersonal relationships as one of many ways to reduce racial segregation and inequality in American life.

These congregations achieve more racial equality between members by focusing on what Marti calls "religious racial integration," or the process by which members gain an identity in, and commitment to, the congregation, in order successfully to attract and retain members. This occurs in three stages in the lived experiences of members. First, members must begin by establishing a connection with the congregation through similar interests or beliefs. Second, persons must reorient their religious identity away from bases that exist outside the congregation and become rooted in the interests, values, and preferences of the congregation. Third, members must integrate their ethnic and racial heritage into a single religious organization. Separate research by Penny Edgell finds that having religious leaders of multiple racial backgrounds and a religious symbolism that is rooted in religious text and tradition promotes this integration.

However, there are significant barriers to the establishment of more racially integrated churches. As described in Chapter 4, most people attend a church close to them. Therefore, racially integrated congregations are more likely to occur in relatively racially diverse neighborhoods or areas. As described above, the races tend to be segregated into different neighborhoods in the US. This residential racial segregation limits the number and location of racially integrated churches.

Figure 12.1 Racially integrated congregations help promote social ties and reduce inequality across racial groups. However, there are significant challenges to establishing and creating these congregations

© Najlah Feanny/Corbis

There are other barriers to achieving this integration, even if the congregation is in a fairly racially diverse area. First, existing congregations often have a tradition, and reputation, of being racially segregated. Therefore, most racially integrated congregations are newly formed. Second, different theological understandings and worship styles across racial groups can create conflict in a congregation. In particular, research by Korie L. Edwards demonstrates that most racially integrated churches do not assemble their own distinctive style of congregational life or balance religious cultures. Instead, they continue to reflect the worship practices, organizational structure, and cultural style of white churches with only symbolic elements representing African American, Latino, and Asian cultures. This dominance can leave many non-white members of the church feeling disconnected from the church or upset that tightly controlled services that dominate in the white tradition do not allow for the Holy Spirit to move within the congregation. Third, the sustained focus on religious racial integration that is necessary to maintain these congregations can be hard to maintain in the long term, particularly for whites who do not have to deal with racial inequality in their everyday lives.

African American religion revisited

Contemporary sociological research has brought other insights into the African American church and mosque. As described previously, African American churches in general are more likely to engage in community and social justice than white churches because of African Americans' historic inability to participate fully in economic, social, and political life. This is particularly true of inner city churches. The African American toolkit, described above, is used to motivate social actions by church members. For example, Mary Pattillo-McCoy, in her ethnographic study of two African American churches, finds that community meetings targeted at curbing youth delinquency, working to close a neighborhood drug house, or inspiring individuals to vote used rhetorical, interactional, and material tools that emphasized the collective responsibility of church members towards an issue.

African American mosques play a similar role in the African American community, especially mosques located in the inner city. In a study of an African American Sunni mosque, Victoria Lee finds that the mosque provides the driving force for change within the community, establishing a multifaceted development program to assist Muslims as well as the community. Importantly, Islam provides African Americans with an opportunity to shape a new identity distinct from an African American Protestant one that is rooted in the history of slavery. Islam also provides religious tools built on highly structured codes, norms, and rituals that address issues important to the inner-city African American community, such as the dissolution of family values, the sexualized stereotype of African American women, and the prevalence of drugs and violence.

However, African American religion is not a monolithic entity that emphasizes uniform issues or concerns. There are substantial class differences in African American religion. The African American church does, in general, bring poor and middle class African Americans together by providing a cultural blueprint for activities with the community. However, upper-class and upwardly mobile African Americans are more likely to become members of churches in white denominations, partly in an effort to conform to their new social status and disaffiliate from an inner-city lifestyle. This helps to perpetuate resource disparities between white and African American churches.

In addition, the African American religious experience, especially in the inner city, is dominated by multiple small "niche" churches. Omar McRoberts finds important consequences of this particularism in his study of the twenty-nine African American churches within a half-mile radius of the Four Corners neighborhood of Boston. These churches do allow people to find a church that aligns with their personal beliefs. However, because many of these churches are located in storefronts, they crowd out small businesses that rely on those spaces to provide a home for their products and services. This contributes to the lack of economic growth in inner city neighborhoods. Additionally, many of these small, storefront churches are run and attended by commuters who do not live in the neighborhood. Thus, religious leaders and members of these churches may have little attachment to the neighborhood, making them less inclined to respond to the needs of the community.

Box 12.2 The role of the African American mosque in the community

Victoria Lee (2010: 154–55) discusses the role that the Mosque she studied played in the broader community:

> The Masjid [Mosque] has emerged as a driving force for change within the local community. A decade ago, the mosque established a multifaceted development program to assist Muslims and the larger community. Its mission statement promotes the development of spiritual, intellectual, and physical resources, the fostering of family stability, and communal and societal advancement. Concretely, it has set up a block watch that meets every month to encourage positive community development, fight crime, and remove trash and blight. It works with the police to prevent drug trafficking as well. The mosque's charismatic leaders have forged a close working relationship with their neighborhood, the nearby hospital, and the mayor of Northeastern City to rehabilitate abandoned houses and revitalize the surrounding area. The Masjid alone has invested in more than a half-million dollar's worth of property to help stabilize the community. Their daily congregational prayers, educational programs, and watchful presence reduce crime and negative activities in the neighborhood. The Masjid also plans to open a high school for Muslim students not only to instill Islamic moral values but also to get young people off the street and to provide them with vocational skills as a way to move forward in a community with limited economic opportunity.
>
> Northeastern City has recognized the Masjid as a positive force in community stabilization. A plaque honoring the Masjid for its community contributions stands at a nearby intersection for visitors to see. However, gaining the city's and neighborhood's trust has not been immediate. Sister Makarim noted that residents were skeptical when the Muslims first arrived in the neighborhood. Neighborhood opinion changed when Muslims, decidedly fed up with the blatant crime surrounding the mosque, lined up on the street, side by side, to keep vigil through numerous nights to fend off the drug trade. Their actions angered the drug dealers, but the residents came to appreciate and welcome the Muslims' presence and contributions to the quality of local life.

Religion and social services

To help alleviate poverty and reduce inequality, many congregations provide social services to the poor and the needy. Social services provided by congregations include homeless shelters, food shelves/pantries, job training, drug and alcohol rehabilitation, family planning, and other services, especially those in urban areas and African American congregations.

Some people argue that religious groups and congregations are uniquely suited to deliver social services and can replace the state in providing these services. In this argument, religious organizations specialize in a more holistic kind of social service

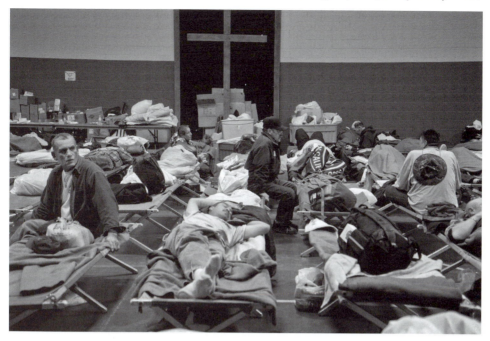

Figure 12.2 Many congregations provide for the short-term needs of the poor and needy. Here, homeless men prepare to sleep at a night shelter held at a church in Glendora, CA

© Marmaduke St. John/Alamy

activity that focuses on personal transformation to provide long-term solutions to people's problems. This holistic approach is thought to be an important alternative to social services delivered by nonreligious organizations, like government agencies, that focus on the short-term needs of clients.

These ideas culminated in the Charitable Choice provision of the 1996 welfare reform law. This provision directs government funding to religious organizations to provide social services through various block grants to state agencies. Funds received through the Charitable Choice initiative must be used to fulfill public social service goals and cannot be used for religious activities, but the government cannot require the providers to remove religious materials from the site. Much controversy surrounds this provision, especially concerns about whether faith-based organizations would be willing to serve anyone without proselytizing and whether there would be religious tests for persons who delivered the services; however, it remains in force today.

Research by Mark Chaves and William Tsitsos from 2001 reveals that the assumptions behind the Charitable Choice provision are flawed, at best. Social services provided by religious groups are most likely to be aimed at meeting short-term emergency needs and require limited contact with needy people. Moreover, government social service programs and collaborative programs are the most likely to engage in holistic service delivery. Finally, as of 2007, according to the National Congregations Study, only 36 per cent of congregations had expressed any interest in using Charitable Choice funds and only 10 per cent had applied for funds.

More broadly, the assumption that religious groups and congregations do a lot to combat poverty or provide social services is flawed. Mark Chaves, using the 1998 National Congregations Study, found that 12 per cent of congregations ran food shelves or other food programs and 4 per cent ran or participated in housing or homeless programs. Overall, 40 per cent did some kind of social service work on an occasional basis, and, on average, only 2 to 4 per cent of a congregation's budget goes toward social service projects. This work is commonly done by a core group of individuals within the congregation, with only 15 per cent of weekly service attenders reporting that they regularly participate in their congregations' social service activities. On a national scale, the volunteerism of religious individuals and groups is laudable and certainly makes a difference in people's lives, but federal, state, and local governments still spend a hundred times more on social services than all congregations in the US combined.

Key points you need to know

- Racial segregation is a persistent feature of American religious life.
- The larger the religious tradition, the more segregated it is.
- The more choices people have of places to worship, the more they choose to be with people who are racially similar.
- There are two major sources of the racial segregation of religion: the legacy of the historical division of African American Protestant and white Protestant churches, and the development of immigrant churches and religions.
- Racial segregation shapes our perceptions of racial others by generating biased ideas of members of racial and religious out-groups.
- Racial segregation creates distinct religious cultures that people use to organize experiences and evaluate reality.
- Racial segregation shapes attitudes towards other racial groups and explanations for racial inequality.
- The effects of the racial segregation of America combine to perpetuate racial inequality by reinforcing disparate social and resource networks, and leading people to favor different solutions for racial inequality.
- Racially integrated congregations may help reduce racial inequality in American life by promoting social ties and the sharing of resources between people of different racial groups.
- There are significant organizational and structural barriers to the success of racially integrated congregations.
- African American religion is not a monolithic entity that emphasizes the same issues or concerns.
- Although religious groups provide many social services in the US, assumptions about their effectiveness and ability to replace the role of the government in social service provisions are flawed.

Discussion questions

1   What are the causes and consequences of the racial segregation of American religion?

2 In what ways does religion provide explanations for, and solutions to, racial inequality?

3 Should religious congregations work to reduce racial inequality? Why or why not?

4 If you had one, was the congregation you grew up in mostly racially homogeneous or racially mixed? Did you ever talk about race issues? What effects do you think the racial composition of your church had on you?

5 Would you go out of your way to attend a racially mixed congregation? Why or why not?

6 What is the role of the African American church and mosque in the community?

7 How does class mobility affect the African American church?

8 Should religious organizations do more to provide social services? Why or why not?

Further reading

Becker, P.E. (1998) "Making Inclusive Communities: Congregations and the 'Problem' of Race," *Social Problems*, 45: 451–72.

Chaves, M. and Tsitsos, W. (2001) "Congregations and Social Services: What they Do, How they Do It, and With Whom," *Nonprofit and Voluntary Sector Quarterly* 30: 660–83.

—— (2001) "Religious Congregations and Welfare Reform," *Society* 38: 21–27.

Christerson, B., Edwards K.L., and Emerson M.O. (2005) *Against All Odds: The Struggle for Racial Integration in Religious Organizations*, New York: New York University Press.

Edgell, P. and Tranby, E. (2007) "Religious Influences on Understandings of Racial Inequality in the United States," *Social Problems*, 54: 263–88.

Edwards K.L. (2008) "Bring Race to the Center: The Importance of Race in Racially Diverse Religious Organizations," *Journal for the Scientific Study of Religion*, 47: 5–9.

Emerson, M.O. and Sikkink, D. (1999) "Equal in Christ, but Not in the World: White Conservative Protestants and Explanations of Black-White Inequality," *Social Problems* 46: 398–412.

Emerson, M.O. and Smith, C. (2000) *Divided by Faith: Evangelical Religion and the Problem of Race*, Oxford: Oxford University Press.

Lee, V.J. (2010) "The Mosque and Black Islam Towards an Ethnographic Study of Islam in the Inner City," *Ethnic and Racial Studies*, 11: 145–63.

Lincoln, E.C. and Mamiya L.H. (1990) *The Black Church in the African American Experience*. Durham, NC: Duke University Press.

McRoberts, O. (2003) *Streets of Glory: Church and Community in a Black Urban Neighborhood*, Chicago: University of Chicago Press.

Marti G. (2009) "Affinity, Identity, and Transcendence: The Experience of Religious Racial Integration in Diverse Congregations," *Journal for the Scientific Study of Religion*, 48: 53–68.

Nelson, T.J. (2004) *Every Time I Feel the Spirit: Religious Experience and Ritual in an African American Church*, New York: New York University Press.

Pattillo-McCoy, M. (1998) "Church Culture as a Strategy of Action," *American Sociological Review* 63: 767–84.

Roof, W.C. and McKinney, W. (1987) *American Mainline Religion: Its Changing Shape and Future*, Camden, NJ: Rutgers University Press.

Tranby, E.P. and Hartmann, D. (2008) "Critical Whiteness Theories and the Evangelical Race Problem: Extending Emerson and Smith's *Divided by Faith*," *Journal for the Scientific Study of Religion*, 47: 341–59.

Wood, R. (2002) *Faith in Action: Religion, Race, and Democratic Organizing in America*, Chicago: University of Chicago Press.

13 Faiths on the margins

In this chapter

This chapter examines the proliferation of religious groups in contemporary America, beginning with discussion of the categories frequently used to describe movements on the periphery of the larger religious culture – sect, cult, alternative religion, new religious movement. It looks at the 1960s, when many new religions – several with an Asian flavor – emerged throughout the culture. That section also probes whether these religions "brainwashed" converts and also efforts to "deprogram" them. The focus then turns to how religion and popular culture become intertwined in new religions such as Scientology. The next section briefly explores religious options based on Satanism. Next comes an examination of charismatic leadership and its sometimes catastrophic results. The final section appraises how new religious movements affected understanding of religious experience and the prospects for new religions when they move into the second and third generations. The discussion in Chapters 18 and 19 will shed additional light on the way the diversity resulting from new religious movements impacts American religious life.

Main topics covered

- How to describe groups on the periphery of religious culture.
- Why some find these categories problematic and others find them useful.
- The fascination in the 1960s with groups rooted in Asian spirituality.
- Why such groups gained plausibility during the civil rights movement and the Vietnam War.
- Reactions of those who found these movements.
- Legal issues and challenges surrounding new religious movements.
- How Scientology illustrates the interaction of religious impulses with popular culture.
- The resurgence of interest in Satanism.
- The nature of charismatic leadership.
- How and why some groups have disastrous consequences.
- The impact of new religious movements on American religious culture.

Sect and cult: problems of terminology

Religions such as Christianity constantly give birth to new groups that draw on the larger tradition, but take on a distinctive quality because of some belief or practice that emerging groups emphasize. Sometimes it is as if a new religion has come to life, remaining only marginally related to the tradition from which it sprang. Sometimes groups split because of disagreement over matters of leadership, over how to interpret and understand sacred writings, or over maintaining standards to preserve authentic belief and practice. Sometimes, too, an individual has a fresh vision of what endows life with meaning, and shapes that vision into a new religion.

A century ago, scholars – including sociologists Max Weber (1864–1920) and Joachim Wach (1898–1955), and philosopher-theologian Ernst Troeltsch (1865–1923) – used several terms to describe such movements. These terms then carried no value judgment as to whether a new movement had a positive or negative character. Those with obvious links to another religious movement were designated as "sects" (think of them as sectors or sections of a larger whole, where all shared common features but also had some unique ones). Weber felt that sects often emerged among persons from the lower end of the socio-economic scale who felt that a religion had become corrupted over time. They wanted to restore its pure essence. In Weber's view, a cult usually (but not always) lacked ties to an existing religion; it usually represented an entirely new religion grounded in an esoteric body of beliefs and practices known only to a few. In this understanding, the Amish might be regarded as a sect of the Christian pietist movement that included the Mennonites and others; ISKCON, about which we will say more in Chapter 18, might be seen as a Hindu sect. The unique teaching of L. Ron Hubbard (1911–86), the basis for Scientology, meets Weber's criteria for a cult – again, without negative nuance attached to the word cult.

Use of these labels gradually became slippery. In the popular mind, sect and cult often became equated. For many, "cult" became a term applied to any religion that one did not like. In other words, the terms took on a negative nuance unintended when they first were used. Some suggested other categories to allow analysis of groups on their own terms and avoid the presumption that new religious approaches were less worthy than existing religions (what Troeltsch called churches, to which others added the category of denominations).

Hence some spoke of alternative religions, since many groups presented themselves as better options than already existing religious communities. Critics felt that this label had negative dimensions since it assumed an existing group was the norm for judging another as an alternative. Others were acutely aware that new religious groups appear all the time. The First Amendment's protection of the "free exercise" of religion means that individuals are free to start new religions as they wish. Some scholars thus preferred to talk about emergent or emerging religions to emphasize how such movements reflected cultural impulses prevailing at their founding. Others called them "new religious movements" (NRMs), although it was not clear when movements might cease being "new" if they lasted beyond the founding generation and developed the standard institutional apparatus of religious groups whose history spanned several generations, even if they remained small.

In our discussion, the label of "new religious movement" will be used most frequently. But none of the terms employed implies a value judgment about the legitimacy of any particular group, although there may be critical appraisal and evaluation. In addition, few who now use these terms accept Weber's conviction that there is direct correlation between any socio-economic status and involvement in a new religious movement. Analysts have found that religious groups attract adherents from across the socio-economic spectrum.

The religious explosion of the 1960s

After the close of World War II, students of American life spoke of a revival of religious interest in the US, for conventional ways of being religious seemed to resonate with millions looking for a new anchor in life. Yet by the later 1960s, several movements that had made their way to the US created what some called a "cult scare." Many had connections with forms of Asian spirituality

In 1965, Swami Bhaktivedanta Prabhupada, founder of the International Society for Krishna Consciousness, arrived in the United States. That same year, a Korean religious figure once imprisoned by the Communists, Sun Myung Moon (1920–), made his first visit to the US. His followers had started seeking American converts as early as 1959. In 1935 Moon had had a visionary experience that led him to found the Holy Spirit Association for the Unification of World Christianity. Popularly called Moonies, Unificationists blend aspects of Christianity (Moon had ties to Presbyterian missionaries in Korea), Buddhism, and indigenous Chinese religious understanding with Moon's own theology. In 1971, a teenage guru called Maharaj ji (1957–) spurred much interest in a Hindu-based group called the Divine Light Mission when he spent time in America. A decade later, another Hindu mystic, who took the title Baghwan Shree Rajneesh (1931–90), arrived in the US, finally organizing a communal-type settlement housing close followers in rural Oregon. A host of other Indian gurus sustained intrigue with Asian spirituality. They often spent time on or near college campuses, seeking converts there. Also fueling interest in Asian religious ways was the widespread interest in Transcendental Meditation, yoga, and other meditation disciplines.

Figure 13.1 Adherents of the International Society for Krishna Consciousness (ISKON), shown here chanting on the sidewalk of New York City's Fifth Ave., illustrate the surge of interest among American young adults in Asian religions during the 1960s

Courtesy of Fred W. McDarrah/Getty Images

Box 13.1 What made new religious movements seem dangerous?

The seeming proliferation of new religious movements in the 1960s produced a backlash, leading many to talk about a "cult scare." What made folks so suspicious?

- Because many of the newer groups had Asian roots, their vocabulary, ways of religious thinking, and practices were unfamiliar. Difference alone made them suspect.
- Several urged adherents to forsake private property and live in communal settings; some seemed to take control of matters of personal choice, such as selecting a marriage partner. This rejection of dominant social patterns made them controversial.
- Leaders appeared to exert dictatorial power over followers. Consequently, outsiders claimed they manipulated members.
- Aggressive proselytizing and fundraising techniques repulsed some who found the style personally intrusive.
- In many cases, rumors of unconventional behavior, from sexual promiscuity to use of controlled substances, added to the popular anxiety.

There is little new about religious teachers promoting their own beliefs and practices in the American environment. The first half of the nineteenth century, for example, witnessed a similar burst of interest in alternative ways of being religious. The communal celibate group called the Shakers flourished then, as did groups like the Oneida Community. In the 1830s, Joseph Smith began to attract a following with his fresh perspective that coalesced into what by the early twenty-first century was one of the nation's largest religions, the Church of Jesus Christ of Latter-day Saints or the Mormons. Spiritualism also attracted much popular attention, as did concern for the end of time, which gave birth to groups like the Seventh-Day Adventists.

But in the 1960s, new religious movements attracted thousands. They also provoked a hostile response. What set these groups apart? One distinguishing feature was that they all had ties to Asian – particularly Indian – religiosity. Hence their understanding of religious truth and belief differed from that of more familiar Christianity and Judaism or even Islam. Difference alone prompted concern; it made some presume that the beliefs and practices had to be sinister, if not dangerous.

Several groups, including Krishna Consciousness and the followers of Rajneesh, lived in communal settings; some Moonies gave their possessions to support the movement. As had been the case with nineteenth-century communal and utopian experiments, abandoning private property and sacrificing control over living arrangements struck outsiders as equivalent to forsaking a lifestyle basic to American society. When ISKCON adherents replaced their given names with Sanskrit ones, not only had they taken on a new identity in ways similar to what Roman Catholic women religious or nuns had often done when they took their final vows, but they also severed ties to their biological families. In turn, some families claimed that the groups prohibited members from contacting their families or speaking with them.

There was more. Many groups aggressively proselytized (sought new converts) and badgered folks to contribute funds to support their ministries. It was amusing, perhaps, to see American men with shaved heads and wearing saffron robes stand on city street corners chanting in Sanskrit, but it was annoying to be targeted by such people in airports, at rest areas on interstate highways, or even at traffic lights and to be pressured to buy a flower or a copy of the Hindu sacred text, the *Bhagavad Gita*. Even some devotees balked; engaging in these activities subjected them to harassment and ridicule.

Sometimes the practices of a group simultaneously attracted curiosity and opposition. Among Unificationists, for example, having Moon personally pair as marriage partners men and women who may not have even met each other and then celebrate their union in mass weddings involving hundreds or even thousands of couples was so different from standard social patterns that non-Unificationists believed it undermined cultural notions of marriage and family.

In addition, all these groups seemed to target persons in late adolescence and early young adulthood, especially college and university students, as the most likely prospects for conversion. Critics claimed they intentionally sought out "loners" or those without a circle of friends, luring them into the group with promises of friendship, companionship, and support. But persons have long dabbled with new religious visions and identities during the transition from childhood, when beliefs reflect those of parents, to adulthood, when they become one's own affirmations. One difference, according to critics, was that those who sought to leave these groups appeared to be constrained from doing so. In other words, there was no easy exit from membership if one became dissatisfied or discontent. All of the groups themselves, however, rejected that claim.

Such controversy raised many questions. A few were legal. Were proselytizing efforts protected by the First Amendment's guarantee of free speech? Some cases were resolved by identifying designated public areas where adherents could promote their religious views. Were converts brainwashed? This question plagued families distraught that their young adult children had opted for striking alternatives to the religious orientations in which they had been raised. Convinced that "no one in their right mind" would make such a dramatic change, they insisted that NRM leaders used brainwashing techniques to instill a new identity in converts. If brainwashing was involved, then allegiance was involuntary and coerced. Some "cult-busters," as they were called, organized interventions to remove NRM members, occasionally by force, and "deprogram" them. That is, they sought to restore an earlier personal and religious identity through tactics equivalent to "reverse brainwashing." Other controversy came when some leaders of the new religious movements faced their own legal challenges. Sun Myung Moon, for example, was convicted on charges of tax evasion based on a claim that he used money donated to the movement for personal gain. He served a short prison term.

All of the contention masks other issues. Most important is that, by and large, those who flocked to new religious movements were legally adults with freedom to practice whatever religion they chose. The First Amendment's guarantee of "free exercise" meant that persons could not be kept from aligning with groups others found unsuitable. Critics also failed to recognize that for millions, traditional ways of being religious had become dysfunctional, thanks in part to shifts in the larger culture such as the civil rights movement, second-wave feminism, and the opposition to the Vietnam

War. Many found in groups such as ISKCON or the Unification Church beliefs and practices that brought coherence and meaning to their own lives, in much the same way as for earlier generations a Methodist, Greek Orthodox, or Reform Jewish approach might have done. In other words, new religious movements functioned as any religion should.

In time, many groups receded from the limelight. Rajneesh left the country, leaving his followers to battle over leadership. Maharaj ji returned to India, where he renounced his former perspective and effectively disbanded the Divine Light Mission in the US. As both ISKCON and the Unification Church moved from the first to the second generation, they confronted the challenges that face any social movement: crafting structures and policies to sustain a group and transmitting what was once a new perspective to a generation nurtured within the movement.

New religions and popular culture: the case of Scientology

In the later twentieth century, other new religious movements emerged that had links to popular culture, especially to worldviews originating in fiction (especially science fiction) and film. Many were intentional parodies of traditional religion. Few have official members; by the end of the century, Internet conversation became the common way those drawn to these religions had contact with one another. These movements include the Church of the Flying Spaghetti Monster, Discordianism, and the Church of the Subgenius. Most seem destined to disappear after the death of their founders, who playfully constructed a religious worldview and attendant practices from fantasies found in fiction and film. For a few, these became faith systems; most knew they were spoofs.

One, however, has moved into a second generation, continuing to attract a following in part because it has developed the necessary institutional apparatus to survive, and in part because several celebrities, including actors Tom Cruise and John Travolta, embraced it. That religion, based on the thought of science fiction writer L. Ron Hubbard, is Scientology. Like the various Asian religious movements, Scientology has aroused controversy. Hubbard first published the work explaining his religious philosophy, *Dianetics: The Modern Science of Mental Health*, in 1950. The title suggests that Hubbard wanted to use psychological constructs to craft a distinctive religion. In addition, designating the approach as science enhanced its appeal to those who sought a rational faith system.

As with most religions, Scientology aims to aid its adherents in finding happiness and meaning in life. Hubbard believed that if life were to have meaning, the mind must unleash its true spiritual nature by eradicating all that was non-spiritual. Scientology developed several techniques, some requiring a fee to access, that enabled one to jettison the psychological detritus hindering full awareness of one's spiritual essence, an essence that brings together mind and body. Not all practitioners achieve this result as they have not mastered the various processes. But Scientologists insist that because their techniques are scientific, they are guaranteed to work if mastered. Mastery may involve use of elaborate machinery (an "E-Meter" or "Hubbard electrometer"). If techniques and the appropriate apparatus do not work, the fault lies with the individual who remains attached to the baggage that impedes realizing pure spirituality or becoming what Hubbard called "clear."

Box 13.2 What is dianetics?

A contemporary edition of L. Ron Hubbard's 1950 work on *Dianetics* that outlines the core beliefs of Scientology begins with a "note to the reader." It explores some key terms and tries to deflect criticism by downplaying claims Scientology's techniques are fraudulent and not scientific at all. Hence the apparatus associated with Scientology, the E-Meter, is called a religious object, not a scientific one. Note as well, in the final paragraph of the excerpt, that the success of the Scientology approach appears very similar to much "self-help" understanding.

> Dianetics (from Greek *dia* "through" and *nous* "soul") delineates fundamental principles of mind and spirit. Through the application of these discoveries, it became apparent that Dianetics dealt with a beingness that defied time – the human spirit – originally denominated the "I" and subsequently the "thetan."
> ...
> The Hubbard Electrometer, or E-Meter, is a religious artifact used in the Churches. The E-Meter, by itself, does nothing and is only used by ministers and ministers-in-training qualified in its use, to help parishioners locate the source of spiritual travail. The attainment of the benefits and goals of Dianetics and Scientology requires each individual's dedicated participation, as only through one's own efforts can they be achieved.
> (From "A Note to the Reader," in L.R. Hubbard,
> *Dianetics: The Science of Mental Health*,
> Commerce, CA: Bridge Publications, 2007, front matter)

Scientology holds regular services that center on readings from Hubbard's writings rather than traditional sermons. It also employs a rich vocabulary to describe the concepts and processes it promotes, functionally equivalent to the theological discourse and related rituals of other forms of religious expression. As a religion, Scientology has ministers and programs to train them. Only those so trained are proficient in using devices such as the E-Meter to assist persons in uncovering the issues that prohibit them from actualizing their genuine spiritual being.

Long-time devotees, like those who chanted to Krishna for years in ISKCON, claim that they have experienced a transformation resulting in genuine happiness and spiritual self-realization. Others, however, have balked at these claims. Some outsiders and some former practitioners insist that no verifiable scientific evidence proves that the E-Meter does or could do what Scientologists claim. Others have insisted that practitioners put pressure on them to forgo medical treatment, being told that their problems stemmed from not yet having rid their "reactive minds" of all that blocked spiritual being from developing. Critics have also condemned the group for charging fees for sessions with those authorized to use the religion's machinery, suggesting that they are attempts to scam more money from the unsuspecting when the desired results do not come. These issues have led to law suits, with some cases settled out of court, some resulting in countersuits to

Figure 13.2 Like other new religious movements, Scientology stirred opponents to see it as a
           dangerous cult.

© Richard Levine/Alamy

demonstrate that Scientology is an authentic religion, and some leading to a muting of
the more extravagant claims about the scientific basis for Dianetics and the certainty
that its techniques would ultimately work.

The rebirth of Satanism

From the 1960s on, the media have promoted the notion that Satanism was growing.
Fueling such speculation were reports of several brutal murders orchestrated by "cult"
leader Charles Manson (1934–) and his followers, known as the Manson Family. The

story of Satanism as a new religious movement, however, is more nuanced than popular perception suggests. For some, Satanism represents a clear rejection of traditions such as Christianity, Judaism, and Islam, which see Satan as the ultimate symbol of evil. Hence, some Satanists accept Satan as a deity, a supernatural power with which to be reckoned. Others do not, instead regarding Satan as representing many natural impulses in human beings that traditional religion seeks to control or dismiss, such as a propensity for self-indulgence.

Several organized Satanic groups have roots in the 1960s. Perhaps the most well known is one that, like some of the religious movements based on science fiction, intentionally parodies traditional religion. In San Francisco in 1966, Anton Szandor LaVey (1930–97), born Howard Stanton Levey, founded the Church of Satan. Three years later LaVey produced the *Satanic Bible*, a guide to his own beliefs in libertine individualism and related rituals. Other groups soon followed, including the Temple of Set, founded in 1975, and the First Satanic Church, set up by LaVey's daughter in 1999 following a schism within the Church of Satan after LaVey's death.

What attracts the greatest publicity and sparks fear of dangerous cult activity are adolescents who use symbols associated with Satanism, such as the pentagram, and indulge in hedonistic activities in places like cemeteries. Some refer to this form of Satanic practice as pseudo-Satanism since it has no order or organization, but emerges from the experimentation of adolescents with socially taboo ideas and practices. Fears that pseudo-Satanism was luring younger Americans into a realm of evil has, since the later twentieth century, prompted some evangelical Christian groups and leaders to condemn the children's holiday of Halloween because of its fantasy celebration of a world of witches, devils, and ghosts.

The charismatic leader within new religious movements

Among common features shared by many new religious movements is having a founding figure or leader whose vision provides the focus for belief and practice. Sociologist Max Weber used the word "charisma" to describe the extraordinary qualities inherent in such persons, although only as others recognize those qualities and become followers is the power of charisma actualized. Weber referred to this individual trait as charisma of person since it resided within the personality of the individual. Other kinds of leaders, according to Weber, exercised similar power and authority, but their charisma derived from the position or office they held. Weber's designation for the authority based on a leadership position was charisma of office. For example, in many religious groups, some persons are set aside ("ordained") as clergy because of special training they have received. As clergy, they have a certain kind of authority regardless of their personalities. Most founders of new religious movements do not need this kind of charisma, but they exhibit a commanding charisma of person that draws followers to them.

Recall the founders of the new religious movements discussed above. Among them are Swami Bhaktivedanta Prabhupada, Sun Myung Moon, Baghwan Shree Rajneesh, L. Ron Hubbard, and Anton LaVey. Each exhibited charisma of person. Some who react negatively towards new religious movements fear the power of such charisma. They claim that such leaders use this inherent power to manipulate followers, forcing them into beliefs and behavior that they otherwise would have spurned. Yet in history figures such as the Buddha, Jesus the Christ, and Muhammad exhibited charisma of

---

Box 13.3 Understanding charisma

The word "charisma" derives from Greek. In the narrowest religious sense, it refers to a "gift" received from God or the gods. For example, Pentecostals regard speaking in tongues or divine healing as charismatic gifts. But charisma also describes a type of leadership. Sometimes that leadership is associated with the position a person holds. The pope, as head of the Roman Catholic church, automatically has this type of charisma. But founders of new religious movements usually exemplify what the German sociologist Max Weber and others have called "charisma of person."

　　Charisma of person:

- is a quality of the individual personality that appears as inherent or "built-in" to the person;
- appears as an innate ability to speak dynamically, voice the concerns of others, and articulate visions for their future with mesmerizing power;
- grows as others look to the individual to use that power for the good of the group and its members;
- has an unstable dimension in that groups formed around a single leader often face tough challenges in transferring leadership to another when the charismatic figure dies;
- occasionally has what some call a "dark side" as leaders spur followers to engage in dangerous activity or behavior.

---

person, sparking controversy in their own day but becoming respected founders of major religious traditions.

　　Those who find charismatic leaders dangerous garner evidence from some extreme cases. Adolf Hitler, for example, exuded a charisma that gave his Nazi movement a religious tone for many. Numerous examples come directly from new religious movements. One that received much publicity was the Peoples Temple led by Jim (James Warren) Jones (1931–78). Following a brief stint working with a Methodist congregation, Jones in 1954 organized his own church in urban Indianapolis. Two years later it took the name of the Peoples Temple. The church for a time briefly affiliated with the mainline Disciples of Christ. Jones eventually moved to California, where he oversaw the formation of around a dozen branches of the Peoples Temple.

　　Jones went well beyond organizing his followers in communal living arrangements. He insisted that his followers, mostly urban and poor, surrender control over their resources to him. In return he provided for their needs, purportedly even healing them of physical and medical problems. However, a series of articles that appeared in 1972 in newspapers in California and Indiana reported cases of sexual misconduct, child abuse, and other improprieties. Consequently, Jones leased land in Guyana in 1974, where he urged followers to join him in a presumed Edenic paradise. Fearing mistreatment of American citizens at the Jonestown, Guyana site, US Congressman Leo Ryan and several others visited in 1978 to investigate. As they prepared to depart, Jones apparently ordered them murdered. Convinced that further investigation and apocalyptic persecution would follow, Jones then led his followers in a mass suicide.

With more than 900 dead as a result, Jonestown became a symbol of all the fears surrounding new religious movements, and Jones himself the epitome of charismatic power turned demonic.

Similar apprehension surfaced two decades later when a much smaller group suicide occurred in California among adherents of a group, Heaven's Gate, influenced by belief in UFOs (Unidentified Flying Objects). Two charismatic persons, Marshall Applewhite (1931–97), who took the name Bo, and Bonnie Nettles (1928–85), known as Peep, led this group. Heaven's Gate expected that the end of time, with the destruction of the world, would come in 1997 with the appearance of the Hale-Bopp Comet at its brightest. To avoid total destruction in the conflagration ending the world, twenty-nine adherents, including Applewhite, released their true selves, their souls, from the physical bodies that they occupied in a communal suicide. Heaven's Gate reinforced the posture of those who thought new religious movements were detrimental and not genuine religions at all.

The challenges and impact of new religious movements

The pervasiveness of new religious movements is a constant of American history. What differs is the extent to which the larger culture is receptive and responsive to them and also the degree to which the new movements appear to contrast with prevailing religious ideas and practices. During times of social stress, such as America encountered in the 1960s, new religious movements spark more criticism. Many of the movements that gained a following in the US during that epoch represented striking alternatives to existing religions. Those that had Asian roots, for example, seemed more radically different because they represented very different ways of thinking about religion than most people held familiar.

The charismatic leader also poses issues, not only for outsiders who may remain suspicious of the intent and integrity of those whose views are markedly different from their own, but even for some within the group. Every new religious movement with a charismatic founder has to grapple with how to transmit leadership to another generation when the charismatic founder dies. Max Weber recognized this problem when he spoke of the "routinization of charisma," by which he meant a process of creating offices and positions of authority so that leadership would continue. However, history reveals that most new religious movements are unable to negotiate this transfer of power. Most fade out when the founder figure and the first generation of devotees die.

At the same time, new religious movements raise questions about the nature of religious experience and what makes a religious belief system plausible. Psychologists have demonstrated how persons who fail to find meaning for their lives in one belief system may undergo a genuine "conversion" or change to another belief system in their search for meaning. Far from being brainwashed, most converts identify with a group because they reap benefits from their association with the group; they gain a sense of identity and wellbeing. In the 1960s sociologist Peter Berger emphasized the importance of plausibility structures in buttressing religious belief and practices. That is, the larger culture as well as personal experience had to support or otherwise provide signals that a particular way of believing and of being religious made sense and was viable. New religious movements create a greater stir when the plausibility structures supporting commonly held beliefs and practices cease to work. So, for example, the civil rights movement, by revealing the depths of racism rampant in

American religion, and second-wave feminism, by exposing the sexism in religious institutions, undermined the plausibility of many religious approaches. They paved the way for fresh ways, for new religious movements, to step in. New religious movements always exist in a dynamic relationship with the larger culture. They become more viable when existing ways no longer seem to work.

Key points you need to know

- The terms used to describe new religious movements can be problematic.
- Beginning in the 1960s, new religious movements with Asian roots flourished in the US.
- The cultural ferment of the era made these movements attractive to many disenchanted with traditional ways of being religious.
- Critics thought many of these groups were dangerous.
- Some believed that "cult" leaders brainwashed converts and consequently sought to "deprogram" them.
- Others insist that identifying with a new religion represents free choice protected by the Constitution.
- Interaction with popular culture, such as science fiction, gave rise to other new religious movements.
- Scientology is among the more prominent and controversial of these groups.
- Satanism, drawing on ancient traditions, has also experienced a resurgence of interest.
- New religious movements often have a charismatic leader or founder.
- Charisma can backfire, leading to disastrous results at times.
- The Peoples Temple and Heaven's Gate are two groups that had disastrous ends.
- New religious movements flourish especially when familiar groups become dysfunctional.

Discussion questions

1 Why are terms like sect and cult problematic? How would you resolve the issues raised by these problems?
2 What characterizes the numerous Asian new religious movements in the US that gained popularity in the 1960s and 1970s?
3 What made these groups attractive to American converts?
4 Why did some persons regard these groups as dangerous?
5 What made some believe that leaders of these groups brainwashed new converts?
6 On what grounds do others dismiss the popular criticism of these movements?
7 What gave rise to Scientology? On what grounds does it make its claim to be a religion? Why do some criticize it?
8 Discuss the similarities and differences between Scientology and Asian groups like ISKCON in terms of their appeal to followers and the criticism from their opponents.

9 How are perceptions of Satanism different from the reality of Satanism as a cluster of new religious movements?
10 What are charismatic leaders? What role do they play in new religious movements?
11 How do Jim Jones and the Peoples Temple illustrate charisma gone awry?
12 What challenges do new religious movements present to American religious culture? What influence to do they have on our understanding of religion in American life?

Further reading

Barker, E. (1984) *The Making of a Moonie: Choice or Brainwashing*, London: Blackwell.

Berger, P.L. (1967; rev. edn. 1990) *The Sacred Canopy: Elements of a Sociological Theory of Religion*, New York: Doubleday Anchor.

Cusack, C.M. (2010) *Invented Religions: Imagination, Fiction and Faith*, Farnham: Ashgate.

Dawson, L.L. (2006) *Comprehending Cults: The Sociology of New Religious Movements*, New York: Oxford University Press.

Gallagher, E.V. and Ashcraft, W.M. (eds.) (2006) *Introduction to New and Alternative Religions in America*, 5 vols., Westport, CT: Greenwood.

Lewis, J.R. (ed.) (2006) *Scientology*, New York: Oxford University Press.

Lucas, P.C. and Robbins, T. (eds.) (2004) *New Religions in the Twenty-First Century: Legal, Political, and Social Challenges*, New York: Routledge.

Mickler, M.L. and Inglis, M. (2000) *Forty Years in America: An Intimate History of the Unification Movement, 1959–1999*, New York: HSA Publications.

Moore, R. (2009) *Understanding Jonestown and Peoples Temple*, Westport, CT: Praeger.

Palmer, S.J (1997) *Moon Sister, Krishna Mothers, Rajneesh Lovers: Women's Roles in New Religions*, Syracuse, NY: Syracuse University Press.

Rochford, E.B., Jr. (2007) *Hare Krishna Transformed*, New York: New York University Press.

14 The Mormon perspective

In this chapter

This chapter looks at many of the trends in American religious life since World War II that we have discussed in earlier chapters, using one religious group – the Latter-day Saints (LDS) or Mormons – to illustrate shifts and changes. It first considers how the LDS began as a new religious movement that became a religious tradition. Then it explores how the LDS moved from the margins toward the mainstream of American religious culture, growing steadily in the decades when mainline Protestant bodies experienced numerical decline. The third section examines how the Mormons responded to the cultural turmoil of the 1960s and movements emerging from that ferment. The chapter also addresses how the Mormons reflect ways in which religious bodies engage themselves in the public sector, echoing the shift from political aloofness to political involvement of many evangelical groups. The chapter concludes with observations about the nature of American religious life in the twenty-first century based on the Mormon experience.

Main topics covered

- Mormonism's experience as a new religious movement in the nineteenth century.
- How the LDS responded to opposition.
- What allowed the LDS to evolve from a new religious movement into a stable religion.
- Ways in which the civil rights era and the liberation movements associated with it had an impact on Mormonism.
- How the LDS experience illustrates ways in which religious groups engage themselves in common life.
- The pulse of American religion in the early twenty-first century.

The Latter-day Saints as a new religious movement

In the early 1820s in upstate New York, a young man named Joseph Smith (1805–44) had a profound religious experience. He believed an angel directed him to hidden golden tablets containing a long-lost revelation from God. Smith published his translation of that revelation as the Book of Mormon in 1830, giving birth to one of many new religious movements that cascaded across the "burned-over district" of New York, an area so named because the fires of revivalism strongly fueled religious enthusiasm there. Smith and his followers were also part of a larger religious effort to recapture or restore American Christianity to its pure, original form. Smith's group took the name of the Church of Jesus Christ of Latter-day Saints. Many know them simply as Mormons. Although adherents today prefer to be called Saints, we shall use the more familiar designation of Mormons.

In the last chapter, we examined some of the hostility new religious movements in the 1960s encountered in the US. The situation for Smith and the Mormons was much the same in the nineteenth century. To outsiders, Smith's beliefs and claims seemed so removed from what they had long accepted that they looked on the Mormon enterprise with suspicion. For example, by elevating the Book of Mormon to the status of scripture, Mormons seemed to outsiders to challenge the sole primacy of the Bible as the basis for religious truth. In addition, Mormons believed that Smith had a near total authority as their leader, an authority given directly by God and evidenced in God's continuing to reveal new truth to Smith. To outsiders, vesting so much power in one individual seemed incompatible with the democratic spirit celebrated by Americans.

When those drawn to Smith began to live in communal arrangements, like the Shakers and other groups of the day, outsiders frowned at the flaunting of social convention. Hostility intensified after the group made its way to Ohio, for there Mormons experimented with abandoning notions of private property and with sharing all material goods in common. Such practice seemed then, as it did with some of the twentieth-century groups that adopted it, to undermine the capitalism that was the foundation of the American economy. Smith also believed that his vision encompassed the whole of a faithful society, a way of life, not simply a religious style. What others might see as the secular realm was for Smith encompassed in a religious world. Non-Mormons, accustomed to seeing "church" and "state" as separate, recoiled at this fusion of the political and the religious.

From Ohio, the group migrated first to Missouri and then to Illinois. There, at a place called Nauvoo, the Mormons received a grant of land over which they had unusual political control, apart from the state. They hoped that within their own enclave, they could fashion a total society based on their religious ideals. However, when Smith received new revelation calling on the faithful to practice what that age called "plural marriage," hostility skyrocketed, and outsiders vigorously protested the special political arrangements the Mormons enjoyed. Yet for Mormons, the practice of men having more than one wife simply replicated patterns recorded in the Hebrew scriptures, the Christian Old Testament, where patriarchs often had scores of wives. Polygamy, however, struck many Americans as undermining traditional marriage and destroying what a later age called family values.

Other beliefs struck evangelical Protestants of the day as contrary to their understanding of Christianity. The Book of Mormon, for example, gives the American continents a mythic past, unrecorded elsewhere, that includes appearances of Jesus Christ in North America following his presumed resurrection from the dead. Mormons also talked about humans having the ability to become gods, leading to the belief that if humans with their material bodies were not only created by God but could become gods, God must also have a material nature rather than being pure spirit. In recent years, however, Mormons rarely emphasized this particular belief. Mormon marriages, properly sealed in a specific ritual event, were thought to endure throughout eternity. More puzzling to non-Mormons was the often-misunderstood practice of baptizing the dead as a means of bringing them into a relationship with God. But, as we saw in the last chapter, distinctive beliefs have always made new religious movements suspect to non-adherents.

A major turning point came after the 1844 arrest of Smith and his brother, not on charges related to polygamy or the conjoining of political and religious authority in the Mormon settlement at Nauvoo, but on charges of having destroyed a printing press belonging to critics of the Mormons. A mob overran the jail, lynching the two. Prosecution of founders of later new religious movements has also occasionally resulted in imprisonment. Sun Myung Moon, the founder of the Unificationist church mentioned in the last chapter, served time in prison after being convicted of income tax evasion

Figure 14.1 After the Saints arrived in Salt Lake City, they erected a large temple in the center of their settlement that remains basic to Mormon self-identity

Courtesy of Shutterstock

Regrouping under the leadership of Brigham Young (1801–77), most of the Mormons embarked on a journey to what is now Utah but then was still Mexican territory. When the US took over the region following war with Mexico, Young became territorial governor, a move that actually gave the Mormons latitude to organize local society around their religious principles. Utah sought statehood and American officials wanted to assure that federal authority superseded Mormon religious authority in political matters, with polygamy among Mormons often serving as the symbol of the divide that separated federal law and American cultural practice from Mormon ways.

Not until Mormon leaders formally renounced plural marriage following a subsequent revelation in 1890 did the necessary steps get underway for the admission of Utah as a state in 1896. By then Mormon growth had ensured that the religion would endure. It had already moved well past the founding generation, an accomplishment shared with few new religious movements, largely because most Mormons accepted the leadership of Brigham Young and his successors and granted them the same power that Smith himself had exercised. In other words, Mormons built religious structures and chains of authority that allowed for survival. However, American Protestant Christians, especially those of a more evangelical posture, remained suspicious, sometimes still calling the LDS a "cult." In reality, by the end of the nineteenth century, the LDS were no longer a new religious movement, but a new religion altogether, with its own body of belief, sacred texts, traditions, and rites. Mormonism had become, as historian Jan Shipps argues, a "new religious tradition."

Box 14.1 The Latter-day Saints as a new religion

Much of the controversy surrounding Mormonism concerns whether Mormons are Christians. Some critics insist the Mormons are cultists. Others emphasize their increasing similarity to forms of evangelical Protestantism. Historian Jan Shipps offers another understanding:

> A major question ... [is] whether Mormonism is or is not Christian. When the obvious LDS behavioral peculiarity disappeared, the members of the Church of Jesus Christ of Latter-day Saints were seen to resemble so closely their evangelical Protestant neighbors that the idea that Mormonism is merely one more slightly idiosyncratic form of Christianity entered popular perceptions of the Saints. All ... from the story of the discovery of the gold plates and the reopening of the canon through the nineteenth-century experience of the Saints and beyond, suggests that ... those perceptions are wrong. And yet the Saints think of themselves as Christians and think of their church as the only legitimate Church of Jesus Christ.
>
> ... While it perceives of itself as Christian, Mormonism differs from traditional Christianity in much the same fashion that traditional Christianity, in its ultimate emphasis on the individual, came to differ from Judaism
>
> ... it becomes as clear as can be that nomenclature notwithstanding, Mormonism is a new religious tradition.
>
> (From J. Shipps, *Mormonism: The Story of a New Religious Tradition*,
> Urbana: University of Illinois Press, 1985, pp. 148–49)

From the margins toward the mainstream

Although suspicion of the LDS has not vanished from American life, in the decades since World War II, the Mormons have demonstrated extraordinary growth and moved increasingly from the margins toward the mainstream of American religious and cultural life. Estimates suggest that in 1950, just under 927,000 Mormons lived in the US. By 2010, the Mormons claimed around six million American members. Figures are elusive, however, as they may include some who no longer consider themselves practicing Mormons, but who remain on membership rolls. Nonetheless, the growth rate is stunning, particularly when one recalls the gradual erosion of mainline Protestant denominations during these years. The LDS now rank among the five largest religious bodies in the nation. Since the migration to Utah, the mountain west has had the heaviest concentration of Mormons, although in recent years other regions have experienced higher growth rates. Globally, by 2010, Mormons counted around fourteen million adherents.

Why have the Mormons grown over the last half century at a rate that exceeds that of most other religious bodies in the nation? One answer lies in their commitment to aggressive proselytizing or seeking converts. Mormon men, for example, are expected to devote two years of their life at their own expense serving as missionaries proclaiming the Mormon truth either in the US or elsewhere before settling into a career and having a family. In recent years, many young women have voluntarily

Figure 14.2 Mormons owe much of their growth in the US and abroad to a volunteer missionary program in which all young men give two years of service to spreading the Mormon vision. Here two such missionaries speak with a woman outside her home in the Pacific island nation of Tonga

Courtesy of Amy Toensing/Getty Images

joined them. Often going door to door, these missionaries enthusiastically speak to folk about the Mormon gospel, the good news they believe contained in both the Bible and their unique sacred texts. In addition, the Mormons have run countless advertisements on television and in other media promoting their practice and belief as offering a viable answer to questions plaguing religious seekers who were still looking for some final truth.

Another reason is the emphasis the Mormon tradition places on social welfare work. In cooperation with other religious and secular agencies, the LDS are often in the forefront of emergency relief efforts nationally and globally when disaster strikes. For example, in 2011 when a tsunami and earthquake struck Japan, Mormons quickly responded by sending not only food and medical supplies, but also new equipment and materials such as refrigerated trucks to Japanese fishermen who lost everything they needed to pursue their careers. Such endeavors enhance the church's reputation, while opening doors for sharing the faith with those who receive assistance. Even within LDS circles, providing for the material needs of the faithful or potential converts remains a priority, with the result that in Mormon enclaves like Utah, a smaller proportion of those in need seek help from government welfare and assistance programs than elsewhere. Mormons do not necessarily oppose government welfare assistance, but their communal ties and bonds create something akin to an extended family that sees looking after fellow believers as a religious obligation the faithful willingly assume.

The notion of family has other importance in Mormon life. Whether they are the large families that resulted from the earlier practice of plural marriage or the nuclear family that is now the norm except among some small splinter groups, family units have served as the primary means of nurturing others in the faith, a matter that we discussed in Chapter 8. Mormons have consistently exhibited a high birth rate, shunning use of artificial means of birth control as do many other conservatively inclined religious groups. The family orientation results not only in a steady, relatively high rate of internal growth as children born to Mormon families themselves become practitioners of the faith, but it also resonates with calls in the larger culture over the last several decades for a renewed commitment to "traditional family values." This allows Mormons to move towards the mainstream of American life.

In addition, despite the rocky relationship with government and political powers in the years when Mormons represented a new religious movement, Mormons have increasingly proclaimed that the core values of the nation are ones they share and enthusiastically endorse. The Mormon commitment to "rugged individualism" and a capitalist work ethic permitted Mormons to transform the Utah desert into their own Eden; it also buttresses their commitment to popular notions of free enterprise shared by many Americans. Once outsiders, Mormons have become renowned for their staunch patriotism. Indeed, some critics find Mormon nationalism itself to be a compromising of prophetic faith, for it seems to equate American governmental policy too easily with the divine will for humanity. Mormon nationalism has also meant that, as among evangelical Christians generally, a disproportionate number of Mormons – some believe as high as 65 per cent – now identify with the Republican Party. John F. Kennedy's nomination as the Democratic candidate for the presidency in 1960 signaled that American Catholics had moved from the margins to the mainstream; likewise, the 2012 Republican presidential nomination of former Massachusetts governor Mitt Romney, a lifelong devout Mormon, indicated that the LDS had achieved broad cultural acceptance.

Roots of Mormon devotion to the nation may lie in the Book of Mormon itself. Recounting a prehistoric past for the American continents, the Book of Mormon gives to the Americas a mythic past as ancient and as riveting as that long associated, for example, with the Middle East or Asian cultures. The Americas become a place for divine action and revelation from before recorded history to the present. Transforming America into sacred space in time has tied the Mormons to American culture. Mormon theology thus served as a catalyst, for it has allowed the LDS to move from the margins towards the mainstream.

The Mormons and the turmoil of the 1960s

Protestant Christians inclined towards separatist fundamentalism or a very conservative evangelical stance retreated from active engagement in the public sphere following the fundamentalist-modernist controversy of the 1920s; so too Mormons remained on the political sidelines after Utah achieved statehood. The exceptions, of course, were in Utah, parts of Idaho, Arizona, and Nevada, and in a handful of communities elsewhere where Mormons enjoyed both religious and cultural hegemony. Yet political activism and involvement in social controversy have marked Mormon life in recent decades, as they have marked that of Protestant evangelicals generally. What brought about the change?

The social ferment surrounding the civil rights movement proved a defining moment within all American religious life. It left its mark on the LDS as well, with long-term ramifications extending into the twenty-first century. Issues of race, paramount in the civil rights era, also challenged the Mormons. Although in the mid nineteenth century the Mormons counted a small number of African American adherents in their number, Joseph Smith shared many of the cultural and religious assumptions of the day regarding the supposed inferiority of African Americans.

Consequently, as the LDS movement grew, African Americans did not receive all the privileges extended to others. Most significant was the exclusion of African Americans from the Mormon priesthood, a phenomenon somewhat different than the priesthood in many other religions. In theory, the LDS tradition operates without clergy, but all males who are found worthy are eligible to become priests. Women were denied access to the priesthood, as were African American men. Other racial minorities were not excluded, and as Mormonism expanded globally, most male converts from a variety of ethnic backgrounds were welcomed into the priesthood. Recall here the discussion of larger links between religion and race in American religion that we examined in Chapter 12.

By the 1960s, the continuing exclusion of African American men from the priesthood led critics to call the religion racist. By 1963, some leading Mormons endorsed extending full political rights to all African Americans, but still insisted on limiting their roles within the church. Among them was Ezra Taft Benson (1899–1994), secretary of agriculture during the Eisenhower administration (1953–61) and later the president of the church, the position that carries the authority once vested in Joseph Smith. However, as the civil rights movement propelled most American religious groups to abandon overt racist and segregationist policies and practices, it also brought change to the LDS. In 1978 new revelation to church president Spencer W. Kimball (1895–1985) opened the priesthood to all males who were found worthy, regardless of race or ethnicity. The change muted charges of racism.

However, because women remained excluded from the priesthood and from other top positions of religious leadership, some claimed the Mormons were sexist. But since rethinking the role of women in religious groups was pivotal for second-wave feminism, resulting in most Protestant bodies sanctioning their ordination to professional ministry and increasing access to other positions of leadership, Mormons have had to wrestle with women's issues. Their experience reflects the many challenges posed by gender that we explored in Chapter 10.

Debates over ratification of the proposed Equal Rights Amendment (ERA) in the 1970s highlight the Mormon struggle with feminism. The patriarchal ethos of Mormonism meant powerful residual support for traditional gender roles and widespread opposition to ratification of the ERA. For the Mormons, as for many evangelical Protestant Christians and Roman Catholics, as we noted in Chapters 5 and 6, the ERA seemed to undermine marriage and family values, thereby further eroding the moral base of American society.

Box 14.2 The role of women in Mormon life

Historian Kathleen Flake has described the role of women within the LDS tradition as follows:

> The status of women within the LDS Church is ambiguous at best. Although women are not formally ordained, the lay nature of Latter-day Saint organization means that they perform virtually all aspects of traditional Protestant ministry, except especially sacramental acts such as baptizing or blessing the sacrament of the Lord's Supper. Women give sermons, organize and preside over a wide range of critical church gatherings, as well as routinely offer prayers of invocation and benediction; teach doctrinal classes; minister to the sick; prepare the dead for burial; and serve proselytizing missions. Nevertheless, there are a number of aspects of church leadership and sacramental practice in which they explicitly cannot participate. These include serving in the policymaking offices of the church and performing any ordinances outside the temple.
>
> (From K. Flake, "Latter-day Saints," in
> *Encyclopedia of Religion in America*, ed. C.H. Lippy and P.W. Williams,
> Washington: CQ Press, 2010, vol. 3, p. 1219)

Not all Mormon women acquiesced to the position of the church or to the second-class status conferred on women. Among them was Dr. Sonia Johnson (1936–), a fifth-generation Mormon. Johnson not only became an outspoken advocate of the ERA, but in the later 1970s helped organize a group called Mormons for the ERA. Johnson and this group stepped up their criticism of the church, insisting that the religion was actively working to defeat ratification of the ERA and thereby engaging in political activity prohibited to any tax-exempt religious organization. By 1979, church authorities took steps to "excommunicate" or expel Johnson from the church. Although it could not stop her feminist activism, the church thus effectively quashed her claim to speak as a Mormon.

One additional issue linked to second-wave feminism that has challenged American religious groups, including LDS, is abortion. Here, too, the posture of the Mormons links them with conservative evangelical Protestants and Catholics. All basically oppose abortion, with few exceptions. The LDS official position mandates that supporting or performing "elective abortion" that is tied to "personal or social convenience" is sufficient grounds for excommunication.

Defeat of the ERA and affirming an anti-abortion stand have not ended all feminist activities in Mormon circles. Although still denied access to the priesthood, women now routinely speak at Mormon conferences, and their leadership roles in ancillary activities, especially those serving other women and children, have received greater attention. Mormon institutions, such as Brigham Young University in Utah, have academic programs in women's studies, and prominent scholars of the LDS tradition include women. But equality with men within the church remains elusive.

Debates surrounding homosexuality have cascaded through Mormonism as through all American religions since the 1960s. Recall our discussion in Chapter 10. Like most evangelical Protestant bodies as we noted in Chapter 5 and the Roman Catholic Church as discussed in Chapter 6, the LDS officially regards homosexual practice as sinful. In several cases, practicing gay men and lesbians have been ostracized, if not excommunicated. Yet like other groups, Mormons have found that grappling with homosexuality remains an undercurrent of twenty-first-century religious life. As early as the 1960s, some homosexuals who refused to relinquish their Mormon identity or their sexual identity organized a group called Affirmation: Gay Mormons United. Known since 1980 as Affinity, the group offers support for gay, lesbian, bisexual, and transgender Mormons and their families, working to bring change to official church policy.

At the same time, the LDS has actively supported efforts to ban legalizing same-gender marriage. Such activity has not been without criticism, however. In June 2008, for example, church leaders called on Mormons living in California to donate money and in other ways to work for the defeat of Proposition 8, an initiative to legalize gay marriage in the nation's largest state. Because the church itself offered no direct monetary support for such political action, it technically did not breach common understanding of the "separation of church and state." However, the outspokenness of church leaders on the matter and the energy devoted to encouraging individual Mormons to act for the proposition's defeat generated much criticism in the popular media. Although media reports suggested that African Americans and Latino Americans disproportionately voted against the proposition, many later claimed that without the aggressive public opposition of the LDS, the proposition might not have been defeated. In 2010, however, a federal judge struck down the voter-approved ban. As courts prepared to hear both advocates and opponents of the ban, those seeking to thwart same-gender marriage in California in December 2011 launched efforts to require a hearing from a different federal judge.

The political dimension of Mormonism continues to cause apprehension among outsiders. In 2012, two church members – Mitt Romney and John Huntsman – actively sought the Republican nomination for the presidency. Their candidacies prompted much media discussion of lingering suspicion of Mormonism. In this case, the concern centered on whether evangelical Protestant Christians, many of whom also identified as Republicans, would support a Mormon for president of the US, regardless of the candidate's political positions. The ambivalence reflected continuing suspicion of the LDS because of its unique teaching in some areas of belief and the conviction among the most theologically conservative Protestants that Mormonism, despite having moved toward the mainstream, was non-Christian at best and a dangerous cult at worst. Yet having two candidates vying for the nomination indicated that Mormons had become part of the fabric of American life.

Box 14.3 The American ambivalence towards the Mormons

As the Latter-day Saints moved toward the mainstream of American religious and public life, ambivalence still prevailed. One analyst explains why non-Mormon Americans are able to combine respect with suspicion in their attitudes toward the Mormons:

> Mormon history has always revealed a tension between adapting to the surrounding culture and emphasizing distinctiveness. In the last 30 years, Mormons have become more like evangelical Protestants in their political leanings ... and even in their theological formulations. There is far more emphasis on grace and on Christ's atonement ... today than there was two generations ago. However, Protestant and Catholic critics are correct when they say that Mormonism remains theologically distinctive ...
>
> Mormons today are likely to stress their distinctiveness in the area of personal and family values. Even those who criticize Mormon theology often express a grudging admiration for the LDS Church's focus on family, teetotaling, tithing and missionary service. Mormon spiritual practices serve as bridge-builders when doctrine is a point of contention.
>
> (From J. Riess, "Normal Mormons,"
> *Christian Century*, 26 Sept. 2011, 28(20), p. 24)

With the exception of opening the Mormon priesthood to men regardless of race or ethnicity, the LDS has held firm in its long-established positions regarding gender roles, matters such as abortion, and homosexuality. Many of its positions illustrate how the LDS shares much of its formal thinking with other groups, especially conservative evangelical Christians and Roman Catholics. Yet to some extent, the LDS has been able to assert its positions without experiencing the same inner turmoil as has come, for example, to the Catholic Church. In the case of American Catholicism, we noted in Chapter 6 how in the wake of Vatican II, the *magisterium* or teaching authority of the church diminished among the rank and file of the faithful. In other words, individuals often ignored church teaching in their own lives, although they still regarded themselves as Catholics. On the surface, at least, the LDS has not experienced the same level of erosion of authority, even if some still work for change.

Why has the Mormon experience been different? One answer lies in the heavy concentration of the Mormons in a cluster of states including Utah, Idaho, Arizona, Nevada, and California. Roughly half the Mormons in the nation live in those states. In some areas, a Mormon aura infuses the culture, influencing both Mormons and non-Mormons. In other words, there is much implicit support for Mormon ways. Another answer is reflected in the way Mormons labor to keep the faithful within the fold, with local congregations or stakes holding activities for men, for women, for youth, and for children, while setting aside one night for family life. In this way, Mormons intertwine their personal lives with the congregation to a greater extent than holds for most religious bodies. Finally, the belief that the president of the church holds authority directly from God and may receive new revelation at any time grants a transcendent power to church leaders. Here there is similarity with the hierarchical structure of the Roman Catholic Church and the notion that the pope is infallible or incapable of error when speaking officially on matters of faith and morals. Mormons, however, have been able to sustain that transcendent aura more effectively, although as the church expands globally it may become more difficult to do so. Mormon faithful in other regions may link authority to perceived efforts to impose western-style patterns on people for whom they are alien.

The ethos of American religion in the twenty-first century

Many sociologists and other analysts of American religious life hypothesized that as the nation became more urban and more industrial, it would also become more secular. That is, the place of religion would diminish, and religious belief and practice would erode. As we have seen, there have been shifts and changes in American religious culture since World War II. Some groups have lost both members and influence. But others have grown and flourish. New religious movements continually appear, adding to the diversity of options available for many people.

At the same time, personal spirituality has become more and more distinguished from organized or institutional religion. Consequently, the pulse of dynamic religion, although still beating strongly, is increasingly difficult to locate and measure. But not all religious expression has become so individualized as to be invisible.

From the time of the civil rights movement into the second decade of the twentieth century, religious folk have stepped up their engagement in the public square. Issues relating to racism, the role or women, and homosexuality have joined with ethical matters ranging from the environment to abortion to inject a religious element into common life, into the political sector as well as the realm of religion.

In many ways, the experience of the Mormons or Latter-day Saints in their evolution from a highly contentious new religious movement in the nineteenth century to a stable religious tradition distinct from others by the twenty-first illustrates the dynamic force propelling American religious life. More diverse and yet more private, more personal and yet more public, religion remains a central ingredient of American culture.

Key points you need to know

- The Latter-day Saints began as a new religious movement, but have developed into a stable tradition.
- In some ways, the Mormons resemble evangelical Protestants and some others in their positions on social issues, but their beliefs remain distinctive.
- As other groups, the LDS has struggled with issues of race, gender, and sexuality in the years since the civil rights movement.

- Mormons have been able to grow steadily and exert authority more effectively than many other religious bodies.
- The Latter-day Saints provide one lens through which to view developments in American religious life since the end of World War II.

Discussion questions

1 How do the Latter-day Saints illustrate the dynamics at work in new religious movements? What prompted early suspicion of the Mormons? How was the LDS church able to move from a new religious movement to a stable religious tradition?
2 How did the Mormons respond to critics who claimed their religion was racist during the era of the civil rights movement?
3 What is the role of women in the LDS tradition? How is it similar to and different from the role of women in other American religious groups? What impact did second-wave feminism have on the Mormons?
4 How have the Mormons wrestled with contemporary issues of sexuality, particularly the religious and cultural conversations over homosexuality?
5 What prompted Mormons to become more politically engaged over the last several decades? Why do outsiders still harbor suspicion of the Mormon religion?
6 Do you think that the religious prejudice directed against new religious movements, religions outside the mainstream, and other non-traditional religious expressions will ever disappear? Why or why not? What forces might help minimize the negative dimensions of prejudice?
7 Using the LDS as a case study, what do you see as the most important trends and changes in American religious life since the end of World War II?

Further reading

Beecher, M.U. and Anderson, L.F. (eds.) (1987) *Sisters in Spirit: Mormon Women in Historical and Cultural Perspective*. Urbana: University of Illinois Press.

Bringhurst, N.G. and Smith, D.T. (eds.) (2004) *Black and Mormon*, Urbana: University of Illinois Press.

Bushman, R. (2005) *Joseph Smith: Rough Stone Rolling*, New York: Knopf.

Givens, T.L. (2002) *By the Hand of Mormon: The American Scripture That Launched a New World Religion*, New York: Oxford University Press.

Shipps, J. (1985) *Mormonism: The Story of a New Religious Tradition*, Urbana: University of Illinois Press.

Yorgason, E. R. (2003) *Transformation of the Mormon Culture Region*, Urbana: University of Illinois Press.

15 Religion and social change

In this chapter

In this chapter, we focus on the complex relationship between religion and broader social changes. We first focus on how and why religion works as a conservative force in society that favors the status quo. We then turn to the conditions under which religion becomes a force for progressive social change, examining the assets of religion that make it a powerful force for social change of any kind, when and how religious groups start or join social movements, and when social movements mobilize religious resources and rhetoric to motivate participation and engagement. We conclude by discussing religious violence, particularly the link between fundamentalism and religious terrorism, as well as delving more deeply into the phenomenon of modern fundamentalism.

Main topics covered

- Religion has a varied and complex relationship with social change. The form of the relationship depends on whether individuals, groups, or a whole society are involved and also on the historical period when it develops.
- Religion often acts as a conservative force in society, favoring keeping things the old way.
- Religious believers have used their faith as the basis for challenging inequality and advocating for progressive social change.
- Sociologists of religion have developed theories to explain what attributes of religion make it a powerful force for social change.
- Modern religious violence is frequently tied to religious fundamentalism, itself a contested phenomenon with multiple definitions and characteristics.
- When religious violence is used by religious fundamentalists, it takes the form of theater and is meant to place religion at the center of political and private life.
- Religious terrorism is distinct from secular terrorism, and religious fundamentalism does not usually lead to violence, especially in democratic societies.

Religion and social change: a complicated relationship

Religion has varied and complex relationships with social change, and its effects depend on the individual, group, society, and broader historical period under examination. In this chapter we will explore three ways in which religion can be a force for social change and the conditions under which it operates in each of these three ways. First, religion can be inherently conservative in favoring the established status quo because religious beliefs and practices help to maintain the political and economic power structure of society. Second, religion can be an agent of progressive social change because religious beliefs and practices provide the motivation and resources to dismantle oppressive and discriminatory political and economic power structures. Third, religion can be a force for division and violence in modern society by fostering fundamentalism and intolerance.

Religion continues to have a large public role in the modern world, even if religious authority is, in general, declining. In other words, we assume that religion is not just a private entity that operates within its own sphere or simply provides meaning to individuals' lives. It does these things, but it also plays a role in supporting or resisting broader social change and popular social movements, which is the focus of this chapter. In previous chapters, we focused on other aspects of the public roles of religion, including the relationship between religion and political behavior (Chapter 9) and the ways in which religion is transmitted (Chapter 8). We also described how religion shapes gender norms and roles (Chapter 10) and racial stereotypes (Chapter 12). In Chapter 19, we explore how religion shapes attitudes regarding national identity and belonging.

Religion as a conservative force

Historically, sociologists of religion and other religious scholars have considered religion to be an inherently conservative force in society, where conservative means aiming to keep society from changing, and thus to "conserve" society. In other words, religious belief and practice help to support and maintain the political, economic, and cultural structures of society. However, the strength of this relationship is weaker in contemporary American life than it has been previously.

In classical theory and research, this conservatism usually takes the form of justifying the actions of the religious, political, and economic elite. Think back, for example, to Marx's statement that "religion is an opiate" because it blinds people to the broader inequalities in society. It is easy to see why this has historically been the case because, like any other institution, religious institutions are dependent upon the favor of those in power. In particular, state-sponsored or mandated religions are unlikely to speak out against the status quo because they usually depend on their tax exempt status, a form of government support, in order to survive financially. Illustrating these doctrines are divine right theologies developed by various cultures that argue the leader of the culture or the civil government has been ordained by God(s) or is a representative of God(s) on earth as a way to justify power. In the contemporary US, many religious institutions work within the political process to achieve their aims rather than believing in the divine right of our elected leaders, as described in Chapter 9.

More recently, analysts claim that religion supports the status quo through its lack of opposition to inequalities in society. For example, many Protestant thinkers teach that inequalities in wealth and poverty and other types of power differential are part of the natural order and will always be part of society. There are also teachings, codified in the public mind by books like *The Secret* by Rhonda Byrne and the emphasis on the Prosperity Gospel in some evangelical denominations described in Chapter 5, that moral, ethical, or proper behavior results in greater life success, including material success. An implication or indirectly stated part of these theologies is that not being successful in life, particularly being poor, is a direct result of immoral behavior. The idea of the relationship between religion, power, and inequality was formalized by Max Weber in his concept of theodicy, or systems of belief that help to explain human suffering, inequality, or other negative aspects of human life and society. Theodicies, when powerful, make it unlikely that religious leaders or believers will actively work to overcome inequality in their society because these inequalities are explained in religious terms.

Box 15.1 Theodicies of suffering and dominance

According to Max Weber, a theodicy is a system of belief that helps to explain human suffering, inequalities, sickness, and other negative aspects of human life and society. Theodicies help to explain the gap between what we believe should happen and what actually does happen, more commonly referred to as the questions of "why bad things happen to good people." There are multiple types of theodicies, but two dominate:

- Suffering theodicies are the religious beliefs that help the lower segments of society come to terms with their position and what they can do to gain redemption.
- Dominance theodicies are the religious beliefs that help the upper segments of society come to terms with their position and any ethical obligations because of it.

Religion as a force for progressive social change

Although religion is usually considered to be a conservative force in society, there are numerous examples where religious believers, leaders, and institutions have used their faith as the basis for challenging existing power structures and inequalities and starting or joining large-scale progressive social movements. Examples of movements in the US that have received support from religions, particularly Protestants of various stripes, include the anti-slavery movement, the temperance movement, and the labor movement in the nineteenth and early twentieth centuries. The role of religious institutions in the civil rights movement, anti-colonialism movements, antiwar movements, the feminist movement, the pro-life movement, and the movement for or opposition to equal rights for alternative sexualities is the subject of much discussion in Part II and Part III of this book. Religious institutions have also been invested in ongoing local movements to combat poverty or hunger, as discussed in Chapter 12, and environmental action. Not all popular movements use religious justification, and some religious groups have opposed or tried to suppress such social movements. For example, Chapter 11 discussed the ways in which religion was used both to justify and to oppose slavery by different stakeholders.

Research on social movements has largely ignored religion for two primary reasons. First, many social movements researchers assume that society is becoming more secular over time and therefore do not consider religion an important area of study. Second, others believe that religion does not influence participation in social movements because they assume that religion largely exists to provide individuals with meaning and create social solidarity. However, sociologists of religion have explored a number of issues related to religion and social movements. These include what attributes or characteristics religion has that make it a powerful force for social change, when religious groups will start or join social movements, and when social movements will mobilize religious resources and rhetoric to motivate participation and engagement.

Christian Smith, in his book *Disruptive Religion*, systematically categorizes all the possible assets (attributes and characteristics) that religion has to mobilize, promote, and assist social movements. Smith places religious assets for social movements in six main categories: transcendent motivation, organizational resources, shared identity, social and geographic positioning, privileged legitimacy, and institutional self-interest. *Transcendent motivation* allows social movements to be rooted in the sacred and define the main goal of the movement as preserving moral imperatives such as love, justice, freedom, and equity. Religion, then, supplies the social movement with icons, rituals, songs, and testimonies of faith in order to motivate members towards social

Figure 15.1 Religion is often used in social movements to provide motivation and common language for protest

action. For example, the hymn "We Shall Overcome" is indelibly linked with the civil rights movement due to its frequent use by protesters. It demands that members are self-disciplined, altruistic, and ready to sacrifice themselves for a greater good, all for the sake of their faith. The extended and long-term focus of many evangelical groups and individuals on abortion illustrates the dedication that religion can encourage in members. This dedication, however, can also lead to extremist acts, which we discuss later in this chapter.

Box 15.2 Religious assets for social movements

Christian Smith, in his book *Disruptive Religion*, systematically categorizes all the possible assets that religion has that are significant for social movement activism. Smith places religious assets for social movements in six main categories:

- Transcendent motivation
    - legitimation for protest rooted in the sacred
    - moral imperatives
    - motivating icons, rituals, or other forms
    - altruistic ideologies and practices.

- Organizational assets
    - trained and experienced leadership
    - financial resources
    - communication channels
    - authority structures.

- Shared identity
    - common purpose among strangers
    - large-scale identifying structures.

- Social and geographic positioning
    - geographic and regional dispersion
    - social diffusion across social boundaries.

- Privileged legitimacy
    - respect for religious leaders
    - freedom of religion.

- Institutional self-interest.

Religious institutions have substantive *organizational resources* because religions have trained and capable leaders readily available as well as financial support from member donations and pre-existing networks of communication for recruits. Believers in the same religion have a *shared identity*, which provides a basis for strangers to unite towards a common purpose and can serve as a foundation for several groups or congregations of people to come together to advocate for a common purpose or goal. Religious institutions, because they are often spread across a region or the whole country, have optimal *social and geographic positioning* in that movements can unite over large distances rather than only in one location. Religion also has the unique ability to cut across social class, occupational, racial, ethnic, and national lines. Additionally, religious officials are often taken more seriously than politicians, social radicals, or others, and religion has more autonomy in the US than many other institutions due to our religious freedoms (the basis for which is described in Chapter 9) giving religion *privileged legitimacy*. The civil rights movement is the quintessential example of each of these assets. As described in Chapter 11, Black Protestant churches served as an organizational and logistical base for the movement, especially in its early days, and these meetings could not legally be interfered with by the civil authorities. The leaders of the movement used religious motivation to appeal to mainline Protestants and Catholics in many parts of the country, in addition to African Americans.

Finally, religion can aid social movements in order to preserve *institutional self-interest* when the state encroaches in areas that religion used to control. For a very recent example, see the controversy among Catholic leaders over the Obama administration's decision in 2012 to require the health care plans of religious organizations to cover contraception for female employees.

While religious groups have tremendous assets and ability to give to social movements, the conditions have to be right before they will start or join social movements. For example, Protestants only began to back the antislavery and temperance movements in large numbers when many preachers began to call on Protestants to engage in personal transformation and public confessions to absolve the special sins of the nation. Additionally, religious groups generally only start or join social movements when a feature or change in society is perceived to be a threat to deeply held religious beliefs or when participation in a social movement is portrayed by the leaders of the social movement as a struggle between good and evil. For example, social movements related to gender, sexuality, poverty, hunger, slavery, war, or the pro-life movement generate a great deal of religious interest because these issues have been a central focus of much religious teaching. On the other hand, environmental activism, anti-globalization, and the labor movement have far less religious support because there are fewer core religious teachings on them. This is slowly changing, however, with the 2011 release of a documentary and lecture in the evangelical Protestant media called *Resisting the Green Dragon*. The backers of this media enterprise developed it in direct opposition to the environmental movement. They believe that the environmental movement is turning into a religion among some young people and, therefore, is a threat to the power of religion.

Religious leaders profoundly affect the likelihood of denominations or particular congregations to start or join social movements. For example, when the governing structure of the denomination or congregation is very hierarchical, as in the Catholic church, members will be far more likely to join social movements if those at the top of the hierarchy advocate participation. Members of more democratically structured congregations or denominations are less likely to listen to those at the top of the hierarchy, but are more likely to join if their clergy advocates for it or if the member personally feels it is important. The age, race, and gender of the religious leader also matter. For example, research reviewed in Chapter 10 shows that female leaders are more likely to take positions that advocate for social movement protest. In addition, younger leaders, leaders who are a racial minority, and those from or in an urban setting are more likely to lead the congregation to participate in social movements.

Secular social movements often try to mobilize religious resources and rhetoric by building coalitions with congregations or religious individuals. It is no surprise that leaders of secular social movements would attempt to do this, given the powerful assets of religion described by Smith, but this mobilization only works under a certain set of circumstances. First, when the majority of those in the movement share a religion, or have closely related religions, the movement will try to draw on religious resources and rhetoric. This is especially likely to be true when the movement is targeted at a dominant structure with a different religion. Second, secular social movements are likely to draw on religion when religious beliefs or leaders are at odds with the status quo or otherwise sympathetic to the movement. These two points are illustrated by the pro-life movement, which unites evangelicals and fundamentalists against what they perceive to be secular political and social forces favoring abortion. Third, secular social movements may attempt to mobilize social movements when alternative organizational structures and political access is not available. For example, Mary Patillo-McCoy and other researchers have found that the African American church continues to be heavily involved in social justice movements and features a more encompassing ministry than white denominations because African Americans are still unable to fully participate in the economic, social, and political life of the country.

Attempts to mobilize religious support into broader social movements can be very powerful in initiating social change. However, there is a limit to this role. Differences in religious beliefs can be an obstacle to mobilizing groups for change, as can differences in race/ethnicity, sexuality, or gender. For example, rather than uniting around views of same-sex relationships, mainline Protestant congregations and individual congregations carve out "niches" for themselves in regards to sexuality, with some being more welcoming and others less so. These congregational niches let members be with those who share the same assumptions about these moral debates. Additionally, official Catholic Church policy endorses very traditional roles; however, it has also (inadvertently) provided spaces, such as social justice organizations, academic institutions, liturgy groups, and parishes with no priest, that have allowed the feminist movement to flourish. Disagreements about appropriate strategies and tactics for action between secular and religious leaders are common and can lead to rifts in social movements. See, for example, the split between the Christian leaders of the civil rights movement, who favored non-violent action, and the secular and Nation of Islam leaders of the Black Nationalist movement, who favored more radical action.

Religion as a force for fostering fundamentalism and violence

Violence motivated by religion is an old and pervasive issue. For example, in 2011, more than fifty people died each day around the world in attacks motivated in part by religion. Religious violence occurs across religious groups, within religious groups, and as acts of religious terrorism. Because religion functions, in part, to define boundaries around social groups, as detailed in Chapter 1, some level of religious violence is likely to be inevitable, especially for groups that define themselves explicitly in opposition to the outside world. There are numerous historical and contemporary examples of religious violence, such as the Crusades, the Thirty Years' War, and the conflict in Northern Ireland. The focus of this chapter is on modern religious violence, usually terrorism, which has been a focus of American religious, social, and political life since the terrorist attacks on New York and Washington DC on September 11, 2001. Terrorism is often tied to religious fundamentalism. In this context, religious fundamentalism refers to the transnational, transcultural version of evangelical fundamentalism described in Chapter 2 and Chapter 5.

Box 15.3 Examples of fundamentalist groups

Beginning in the 1970s, fundamentalist groups emerged in many of the world's major religions. Below are examples of some fundamentalist groups. The Christian fundamentalist groups active in the US are described in Chapters 2 and 10.

- Christian fundamentalist groups:
  - the Moral Majority
  - the Christian Coalition
  - fundamentalist LDS movements.

- Islamic fundamentalist groups:
  - Islamic theocracy in Iran
  - Hamas and Hezbollah
  - the Muslim Brotherhood.

- Buddhist fundamentalist groups:
  - Nichiren Buddhism
  - the New Kadampa Tradition and the Dorje Shugden.

- Hindu fundamentalist groups:
  - Hindutva and Hindu Nationalism.

- Jewish fundamentalist groups
  - Haredi (ultra-Orthodox Judaism).

In the 1970s and 1980s, fundamentalist movements emerged, or re-emerged, in most of the world's major religions nearly simultaneously. Examples include the Christian Coalition in the US, Hamas and Hezbollah in Palestine, and Hindutva in India. Michael Emerson and David Hartman, in their review of the sociological literature on fundamentalism, state that sociologists were unprepared for this emergence. This means that religious fundamentalism is a recent area of focus in the sociology of religion. As a result, there is much we still do not know about the reasons for the global emergence of fundamentalism when it did or how best to measure it.

Box 15.4 What is fundamentalism?

Scholars have wrestled with trying to define fundamentalism precisely. Here are some of their attempts:

- Martin Riesebrodt (1990): "an urban movement directed primarily against dissolution of personalistic, patriarchal notions of order and social relations and their replacement by depersonalized principles."
- Gabriel A. Almond (2003): "a discernible pattern of religious militancy by which self-styled 'true believers' attempt to arrest the erosion of religious identity, fortify the borders of the religious community, and create viable alternatives to secular institutions and behaviors."

Even defining fundamentalism is a contentious issue, but there is consensus that fundamentalism is a contextual phenomenon and cannot be defined without understanding the social reality that surrounds it. In particular, fundamentalism cannot be understood apart from modernity nor exist outside of modernity, a notion described in Chapter 2. Most simply, fundamentalism can be defined as the rejection of some aspects of modernity on religious grounds. Fundamentalists, then, define themselves in opposition to modern society and attempt to stop what they believe is the destruction of values, social ties, and meaning caused by modernity. On the other hand, from a modernist viewpoint, fundamentalists are religious reactionaries attempting to restore oppression, patriarchy, and intolerance.

A number of researchers have tried to define the characteristics of fundamentalist groups and movements. Martin Riesebrodt compares the fundamentalist movements in the US, as described in Chapter 5, and the rise of the Shi'ite fundamentalist movement in Iran, culminating in the rise of a theocracy. He finds similarities in terms of the ideological characteristics of the two movements. Both movements reacted to what they perceived to be the *marginalization of religion* in their society. Using these similarities, Riesebrodt characterized fundamentalism as having an organic social ethic based on *statutory ethical monism*. This means that the only source of morality in fundamentalism movements is the one revealed by God and contained in the holy texts of divine law; other notions of morality are rejected. Fundamentalists believe that their ethical and moral rules are universal in that they apply to all people in all times and cultures and regulate all situations and spheres of life. Thus, fundamentalism is religious republicanism, which is the attempt to realize divine law, the adherence to one's own religious roots, and the rejection of non-religious influence in all spheres of life. Religious republicanism, then, had a *selective and dualistic worldview* in that it divides the world into two opposing viewpoints: God and Satan. Riesebrodt also identifies *millennialism and messianism* as characteristics of fundamentalist movements. In other words, fundamentalists believe that they herald the coming end of the world in which there will be a victory over evil and true believers will be ushered into the spiritual realm by a savior or messiah.

Riesebrodt also identified other similarities in the two movements. For example, both featured *patriarchal moralism* such that female bodies were seen as seducers of men and women's appropriate role within society is as mothers and housekeepers.

Fundamentalist groups in both countries also rejected organized welfare, instead focusing on the moral and voluntary obligation of the rich to give to the poor.

Box 15.5 Characteristics of fundamentalist groups

Riesebrodt and Almond, Appleby, and Sivan compare fundamentalist groups across countries. They identify several ideological and organizational characteristics that fundamentalist groups have in common.

- Ideological characteristics:
  - reaction to the marginalization of religion
  - statutory ethical monism
  - selective and dualistic worldview
  - millennialism and messianism
  - patriarchal moralism.

- Organizational characteristics:
  - select, chosen membership
  - sharp ideological or physical boundaries
  - authoritarian organizational structure
  - behavioral requirements.

Almond, Appleby, and Sivan compare eighteen fundamentalist movements throughout the world. They find similar ideological characteristics among them, as did Riesebrodt, but also outline some common structural or organizational characteristics of these movements. They find that fundamentalist movements have a *select, chosen membership* in which members believe that they are divinely called to the group. They also find that fundamentalist groups draw *sharp ideological or physical boundaries* to separate themselves from sinful society and achieve high levels of group solidarity and cohesion. Third, fundamentalist movements usually have an *authoritarian organizational structure* led by a charismatic leader or leadership. Finally, fundamentalist groups usually have elaborate *behavioral requirements* in order to create a powerful, conforming dimension among followers. Such behavior includes distinctive music, rules for dress, and censorship of reading materials. Given this set of characteristics, Christianity, Judaism, and Islam are more likely than other religions to have strong fundamentalist movements, although they do exist across religions.

In the US, fundamentalism seemed to disappear from the religious scene in the 1920s, as described in Chapter 5. However, the historian Joel Carpenter presents a convincing case that fundamentalists didn't disappear completely, but instead retreated from the public arena. They formed a vast network of agencies that linked them together, including publishing houses like Scripture Press and independent Bible schools and colleges such as the Practical Bible Training School and Bob Jones University. Within these networks, US fundamentalists eschewed politics and most of the trappings of society as polluted by sin and otherwise tainted. They were content to remain apart so long as American culture maintained a veneer of Christian religiosity: to give some examples, the addition of "under God" to the Pledge of

Allegiance, placing "In God We Trust" on all coins and currency (described in Chapter 4), the fact that children in public schools across the nation engaged in prayer before the start of the school day, and public school assemblies often began with reading a passage from the Bible. However, the 1960s and ensuing decades brought about challenges to this Christian veneer, with the Supreme Court decisions forbidding devotional prayer, Bible reading in public schools, and *Roe v. Wade* (described in Chapter 5 and 9), increasing religious pluralism (the focus of Chapters 18 and 19), and decreasing religious affiliation (the focus of Chapter 16). These changes spurred fundamentalists to action, with major fundamentalist leaders, such a Jerry Falwell and Pat Robertson establishing powerful organizations meant to influence public life.

Fundamentalist movements are of interest to sociologists of religion because, in part, they are thought to lead to religious violence and religious terrorism. Mark Juergensmeyer's volume on religious terrorism is the seminal sociological volume on the topic. He first demonstrates that most fundamentalist groups are not violent, although some are, and that not all religiously based violence is carried out by fundamentalists, although religious terrorism is. He then argues that fundamentalism can turn to violence because it provides the ideology, motivation, and organizational structure for individuals to commit violent acts.

Religious violence takes a particular form when committed by fundamentalists. Religious terrorism is used as a theatrical form of violence; in other words, it is as a symbolic act. It uses images of a cosmic war between good and evil or martyrdom and is performed to dramatize a cause. Religious violence is meant to place religion at the center of political and private life and oppose the secularization of society. By looking at terrorism through the lens of the theater, Juergensmeyer examines the stage where terrorist attacks occur, the symbolic meaning behind the target of the violence, the time or date when the "performance" is done, and how the audience perceives the event. For example, the terrorist attacks on September 11, 2001 targeted the World Trade Center, a symbol of American economic power, the Pentagon, a symbol of American military power, and (unsuccessfully) either the US Capitol building or the White House, the seat of American political power. The attackers chose that day because the weather would be clear, ensuring a maximum number of people would see the attacks. The stated motivation of the attackers was to end the US presence in Saudi Arabia, end the American support of Israel, and to end US sanctions against Iraq. Osama Bin Laden declared a holy war and the killing of American civilians until such aims were met. A key element of this type of violence is that it is unlikely to end due to compromise on the part of fundamentalists because it is based on absolutist moral values and seen as morally justified. The long nature of the "war on terror" illustrates the duration of these conflicts.

Because religious terrorism is a form of theater, there are differences between religious terrorism and secular terrorism. Religious terrorism draws from religion in ways that provide divine motives or duties, is more likely to target civilian populations, and uses violence as an end in and of itself, with limited or incoherent political goals. Again, the September 11 attacks are an excellent example of these characteristics. Secular terrorism, on the other hand, tends to draw from feelings of oppression or exclusion as a justification for action, to target government or military targets, and to have coherent or explicitly political, social, or economic goals. For example, the Oklahoma City bombing was an attack on a federal office building in Oklahoma City, OK, by Timothy McVeigh in 1995. The attacks were motivated by a desire to retaliate

Los Angeles Times

On The Internet: WWW.LATIMES.COM   WEDNESDAY, SEPTEMBER 12, 2001   Copyright 2001/CCV/108 Pages   50¢ Designated Areas

TERRORISTS ATTACK NEW YORK, PENTAGON

Thousands Dead, Injured as Hijacked U.S. Airliner Ram Targets; World Trade Towers Brought Down

Tragedy: Assault leav
Manhattan in chaos.
Three of the flights w
en route to L.A., one
San Francisco. Presid
Bush puts military or
highest alert, closes
borders and vows to
'find those responsib

By MATEA GOLD
and MAGGIE FARLEY
TIMES STAFF WRITERS

NEW YORK—In the wor
rorist attack ever again:
United States, hijackers str
the preeminent symbols of t
tion's wealth and might Tu
flying airliners into the 1
Trade Center and the Pen
and killing or injuring thousa
people.

As a horrified nation watcl
television, the twin towers
World Trade Center in lowe
hattan collapsed into flamin
ble after two Boeing 767s ra
their upper stories. A third ai
a Boeing 757, flattened one
Pentagon's five sides.

A fourth jetliner crashed ir
ern Pennsylvania. Authoritie
the hijackers might have be
ing to aim the plane at the
dential retreat at Camp Davi
the Capitol or other targ
Washington.

The assaults, which stirre
and anxiety across the count
evoked comparisons to Pear
bor, were carefully planned a
ordinated, occurring within 5
utes. No one claimed respons
but official suspicion quickly
Saudi fugitive Osama bin I
Unexplained was how the ter
boarded the jets and overpo
the crews.

Federal law enforcement s
said the FBI conducted se
and served subpoenas, ro

AP photo : CARMEN TAYLOR via KHBS-KHOG-TV
United Flight 175, above, heads for the south
tower of the World Trade Center in Manhattan,
then explodes on impact while the north tower
burns from an assault about 20 minutes earlier.

NEWS ANALYSIS
Real Test   **In New York, a Day of Fire and Fear**

Figure 15.2 Religious terrorism can be understood as a theoretical form of violence. The 9/11 terrorist attacks occurred during clear weather, so they could be easily seen, and against targets that represented America's economic, military, and political power

against the Federal Bureau of Investigation, the Bureau of Alcohol, Tobacco, Firearms, and Explosives, and the Drug Enforcement Agency. The building was specifically selected to maximize causalities among these agencies and minimize causalities among nongovernmental employees.

Sociologists of religion have also explored why fundamentalism leads to violence in some cases but not in others. This research finds that violent religious groups are more likely to arise in places where the state tries to regulate or suppress religious freedom. For example, Islamic terrorist groups are largely active in countries in the Middle East and Southeast Asia, which are often heavily security oriented with little religious or civic freedom. On the other hand, violent religious groups occur far more rarely in democratic societies because fundamentalist groups work through political avenues. Religious terrorism is particularly rare in the US because many fundamentalist groups work through the political system, instead of trying to overthrow that system.

By way of review, we discussed three potential relationships between religion and social change. We first discussed the default position of many sociologists of religion, namely that religion works as a conservative force in society that supports societal elites or otherwise favors the status quo. Next, we discussed historical examples of and conditions under which religion becomes a force for resisting or even overthrowing the status quo. Finally, we discussed religious violence and the link between fundamentalism and religious terrorism. It is worth noting that all of the topics in this chapter indirectly involve the government. As discussed in Chapter 9, the most common way in which religious groups try to instigate social change in democratic societies is through the electoral and policy process.

Key points you need to know

- Religion can either stop social change, act as a force for progressive social change, or be a source of fundamentalism and violence.
- Religion can act as a conservative force in society that helps to support and maintain the political, economic, and cultural structure of society.
- Religious believers, leaders, and institutions have also used their faith as the basis for starting or joining large-scale progressive social movements.
- Religious institutions have numerous attributes and assets that are significant for social movement activism, particularly transcendent motivation.
- Religious groups will start or join social movements when religious leaders and believers are personally invested in the social change.
- Secular social movements will mobilize religious resources and rhetoric by building coalitions with congregations or religious individuals in communities.
- Modern religious terrorism is tied to religious fundamentalism.
- Fundamentalism can be defined as the rejection of some aspects of modernity on religious grounds.
- Religious violence takes the form of theater in which violence is committed as a symbolic act. This makes religious terrorism distinct from secular terrorism.

Discussion questions

1 How do religious groups support the status quo and act as a conservative force on social change?
2 What do religious institutions and believers have to contribute to social movements?
3 Why do religious institutions, leaders, and believers support some social movements and not others?
4 What are some limits on religious participation in secular social movements?
5 What is religious fundamentalism? Why is defining it difficult?

6 What are the key ideological characteristics of religious fundamentalism?
7 In what ways is religious terrorism an act of theater?
8 How is religious terrorism different from secular terrorism?
9 Why do some fundamentalist groups turn to violence and others do not?

Further reading

Almond, G.A., Appleby R.S., and Sivan E. (2003) *Strong Religion: The Rise of Fundamentalisms around the World*, Chicago: University of Chicago Press.

Casanova, J. (1994) *Public Religions in the Modern World*, Chicago: University of Chicago Press.

Emerson, M.O. and Hartman, D. (2006) "The Rise of Religious Fundamentalism," *Annual Review of Sociology*, 32: 127–44.

Hoffman, B. (2001) "'Holy Terror': The Implications of Terrorism Motivated by a Religious Imperative," *Studies in Conflict and Terrorism*, 18: 271–84.

Juergensmeyer, M. (2000) *Terror in the Mind of God: The Global Rise of Religious Violence*, Los Angeles: University of California Press.

Katzenstein, M.F. (1998) *Faithful and Fearless: Moving Feminist Protest inside the Church and Military*, Princeton, NJ: Princeton University Press.

Moon, D. (2004) *God, Sex and Politics*, Chicago: University of Chicago Press.

Pattillo-McCoy, M. (1998) "Church Culture as a Strategy of Action," *American Sociological Review*, 63: 767–84.

Peterson, R.A. and Demerath, N.J., III (1942) "Introduction," in L. Pope, *Millhands and Preachers*, New Haven: Yale University Press, xvii–1.

Riesebrodt, M. (1993) *Pious Passion: The Emergence of Modern Fundamentalism in the United States and Iran*, Berkeley: University of California Press.

Robinson, L.W. (1987) "When Will Revolutionary Movements Use Religion?", in T. Robbins and R. Robertson (eds.), *Church-State Relations: Tensions and Transitions*, New Brunswick, NJ: Transaction Books, 53–63.

Smith, C. (ed.) (1996) *Disruptive Religion: The Force of Faith in Social Movement Activism*, New York: Routledge.

Wellman, J.K. and Tokuno, K. (2004) "Is Religious Violence Inevitable?" *Journal for the Scientific Study of Religion*, 43: 291–96.

Wilde, M. (2004) "How Culture Mattered at Vatican II: Collegiality Trumps Authority in the Council's Social Movement Organizations," *American Sociological Review*, 69: 576–602.

Young, M.P. (2002) "Confessional Protest: The Religious Birth of U.S. National Social Movements," *American Sociological Review*, 67: 660–88.

Zald, M.N. and McCarthy, J.D. (1987) "Religious Groups as Crucibles of Social Movements," in M.N. Zald and J.D. McCarthy (eds.), *Social Movements in an Organizational Society*, New Brunswick, NJ: Transaction Books, 67–96.

Part IV

Where American religion is heading

16 Spirituality's challenge to religion

In this chapter

This chapter examines claims that more Americans than ever before are not affiliated with any organized religion. It then considers the idea that in complex, urban, industrial societies the heart of religion becomes increasingly invisible and privatized, not linked directly to religious institutions. Next the focus turns to those Americans who claim to be "spiritual, but not religious" and what this phenomenon means for American religious life. Discussion of "hybrid" religiosity or spirituality follows, before "New Age" religious expressions, Wicca, and the metaphysical religious tradition receive attention. The final section appraises the import of these phenomena for American religious life.

Main topics covered

- Why a larger proportion of Americans are not formally affiliating with organized religion.
- Where this trend appears most prevalent.
- How such persons find their spiritual needs fulfilled in venues from the Internet to self-help groups.
- Theories that religion becomes increasingly invisible as a society becomes more complex.
- What it means when people claim to be "spiritual, but not religious."
- The nature of highly personalized spirituality.
- The renewed interest in "New Age" spirituality.
- The fresh appreciation of Wicca in contemporary spirituality.
- The renewed vitality of the "metaphysical tradition."
- The way spirituality augments the pluralistic style within American religion.

Religiously unaffiliated Americans

The American religious landscape includes those who do not formally affiliate with religious groups or who do not identify themselves as religious. In recent years, analysts have suggested that the proportion of religiously unaffiliated Americans has steadily risen. Precise figures to support this claim are difficult to obtain and assess. Some surveys indicate that roughly 40 per cent of Americans do not hold membership in any religious group, a figure that has been relatively constant for decades. This figure is based primarily on membership data reported by organized religions, not individual self-identification. Nor does it necessarily reflect the movement from one group to another ("denominational switching") that has increased markedly since World War II. The figures, then, are tentative at best. Adding to the dilemma of pinning down accurate numbers are differences in defining membership. Not all groups count members the same way; some new religious movements, as we have seen, may not count them at all.

However, a much higher proportion of Americans give themselves a religious label when asked than the proportion religious groups claim as members. For example, the 2007 Religious Landscape Survey conducted by the Pew Forum on Religion and Public Life indicated that only 16 to 17 per cent had no particular religious identity or did not indicate one. So self-identification yields a different picture than formal membership data.

The Pew study also demonstrated that the majority of those who claimed no religious affiliation – including those self-identified as atheists or agnostics – had during their childhood been part of organized religion, having shed their affiliation later, most likely because of some personal disagreement with the doctrines or ethical positions taken by the group. Pew researchers found two ramifications of these figures especially important. First, they expressed surprise that the figure was so low. Surveys in other industrialized nations – especially nations in Europe – show that the inroads of secularization result in a far higher percentage claiming no religious identification; since the US is among the most industrialized nations, many expected that secularization would have also dramatically diminished the size of the religiously affiliated population in America. Second, more than one-third of those who self-identified as unaffiliated still regarded themselves as religious. The Pew study found that only about one-quarter claimed to be either atheists or agnostics, while the rest saw themselves simply as secular. In other words, the largest cluster of those who had no formal religious ties retained a personal faith replete with religious beliefs and often with religious practices.

Common threads link those who are not formally part of any religious institution. One is age. Those in late adolescence and early young adulthood are more likely to eschew affiliation or identification. Historically, most of those returned to some sort of religious group once they had married and had families – until the generation that came of age during the 1960s, the so-called baby boomers. That generation broke the pattern. A much larger proportion remained unaffiliated and therefore less inclined to provide their children with any religious nurture or instruction.

Another recurring feature was region. In the proverbial "Bible Belt" of the southern US, formal affiliation and participation remain higher than elsewhere, although even here the number of those not engaged with a religious group is on the rise. The Pacific northwest historically has evidenced the lowest rate of membership or other formal affiliation. Analysts sometimes refer to this area as the "none zone" because of the higher proportion of respondents there who would check "none" on surveys asking for religious identification. The Pew Forum study in 2007, however, revealed that one other region is approaching the levels of the Pacific northwest for low rates of affiliation. That region is New England, centuries ago the bastion of Puritan Protestantism.

The tentativeness of these figures makes what they tell us about religious life in contemporary America elusive. Understanding their import is complicated by suggestions that many Americans, when asked about religious affiliation, will offer one or select one from a list, whether or not they actually have any connection to the group. Because American society remains more religious, at least on the surface, than the societies of other industrialized nations, claiming a religious identity is as much a sign of social respectability as an indicator of a deep commitment. Recall the sociologist Will Herberg's argument noted in earlier chapters and to which we shall return in Chapter 19. More than half a century ago, Herberg insisted that most Americans found any form of Protestantism, Catholicism, or Judaism equivalent to any other in offering moral guidance to make people good citizens. In the twenty-first century, Herberg's hypothesis suggests that Americans claim a religious identity because they think that it goes with being moral and upright citizens. Hence many believe that the actual proportion of those who have no religious affiliation or identity is much higher than survey figures using self-identification indicate. After all, if one uses membership data supplied by religious groups, close to half the population may not actually hold formal affiliation with any religious group.

In addition, sociologist Robert Bellah and his associates noted in the 1980s that the generation then coming of age – the later baby boomers and the first of those who followed them – was reluctant to enter into formal commitments of any kind. Hence the proportion of those not officially identified with a religious group rises as one looks at younger segments of the population. These folks are also more likely than others to turn to new religious movements that do not keep official membership rosters but rely on chat rooms and other communications media offered through the Internet to build loose associations among those attracted to the group. What cannot be determined precisely, however, is whether these same persons may follow multiple religious groups online, without seeing any single one as the religion to which they are committed. Others may simply go to Internet web sites in search of inspiration or spiritual guidance. We examined many of these issues from a more self-consciously sociological perspective in the last chapter.

Religion becomes invisible

Much of this discussion relies on a theory advanced by the sociologist Thomas Luckmann in his 1967 book *The Invisible Religion*. Luckmann argued that modern societies were becoming more urbanized and industrialized, more reliant on science and technology, and more dependent on expanding networks of secondary and tertiary relationships. As societies thus become more complex, religion becomes more difficult to pinpoint, or invisible. In other words, religious institutions (churches, synagogues, temples, mosques, etc.) and religious professionals (ministers, priests, rabbis, imams, gurus, and so on) represent just one aspect of the religious world of ordinary people. The teachings of organized religions in turn inform only part of the personal belief system on which people draw to try to make sense out of life. Rather, people look to a broad range of options – some of which at first might not seem really religious at all – in constructing an individualized world of meaning. They may have connections to with one or more religious groups, but do not rely solely on them for their customized beliefs and practices.

Self-help groups offer one illustration of how religion becomes invisible. Since the 1960s, Americans have sustained a fascination with self-help programs. Bookstores began to stock large selections of self-help materials, often placing them next to more overtly religious titles. Some self-help approaches had religious roots. Several had ties to the "positive thinking" advocated by the mainline Protestant pastor Norman Vincent Peale in the 1950s. Robert Schuller (1926–), beginning with his *Way to the Good Life* (1963) which promoted "possibility thinking," echoes Peale's approach. Self-help principles undergirded the rapidly expanding "anonymous" groups patterned after Alcoholics Anonymous (AA), which was founded in 1935 but has experienced considerable growth from the 1950s onward.

Although these groups do not purport to be religious congregations, they provide participants with support networks of family and friends. AA members, for example, may or may not be part of more traditional religious congregations. Each "anonymous" group – whether AA, Narcotics Anonymous, Overeaters Anonymous, or any other – is a cluster of people who reinforce each other as they attempt to change their behavior. In addition, groups modeled after AA use language with religious connotations, although individuals decide how to define specific terms. For example, changing behavior involves accepting help from a "higher power." Many identify that "higher power" with God, but the groups do not make that identification explicit.

Box 16.1 Self-help and spirituality

Although self-help groups such as Alcoholics Anonymous, Narcotics Anonymous, and Overeaters Anonymous are not explicitly religious, they often take on a spiritual quality in that:

- they offer participants the same kind of nurture and support as a religious congregation;
- their techniques call for reliance on a "higher power" that many identify with God;
- they provide members with a sense of meaning and purpose for their lives and a sense of connectedness with other kindred people;
- they may or may not replace engagement with a more traditional religious group.

In these ways, self-help illustrates Thomas Luckmann's claims that in a highly complex, industrialized society, religion becomes increasingly diffuse, almost to the point where it becomes invisible since it is not linked only to religious institutions and traditions.

At the same time, these groups function like religious communities for participants, who receive from group members nurture and support equivalent to that provided by congregations. They do not replace congregations for all, but some do not associate with congregations and look to these groups for those human associations that help provide meaning in life. Success comes when individuals abandon destructive behavior and find happiness, but also when religious institutions themselves use similar groups to help people build affective ties to the congregation.

By the 1990s, small groups had become so prevalent that the sociologist Robert Wuthnow edited a collection of essays arguing that the small group was transforming American religion, becoming the primary mode by which individuals developed ties to a larger congregation or religious community. Congregations of every theological persuasion and religious heritage offered divorce support groups, singles' groups, groups for young mothers, and an array of cognate options. Other groups catered to atheists, agnostics, and skeptics. Many who "belonged" to groups sponsored by a religious congregation were not actually members of the congregation. Nevertheless, they found guidance in their quest or search for meaning in the support received from the group itself. The groups thus provided social support as well as religious support.

Spiritual, but not religious

Other examples of how the pulse of religion moves beyond religious institutions and becomes increasingly invisible come to light in examining the trend within American culture, evident from the 1980s on, to replace "religion" with "spirituality" in popular discussions about faith and practice. Robert Wuthnow has studied this trend away from religion towards spirituality. Numerous others, such as the sociologist Wade Clark Roof, have also emphasized this phenomenon. In *After Heaven: Spirituality in America since the 1950s*, Wuthnow documented the movement away from spiritual life oriented around what he called a "dwelling" and towards a vaguely defined "seeking." Similarly, Roof suggested that baby boomers were a "generation of seekers" whose spiritual quest redirected the course of American religious life.

Both highlight how more Americans shun engagement with organized religion without shedding interest in religious belief or practice. Individuals increasingly refuse to let religious institutions and traditions define their personal beliefs and how they put them into practice. For example, persons raised as Catholics may ignore church teaching prohibiting the use of artificial means of birth control and attend Mass only

---

Box 16.2 What is hybrid spirituality?

Many who call themselves "spiritual, but not religious" develop a hybrid spirituality. They construct a personal, customized set of beliefs and practices that serve as an anchor in understanding their own life experiences. This hybrid, individualized spirituality often:

- draws from many religious traditions and belief systems as well as from nonreligious sources;
- affirms the reality of supernatural power and the ability of humans to access that power;
- reflects the individualism characteristic of American culture;
- may be "added on" to association with an organized religion or congregation;
- has a generic quality rather than an obvious tie to any one style of doctrine or practice;
- has a practical focus in that it acts to provide meaning and direction to life;
- assumes that there is more to life than what is found in empirical reality.

occasionally, but still regard themselves as Catholics, though Catholics who determine their beliefs for themselves. Seekers create customized sets of beliefs and practices just for themselves.

Wuthnow's image of the dwelling reflected the presumed religious revitalization of the 1950s, when denominational publishing houses churned out literature ranging from monthly magazines to devotional guides to help the faithful be religious and when religious life centered on churches, synagogues, and temples. Fixed religious authorities – churches or rabbis, theologians or congregations – set the bar for spirituality and guided its course.

Spirituality as seeking or a journey toward an elusive destination also echoes Luckmann's claim that religion becomes more invisible as society becomes more complex. But there is more. Recall the study by Robert Bellah and his associates on changes in attitudes toward commitment among Americans in the later twentieth century. The early baby boom generation, coming of age in the 1960s, developed an aversion to any kind of commitment, whether to a religious group, a political party, or even a life-long career. Religious groups marked by racism and sexism no longer provided a spiritual fulcrum. Those who assumed that science and its attendant rationalism brought happiness faced disappointment. The horrors of the Vietnam war, seen daily on the evening news, in one sense undermined the idea that science and technology, which brought napalm and new weapons to the battlefields of southeast Asia, could transform society into paradise. Some were drawn to Asian religious options because traditional religious options seemed complicit in society's anguish. Recall, too, how Vatican II for American Catholics opened doors for questioning the teaching authority – the *magisterium* – of the church. Added to all of this by the end of the twentieth century were the myriad opportunities to explore new ideas through the Internet.

Together these forces propelled the baby boom generation and those who came after to jettison organized religion, even if they maintained formal religious affiliation or responded to surveys with a religious identification. They were more inclined to construct a personal, often hybrid set of beliefs. In keeping with the popular mythology of Americans as rugged individualists, hybrid spirituality placed final authority in matters of belief not in organized religion, but in individual seekers themselves. Persons freely determined for themselves what to believe and how they wished to live that belief. Hybrid spirituality became the epitome of what others, in a different context, called "lived religion." So, for example, women who explored spirituality oriented to the goddess, whether identified with Wicca or not, were looking to their experience as women as the foundation for spirituality, not to the doctrines and practices of a formal religious tradition.

What also sets this hybrid spirituality apart from more traditional understandings of disciplines of prayer, study of sacred texts, etc. is its blending of practices and ideas from multiple religions. For example, individuals may self-identify as Christian, but also practice Eastern meditation disciplines such as yoga; they may attend religious services at one congregation, but gain spiritual nourishment from television preachers whose religious affiliations are very different.

In addition, much that informs a personal, hybrid spirituality has a generic quality. In the 1990s, for example, a series of spiritual guides all bearing the words *Chicken Soup* in the title were strong sellers in book stores. Volumes targeted particular audiences, from teenagers to wives to pet lovers, with stories intended to inspire. None

Figure 16.1 Many who see themselves as "spiritual, but not religious" create a hybrid expression of personal spirituality that draws on many sources. Here a woman practices yoga, a traditional Asian religious discipline, but with a Christian flavor since she is part of a group meeting at a Christian church in New York City

© Emily Anne Epstein/Corbis

carried denominational endorsement; all avoided intricacies of theology and doctrine. *Chicken Soup* books provided simple inspiration; readers could take from them whatever met their needs at the moment. They could also interpret any specific religious statements however they chose.

Even the religious magazine *Guideposts*, established by Norman Vincent Peale to advance his "positive thinking" approach, carries material that draws from multiple formal religious approaches. Like the vignettes in the *Chicken Soup* books, *Guideposts* stories illustrate the practical bent of hybrid, individualized spirituality. A typical issue might include articles on exercise and weight loss, lessons to be learned from pets, and testimonies about personal growth from celebrities, along with extracts from the writings of Peale and his associates. Books published by *Guideposts* have addressed topics such as sightings of angels and messages from the "hereafter." These illumine two other features of this highly individualized, personal spirituality: a keen sense of the supernatural, though not always defined in traditional terms or limited to belief in God, and the conviction that there is more to life than simply physical existence. To be sure, such ideas and beliefs are part of more traditional religion as well, but hybrid spirituality leaves it to individuals to construct their own understandings of what beliefs "work" for them, regardless of the sources from which they draw.

Material in *Chicken Soup* and *Guideposts* is not the only way the sense of the supernatural represented by angels penetrates popular spirituality. Jewish, Christian, and Muslim scriptures all describe some angelic beings; unseen spiritual forces are common to native American and African tribal religiosity and also to strands of Asian traditions. Yet spirituality owes much of the contemporary passion for angels to mass culture, not to the sacred texts and teachings of religious traditions. The still popular (though not highly critically acclaimed) movie *It's a Wonderful Life*, released by prominent filmmaker Frank Capra in 1946 when America was recovering from World War II, offered a vision of beneficent angelic beings who helped rid society of evil and vice by enabling ordinary people to discover and act on an inner altruism.

More influential have been two television series, *Highway to Heaven* (1984–89) and *Touched by an Angel* (1994–2003). Both continue to inspire cable television audiences in the twenty-first century through reruns. As a result angels became seen as benevolent protectors ("guardian angels"), supernatural forces guiding believers in their spiritual quest. Sometimes anthropomorphized or shown as human, angels remain a staple of hybrid spirituality's affirmation of supernatural power and the ability of humans to access that realm of power.

Into the "New Age" and beyond

In casual conversation, many persons equate hybrid spirituality with what is called "New Age" religious expression, but New Age refers to another distinctive way of being religious, one that encompasses an extraordinarily diverse range of ideas and practices. Some are not new in that many who began to use the New Age designation in the 1960s and 1970s drew from earlier religious and social movements, including Theosophy and spiritualism. Some also adapted ideas found in ancient philosophies such as Neoplatonism.

One barometer to mark New Age's becoming part of the spiritual quest is the launching of the *East West Journal* in 1971. By the second decade of the twenty-first century, numerous websites (including the "e-zine" *New Age Journal*) provided the major way for persons interested in this approach to spirituality to establish contact with others who had similar spiritual interests as well as to learn of seminars and retreats for practitioners offered by a host of self-proclaimed and self-trained New Age teachers.

Lacking sacred texts and formal doctrines, New Age represents an amorphous approach to spirituality, but generally manifests all the qualities of hybrid spirituality noted above – expecting some practical results, accepting belief in a supernatural realm, assuming that a spiritual realm (a "hereafter") interacts with empirical reality, and fusing ideas and practices drawn from Western and Eastern religious traditions. Most who identify with New Age are convinced that humans have an innate spiritual nature that transcends time. Techniques such as meditation allow that inner spiritual nature to release its power. Some insist that this spiritual nature can "channel" the essence of other beings, most of whom lived in some past era. In this vein, some intrigue with New Age perspectives comes from their association with celebrities such as Shirley MacLaine.

Another feature common to much New Age expression, but also found in other religious orientations, is the conviction that living in harmony with unseen natural forces – the rhythm of the universe – facilitates realization of one's inner spiritual nature. This aspect of New Age spirituality fostered interest in ecology and the environment because it cultivates a sense of oneness with the natural world. It has affinities with holistic medicine, which is perceived to be more attuned to nature than

---

Box 16.3 Understanding the "New Age"

Religious expressions that carry the label "New Age" are many and varied. Here is one scholar's attempt to show how to recognize New Age religious phenomena:

> The New Age movement was a discourse community because its adherents adopted a coherent yet diverse set of spiritual and social values and used a common language to communicate with each other. Put another way, New Agers knew they were in the company of fellow travelers when they heard certain key terms and concepts – for example, *energies, auras, channeling, transformation,* and *empowerment.* Many New Agers were mistrustful of institutions and preferred biodegradable organizational forms that emerged and disappeared as needed. The weekend seminar, the weeklong retreat, workshops, lectures, newsletters, and magazines were the preferred modes of interaction and communication for New Agers.
>
> (P.C. Lucas, "New Age Religion(s)," in C.H. Lippy and P.W. Williams (eds.), *Encyclopedia of Religion in America,* Washington, DC: CQ Press, 2010, vol. 3, p. 1544)

---

medical protocols that rely only on manufactured drugs. These interests also tap into scientific understanding, since many attracted to New Age ideas believe that physics, biology, and other scientific fields enable one to understand more profoundly the interconnectedness of all reality and hence how the spiritual essence within humans is the same as the essence within all things. This perspective also echoes ancient ideas of monism, or the sense that all reality is at root a unified, single (mono-) whole.

New Age efforts have critics, even among sympathizers, who find it simplistic. Emphasizing the inner self, claim some, borders on narcissism, while the celebration of a single unity in all reality that is good seems to others to minimize human weakness leading to evil. Just as some have qualms about whether the evangelical seekers associated with Protestant megachurches and new worship styles minimize the altruistic and prophetic dimensions of traditional understandings of Christianity, some insist that the self-absorbed ecstasy of New Age practice eliminates social action to combat injustice and transform society. In other words, New Age's inward gaze can easily ignore a passionate concern for others and for social change.

Part of New Age's appeal is the contrast it offers between inner spirituality and an external world in which racism, sexism, and war undermine all that is spiritual. At the same time, because there are no membership requirements to be part of the New Age, many embrace New Age ideas and practices in their own hybrid spirituality, including some who retain affiliation with more traditional religious groups.

Other movements also rekindled interest in the inner life, including spiritual "cousins" of New Age phenomena. Often they are grouped together as metaphysical religions. Some consider religious expressions that emphasize the occult, such as Wicca, to be metaphysical religions. As with New Age, the metaphysical tradition has a long history, stretching back to ancient philosophical schools. Over the centuries, it helped give birth to spiritualism, the nineteenth century literary and religious movement known as Transcendentalism, Theosophy, new religious movements such as Heaven's Gate, and even some self-help groups.

The distinguishing feature of metaphysical religious expression is its emphasis on the mind. The mind, not necessarily an inner spiritual essence as in New Age thinking, links humanity to all reality. For some, the mind represents a divine spark present in all reality. Many, but not all, metaphysical understandings suggest that some sort of mystical experience or a sense of the union of the individual mind with Mind itself (traditional God-language is often avoided) is the goal. As with New Age, meditation practices and similar ritual activities facilitate bringing about this experience. Most critical is the way meditation offers insight into the true nature of all reality. Because insight is apprehended in the mind, the designation of metaphysical remains appropriate.

In many Christian circles, part of the fascination with the Gnostic gospels, most of which were found in Egypt in 1945 just after the end of World War II, stems from their teaching that a divinity within the individual may be tapped through right knowledge (gnosis). Since 1975, when the translated materials became widely available, intrigue has mounted. Many believe that Gnostic teaching was unfairly quashed in the early centuries of Christian development and represents as authentic an understanding of early Christian thinking as that found in the traditional Bible.

One increasingly popular expression of Buddhism belongs as much to the metaphysical tradition as to the Theravada strand of Buddhism that gave it birth. Known as Vipassana, this expression has an affinity with the metaphysical tradition in its conviction that mastery of particular meditation techniques enables one to grasp the true nature of reality. Some link this with the elusive, but traditional Buddhist notion of nirvana. However, it is an awareness that is accessible to devotees of Vipassana techniques, whether or not one affirms the range of Buddhist teachings.

As with New Age understanding, it is difficult to indicate precisely how many Americans identify with metaphysical ideas. A metaphysical orientation and even practices of meditation leading to mystical experience may be added on to more traditional forms of religion. Some scholars suggest that Vipassana is the fastest growing form of Buddhism in twenty-first century America, but there are no membership data. Like those who move from one Protestant denomination to another or to a group that eschews denominational affiliation, persons move freely among New Age and metaphysical expressions as they search for the key to meaning in life. They may experiment with several possibilities, yet never abandon association with more traditional forms of religion. All become part of the hybrid spirituality characteristic of belief and practice in complex societies where religion becomes increasingly invisible.

Another thread of spirituality, one on the margins of both traditional religion and New Age and metaphysical approaches, is Wicca. Two primary forces account for the renewed interest in Wicca since the 1960s. One is second-wave feminism's concern for the role of women and the place of women's experience in religion. The other is the growing awareness of ecology and environmental issues.

Often popularly equated with magic intended to produce evil results and with witches who personify malevolence, Wicca provokes the same fears and negative images as many new religious movements. However, at base, Wicca is not nefarious, nor are its practitioners committed to reprehensible behavior. Rather, Wicca celebrates the processes of nature, especially those associated with fertility. It looks to the goddess as supreme because of the logical connection these processes have with women, whose

Figure 16.2 At this Wiccan center in Hoopeston, IL, students are learning how to perform a lunar ritual. The center offers instruction in the beliefs, traditions, and practices of Wiccans

Courtesy of Scott Olson/Getty Images

fertility sustains the human race. In Wicca, harmony with natural rhythms of the universe, achieved through ritual activity and devotion to the goddess, results not only in personal wellbeing but also in the wellbeing of the planet and all forms of life.

Most religious groups have ignored female experience, promoting the idea that dominion over nature means control and exploitation. Wicca appeals to many women whose unique experience from menstruation through menopause echoes currents at work in nature itself. Women's bodies – and hence the goddess – nourish the world and the environment. Many principles behind Wicca pre-date Christianity. Hence adherents and critics both refer to Wicca as pagan. For adherents, this designation distances Wicca from Christianity and all traditional religion; for critics, the word carries a negative nuance.

Leaders of the movement, such as Hungarian-born Zsuzsanna Budapest (1940–), originally known as Zsuzsuanna Emese Mokcsay, and Starhawk (1951–), the name taken by Miriam Simos, have organized all-female covens (congregations of Wiccan witches). They have crafted rituals celebrating women's experience and the goddess, helping the movement develop a body of belief. Some Wiccan groups attract both women and men. Beyond covens, many more identify with Wiccan ideas through the Internet.

Because of popular suspicion, Wicca has maintained a low profile. Yet some Wiccan writings have attracted a wide readership: Starhawk's *A Spiral Dance* (1979) has sold more than 300,000 copies, a figure in excess of estimates suggested for the number of coven members in the US. Hence many analysts insist that just as thousands of

Christians, for example, may practice forms of meditation associated with Asian religions but not self-identify as Hindus or Buddhists, so thousands incorporate aspects of Wicca into their personal spirituality. Other dimensions of female spirituality came under examination in Chapter 10.

For some, New Age, metaphysical, and Wiccan practice serve as religions. For others they are among a range of sources that shape an eclectic personal spirituality. Often lacking the structures and institutions that people associate with religion, they remain fluid but vital dimensions of American spirituality in the twenty-first century.

The impact of spirituality for American religion

"Spirituality" sections of bookstores and the content of religious magazines oriented to a mass audience provide ample evidence of the diffuse nature of the contemporary religious quest. The mixture of Asian ideas with more traditional ones likewise demonstrates how the new pluralism in American religion has penetrated every aspect of religious consciousness. But there are other implications.

Many, especially the so-called "unchurched" or unaffiliated, see spirituality as an alternative to religion, something more personal and more meaningful than doctrines and rituals linked to presumably arid traditions. But the relationship is more complex. The complexity involves determining whether the presumed intrigue with customized spirituality is new to the American religious landscape or awareness of a substratum that has a long history. Have Americans always constructed private, personal worlds of meaning?

The answer to that question is affirmative. Historians have demonstrated, for example, that those mythic prototypes of strict religion, the Puritans who settled seventeenth-century New England, were as intent on reading almanacs for astrological forecasts as they were in poring over scripture. Both shaped their world of meaning. Studies of immigrant Catholic communities reveal the intertwining of local folk belief and practice with formal church doctrine and ritual, especially in the host of religious festivals still celebrated in parishes that once served a particular ethnic constituency. African American religious life likewise has long layered an acquired Christian heritage onto African tribal spirituality, crafting understandings that defy neat categorization. One example that captured public attention in the 1990s, as Caribbean immigration grew, was Santeria, a hybrid expression that draws not only on things African and Catholic – Santeria literally means the "way of the saints" – but also on a spirituality indigenous to Caribbean culture.

What may be "new" about trends in spirituality as a quest, a search for meaning, is the recognition by religious leaders and analysts alike of a phenomenon that has long existed, not the phenomenon itself. Hence evangelical megachurches trumpet their "seeker services" that offer practical advice for living without an overlay of tradition, allowing participants to craft their own belief systems (even if a particular megachurch has a denominational affiliation), but Americans have done that for centuries. What may also be new is the opportunity to tap into a wider array of spiritual resources, given the new pluralism that has transformed American religious life. Asian approaches, for example, are no longer confined to intellectual circles or new religious movements targeting the young; even mainline churches offer instruction in yoga and other Asian meditative disciplines. As religious life becomes increasingly globalized, then, spirituality will continue to become more hybrid, and "pure" traditions will be harder to locate.

Key points you need to know

- Several polls show that more and more Americans are not affiliated with religious organizations.
- A religious seeking has for many replaced association with a single religious institution as the basis for personal spirituality.
- Certain areas of the country, such as the Pacific northwest, have a higher proportion of the population religiously unaffiliated.
- Thomas Luckmann hypothesized that as societies become more complex, religion becomes increasingly invisible.
- Self-help groups, such as Alcoholics Anonymous, may take on religious dimensions.
- Today many Americans describe themselves as being "spiritual, but not religious" to show they hold religious beliefs, but do not identify with a religious institution.
- Many people create a hybrid spirituality that draws on many resources.
- Popular belief in angels illustrates one feature of hybrid spirituality, a belief in supernatural forces and power.
- Some Americans link personal spirituality to "New Age" expressions, to the metaphysical tradition, or to Wicca.
- Spirituality expands the pluralistic character of American religious life.

Discussion questions

1 What is the basis for the claim that more and more Americans have no religious affiliation? Are Americans becoming less religious?
2 How would you account for the reluctance of Americans to take on a formal commitment to or membership in a religious institution?
3 How and why does religion seem to be increasingly invisible in contemporary society? If religion is invisible, does it cease to exist as a social force within the larger culture?
4 How do self-help groups take on a religious dimension?
5 What do people mean when they say that they are "spiritual, but not religious"?
6 Describe "hybrid spirituality." Why is it attractive to contemporary Americans?
7 How would you describe "New Age" religious expression?" What about it is "new"? What is not so new? What gives New Age plausibility in contemporary America?
8 Explain what is meant by metaphysical religions. How would you account for the renewed interest in this approach to being religious?
9 How would you explain Wicca and its appeal, especially to women, in recent decades?
10 What long-term impact are current trends in spirituality likely to have on American religious culture?

Further reading

Albanese, C.L. (2008) *A Republic of Mind and Spirit: A Cultural History of American Metaphysical Religion*, New Haven, CT: Yale University Press.

Ammerman, N.T. (2007) *Everyday Religion: Observing Modern Religious Lives*, New York: Oxford University Press.

Bellah, R.N., Madsden, R., Sullivan, W.M., Swidler, A., and Tipton, S.M. (1996) *Habits of the Heart: Individualism and Commitment in American Life*, rev edn, Berkeley: University of California Press.

Berger, H.A. (1999) *A Community of Witches: Contemporary Neo-Paganism and Witchcraft in the United States*, Columbia: University of South Carolina Press.

Fuller, R.C. (2001) *Spiritual, but not Religious: Understanding Unchurched America*, New York: Oxford University Press.

—— (2004) *Religious Revolutionaries: The Rebels Who Reshaped American Religion*, New York: Palgrave Macmillan.

Gardella, P. (2007) *American Angels: Useful Spirits in the Material World*, Lawrence: University Press of Kansas.

Lippy, C.H. (1994) *Being Religious, American Style: A History of Popular Religiosity in the United States*, Westport, CT: Greenwood.

McGuire, M.B. (2008) *Lived Religion: Faith and Practice in Everyday Life*, New York: Oxford University Press.

Orsi, R.A. (2005) *Between Heaven and Earth: The Religious Worlds People Make and the Scholars Who Study Them*, Princeton, NJ: Princeton University Press.

Pike, S.M. (2001) *Earthly Bodies, Magical Selves: Contemporary Pagans and the Search for Community*, Berkeley: University of California Press.

Roof, W.C. (1994) *A Generation of Seekers: The Spiritual Journeys of the Baby Boom Generation*, San Francisco: HarperSanFrancisco.

Schmidt, L.E. (2005) *Restless Souls: The Making of American Spirituality*, San Francisco: HarperSanFrancisco.

Stanczak, G. (2006) *Engaged Spirituality: Social Change and American Religion*, Rutgers, NJ: Rutgers University Press.

Wuthnow, R. (1998) *After Heaven: Spirituality in American since the 1950s*, Berkeley: University of California Press.

—— (ed) (1994) *"I Come Away Stronger": How Small Groups Are Changing American Religion*, Grand Rapids, MI: Eerdmans.

17 Contemporary religious thought
From tradition to experience

In this chapter

This chapter explores how American religious thought (theology) has changed since the end of World War II. It opens with a discussion of how religious thought has traditionally been understood. Then it looks at some new expressions in which the lived experience of people is primary. The first of those is African American or black theology. Consideration of feminist thought and then of gay and lesbian theology follows. The next section looks at voices that still seemed unheard, particularly those of African American and Latina women. Attention then turns finally to how contemporary ethical issues, from environmental concerns to biomedical matters, have added new dimensions to religious thinking. Our emphasis falls on movements in religious thought that have direct ties to many of the social and cultural currents whose impact have shaped the discussion of movements, groups, and traditions in earlier chapters. To that extent, we omit consideration of other significant intellectual ventures, including, for example, the renewed interest in intellectual currents rooted in the Anabaptist heritage represented by John Howard Yoder, the popular "postliberal" theology of Stanley Hauerwas, or the fresh appreciation of the Christian Realism of Reinhold Niebuhr that followed on Barack Obama's election to the US presidency in 2008.

Main topics covered

- The traditional construction of religious thought.
- Why the starting point for religious thought changed from received doctrine to personal experience.
- How new trends relate to postmodernism and changing approaches to spirituality.
- Major themes and figures in black theology.
- The nature of feminist thought.
- Ways Latino theology celebrated ethnicity and community.
- Why African American women felt it necessary to construct an alternative in Womanist theology and Latina American women an alternative in Mujerista theology.
- How gay and lesbian theology made sexuality central to religious thinking.
- Ways ecology, environmental ethics, bioethics, and other ethical issues pushed religious thought in fresh directions.

The Christian theological heritage

Thus far, our consideration of religion in American culture since World War II has looked primarily at developments from the perspective of traditions such as mainline Protestantism or American Catholicism, institutions such as denominations and churches, and movements such as new religions. Following some sociologists and historians who emphasize lived religion as foundational, we have also examined religion from a very individual point of view, examining shifts in personal spirituality and its increasingly hybrid, eclectic nature. Yet another way to see the dynamics at work in American religion is to look at religious thought or theology. Although theologians may have some identification with traditions such as Protestant Christianity or Judaism, their efforts to examine rationally the nature of belief and how belief relates to life is by no means restricted to a single tradition or institution. Thinkers offer their ideas to all, regardless of religious identity, although their positions may be grounded in one tradition. Because religious thought cuts across all the ways we have looked at religion in contemporary America, a chapter devoted to changes and trends in thinking adds another means of understanding and analyzing American religious culture.

Much of contemporary American religious thinking has ties to the Christian tradition and its theological heritage. At least from the time of Thomas Aquinas in the thirteenth century, Christian theologians organized their thinking in systemic fashion, proceeding carefully from one doctrine to another. This method and the idea that theology addressed a received body of doctrines examined systematically remained the norm until the later twentieth century. For Catholics, even Thomas's explanation of doctrine remained authoritative until Vatican II. For Protestants, starting with the Reformation giant John Calvin (1509–64), theologians struggled to reinterpret doctrines to keep pace with the times. But the old categories remained in place. For example, religious thinkers probed the nature and sources of religious knowledge (revelation), the doctrine of God, Christology (teaching about Christ), ecclesiology (the nature of the church), and eschatology (end times), among others. They wanted to move logically from one to the next, showing how each doctrine related to the others. Topics for discussion seemed a given, with received categories not to be altered.

After World War II, several Christian theologians produced new interpretations taking into account modern intellectual and scientific developments. The German immigrant and philosophical theologian Paul Tillich (1886–1965), for example, published a widely acclaimed three-volume *Systematic Theology* between 1951 and 1963. His approach drew on both earlier liberalism and the neo-orthodoxy that tried to correct liberalism's excesses, filtered through the German philosophies he imbibed as a student. But Tillich employed the standard categories and sought to interweave every doctrine and idea. The evangelical theologian Carl F.H. Henry (1913–2003) devoted six volumes to a similar task, but from a more orthodox perspective than Tillich. The first volume of his *God, Revelation, and Authority* appeared in 1976; the last in 1983.

Yet even before Tillich had finished his *magnum opus* and Henry had published the first of his six volumes, events in American society and in global religious life began transforming the theological enterprise. The civil rights movement, for example, raised questions about whether the Christian theological heritage in America reflected only the white experience, not the racial and ethnic diversity of the nation. Many questioned whether the received theological tradition spoke at all to the people whose history included enslavement, discrimination, segregation, and racism.

American religious thinkers in the 1960s were aware of movements elsewhere that rooted theology in the lived experience of oppressed peoples, although their stories differed from those of African Americans. In Latin America, economic disparities often pitted organized churches against the masses, since the churches were part of an economic and political power elite. Consequently some priests and other thinkers began to talk about liberation theology. They found the heart of the Christian message not in doctrines passed down over the centuries, but in a message of freedom – liberation – from all forces (particularly economic ones) that kept humans from realizing their full potential. African American thinkers quickly applied the same ideas to the lived history of descendants of slaves who still lived in a racist society. They, too, responded to a message of liberation and freedom, giving birth to black theology.

African Americans were not alone in finding a theology or belief system grounded in liberation relevant. Feminist thinkers began to draw on these ideas, constructing a perspective grounded in women's experience, a lived history that reflected the oppression of sexism and denial of access to positions of power and influence in both religious and societal circles. When gay and lesbian Americans called for an end to oppression based on sexual orientation, some saw that the received theological heritage was not only white and patriarchal in its focus, but heterosexist as well. In time, other voices spoke, as African American and Latina women found these new ventures wanting when it came to linking beliefs to the lived realities they encountered.

What these efforts to rethink the theological heritage shared was making personal experience – whether of African Americans, women, gays, Latina women, or others – the starting point for theological reflection. Lived experience replaced received doctrine, and even the categories that had informed theological heritage for centuries. Using lived, personal experience as the springboard for constructing religious thought resonated with what philosophers, theologians, and literary critics called postmodernism, a term difficult to define or to describe precisely. Postmodernism rejects any absolute authority outside personal experience. Individuals and what they encounter in their daily lives become the authority – not a sacred text, not a theological heritage, not a religious professional. There are no fixed standards. What is accepted as truth fluctuates as experience changes. The earlier discussion of spirituality's moving from expressions offered by religious institutions to a personal, individual quest also illustrates this aspect of postmodernism. Making lived reality the foundation for formulating and interpreting belief has transformed religious thought.

Black theology and the lived experience of African Americans

As mentioned earlier (especially in Chapter 11), the civil rights movement was one catalyst sparking extraordinarily creative endeavors in African American religious thought. By the end of the 1960s, several writers offered fresh, original works clustered together as "black theology." Among the most prominent was James M. Cone (1938–), an Arkansas native who lived through the horrors of segregation as a child. Cone received a classical education in theology at Northwestern University. When he began teaching systematic theology, he realized that the western theological tradition had little bearing on the lived experience of African Americans. The history of slavery and racism required a radically different approach in order to make the Christian message germane to what African Americans encountered in their collective past and their present daily lives. Recall here also the discussion of the interplay between race and religion discussed in Chapter 12.

Inspired by Latin American liberation theology, Cone called for a black theology of liberation that would join with black power to vanquish the sin of white oppression. For him, the Christian message proclaimed freedom from every force and power that kept men and women from realizing their full potential. Oppressive structures that thwarted self-actualization were enemies of faith; persons of faith needed to demolish them.

Box 17.1 James Cone's black theology of liberation

African American theologian James Cone adapted constructs from liberation theology to develop a perspective that he believed spoke directly from and to the lived experience of African Americans. Central to Cone's thinking is the idea that the God of the Bible is always the God of those who are oppressed, regardless of the type of oppression encountered. In an interview, Cone reflected on his theological formulation:

> The assertion that "the gospel is liberation" is not an arbitrary statement. It is an assertion based on faith in God's revelation in history as made known in the Exodus and the appearance of Jesus Christ ... The concept of liberation is not one among many themes in the biblical tradition; it is rather the essence of God's revelation in history ...
>
> This means that I cannot be free until all men are free. And if in some distant future I am no longer oppressed because of blackness, then I must take upon myself whatever form of human oppression exists in the society, affirming my identity with the victims. The identity must be made with the victims not because of sympathy, but because my own humanity is involved in my brother's degradation.
>
> (From W. Hordern, "Dialogue on Black Theology: An Interview with James Cone," www.nathanielturner.com/dialogueonblacktheology.htm, accessed 12 November 2010; first printed in the *Christian Century*, 15 September 1971)

Some critics found Cone's stance troubling. It seemed to endorse use of violence to end oppression. Most appraisals suggest that Cone captured the essence of the biblical message when he saw the gospel as a mandate to rid society of structures that denied the full humanity of its people. Feminists, especially African American women, at first thought Cone failed to appreciate the double oppression they felt as victims of discrimination based on race and on gender. But Cone came to realize that liberation knew no boundaries. Consequently, he supported full inclusion of gays and lesbians in religious and social life and also the inclusion of persons of all ethnic persuasions, especially Latino/a Americans, who often encountered discrimination as new immigrants akin to that faced by Catholic and Jewish immigrants generations earlier.

Feminist religious thought

In Roman Catholic circles, the ferment generated by the Second Vatican Council that we mentioned in Chapter 6 joined with second-wave feminism to pave the way for new approaches to understanding doctrine. Catholic feminist theologians urged more concerted efforts to end sexism within the church and to examine doctrine through the lens of women's experience. Among the earliest and most strident was Mary Daly (1928–2010), whose *Beyond God the Father* (1968) and *The Church and the Second Sex: Toward a Philosophy of Women's Liberation* (1973) stirred the passions of many women, Catholic and non-Catholic. A long-time faculty member at the Jesuits' Boston College, Daly became embroiled in controversy when she attempted to forbid men to take her classes or to speak in them if they did. In time, Daly's feminism became decidedly anti-male, and she finally ended her association with the church.

Figure 17.1 Mary Daly was a pioneer but controversial advocate for a feminist theology rooted in Roman Catholic thinking, although she later abandoned her ties to the church

Courtesy of the Sophia Smith Collection, Smith College Archives

Others, such as Rosemary Radford Ruether (1936–), remained in the Catholic Church, although Ruether spent her academic career primarily at Protestant or interfaith theological schools. Drawing on her early work exploring how Christian anti-Semitism distorted theology, Ruether recognized that the same distortions allowed a patriarchal denigrating of women to take hold. Later Ruether linked women's experience with ecological/environmental concerns. She understood, as did some practitioners of Wicca, that what women experience in their bodies mirrors rhythms of the natural world.

Highly influential not only in Catholic theological circles, but in Christian feminist circles generally is the German born and educated Harvard professor Elisabeth Schüssler Fiorenza (1938–). Schüssler Fiorenza's, *In Memory of Her* (1983), turned a feminist eye to early Christianity, both within and beyond the New Testament. She demonstrated that careful reading of surviving texts and other evidence required shedding patriarchal images and assumptions that shaped much of Christian history.

Scores of Protestant women also began to produce significant writings that redirected the course of Protestant religious thought. Historian Nancy A. Hardesty (1941–2011), for example, tackled the issue of gender-based language in her widely reprinted *Inclusive Language in the Church* (1987), showing that rigorous analysis of biblical texts did not support exclusive use of male terms for deity. Many who were resistant to accepting women in professional ministry based their opposition on such male referents. With Letha Dawson Scanzoni (1935–) Hardesty co-authored a study, *All We're Meant To Be* (1974), which built a solid biblical foundation for many of the claims made by second-wave and third-wave feminists about women's equality.

Box 17.2 A feminist thinker argues for theology based on experience

The shift from a received body of doctrine and tradition to lived experience that characterizes recent American religious thought received a strong endorsement in the writing of feminist theologian Sallie McFague. In the preface to her *Metaphorical Theology*, she argued that today it was impossible to write a "complete theology" but only theology that reflected a particular tradition and the experience (she calls it "sensibility") of the individual theologian:

> Our age, which has pressed home the lessons of historical relativity and pluralism, has also become aware of the relativity and pluralism of theology's resources: Scripture and tradition. Different perspectives and interpretations are not necessarily incorrect because they are different. Limitation and variety are endemic to theological reflection given its subject matter – the meaning of human life in light of the transforming activity of God. In short, there is no *one* way to express the event as there is no *one* perspective from which to approach it ...
>
> In other words, no one writes the full, complete theology. As [theologian David] Tracy rightly points out, each theology is an intensification of a particular, concrete tradition and sensibility. It *should* be thus, as long as other ways are kept in view and the limitations of one's own way acknowledged.
>
> (From S. McFague, *Metaphorical Theology: Models of God in Religious Language*, Philadelphia: Fortress, 1982, p. viii)

By the early 1980s, other mainline Protestant feminist writers, often faculty at mainline theological schools, pushed feminist reinterpretations of Christian theology further. The liberation thinking informing black theology was a seminal influence on them. Many first tackled issues of religious language, in particular the lack of feminine images with reference to God in most of the Christian theological tradition. Until the language issue was resolved, patriarchal dominance would continue in religious institutions and in society.

Letty M. Russell (1929–2007), an ordained Presbyterian who taught at Yale Divinity School, delved deeply not only into liberation theology, but into the lived experience of Third World Christians in her efforts to undo centuries of patriarchal biblical interpretation and to offer a fresh feminist understanding. Sallie McFague (1933–), long-time Vanderbilt Divinity School professor and dean, devoted much of her writing to arguing that all religious language was metaphorical, not literal. If that were so, one could build as strong a case for identifying God as Mother as most of the tradition did for identifying God as Father. In addition to issues of language, Rebecca S. Chopp (1952–), in *The Power to Speak: Feminism, Language, and God* (1989), drew on the economic aspect of Latin American theology to insist that only if women in industrialized nations resisted economic oppression based on their being underpaid and mistreated could humanity experience emancipation from all repression and oppression, the core of the Christian message for her.

A host of ethical issues directly affecting women also cried out for analysis from the experience of women. Foremost was abortion. Beverly Wildung Harrison (1932–2012) crafted a strong feminist theological argument supporting legalized abortion under certain conditions in *Our Right to Choose: Toward a New Ethic of Abortion* (1989). Other debates surrounding abortion received attention in Chapter 9.

Feminist theologians were also instrumental in encouraging Protestant theological schools to rethink how they trained persons for professional ministry when women came to outnumber men in their student populations. Just as black theology found the larger tradition wanting because it did not speak to the lived experience of African Americans, feminist theology was both critique and corrective in insisting that religious thought looked very different if the starting point was the lived experience of women, not of white men. By the 1980s, both black theology and feminist theology had become integral to the larger American theological heritage. But the task was far from complete. As soon as black theology and feminist theology made their mark, other voices began to speak, claiming that even these reformulations lacked relevance to the lived experience of other groups.

One fresh current came from African American women, who developed Womanist theology, a term taken from author Alice Walker. These thinkers found that black theology retained a male focus that overlooked the experience of African American women as women. They rejected feminist thought emerging in white Protestant and Roman Catholic circles because it neglected their experience as African Americans. In other words, Womanist thought responded to both racism and sexism.

Theologians such as Katie Cannon (1950–), the first African American woman ordained in the mainline United Presbyterian Church (USA) and Delores S. Williams, one-time colleague of Cone on the faculty of New York's Union Theological Seminary, offered a new approach. Both believed black churches fostered a dangerous sexism because they made it difficult for women to serve as pastors or as lay leaders in other than ancillary organizations. For Womanist thinkers, sexism within the black church was as dehumanizing as sexism in society. It had to be demolished, as did the racism that Womanist theologians experienced because of their African American identity.

Other currents of feminist religious thought began to appear by the dawn of the twenty-first century, but because they addressed traditions such as Judaism and Islam, which were numerically smaller than the broader Christian heritage, they attracted less attention. Some female rabbis, for example, began to rethink the ways in which ancient practices regarding women that many found oppressive might actually become liberating by elevating women to a unique place within Jewish life. Muslim feminist thinkers sought to counter popular perceptions that Islam denigrated women, finding in the Qur'an a basis for the dignity and rights of women. All these endeavors provide yet another perspective on the close ties between gender and contemporary American religion that we explored in Chapter 10.

Ethnic community in Latino and Mujerista religious thought

The surge in Latin American immigration following immigration law reform in 1965 (about which we shall say more in Chapters 18 and 19) added other dimensions of lived experience to the theological enterprise. Latino thinkers, when they addressed issues of oppression of an economically disadvantaged minority and an ethnic group subject to discrimination, found resources in black theology and the liberation theology originating in Hispanic circles. They also engaged in conversation with the larger theological tradition, despite its Eurocentric bias. The result was a Latino theology that made ethnic identity the starting point. Thinkers such as Roberto S. Goizueta and Alejandro García-Rivera (1951–2011) emphasized the sense of community central to American Latino/a ethnic identity as a basis to talk about not only human relationships but also theological constructs such as the kingdom of God. Highlighting community did not mean minimizing diversity. On the contrary, in part because they were aware of the rich diversity among Latino immigrants and their native cultures, they used community as a metaphor for a place that sheltered and honored diversity rather than eradicating it. The resulting diversity amid unity becomes a thing of beauty, even as God's reign is a thing of beauty.

Historical theologians began to redirect understanding of how Christian thought might look if the starting point were the Hispanic experience, not the long dominant Eurocentric one. Justo L. González (1937–) has been at the forefront of efforts to refract theology through a Hispanic prism. Much of González' work captures the standard story of the history of Christianity and of Christian thought, but more recent efforts have turned traditional interpretation upside down by making a Third-World perspective the norm for exploring both history and thought.

The popular mind links Latino culture with images of macho men and subordinate women. Consequently Latina women argued that even Hispanic theology cannot speak to the experience of women if it makes the Latino male posture normative. The result is Mujerista theology. Ada María Isasi-Díaz (1943–2012), an early advocate of Mujerista thought, insists that the daily lives of women, including childrearing and homemaking along with other labor, present the most fruitful starting point for a theology that honors the Latina experience. In much Mujerista thought, family becomes the model for community, and the critical role of women in sustaining family life in turn becomes the crucible in which genuine community – the reign of God – is found.

Latino and Mujerista thought is poised to push religious thought in new directions in the twenty-first century. Census figures indicate that persons of Latino/a origin and descent constitute the largest ethnic minority in the US, with African Americans now the second largest. As immigration continues to swell the ranks of the Latino/a population, a matter to which we shall return in Chapter 19, the centrality of this ethnic cluster to American life will increase. So too will efforts of Latino and Mujerista theologians to make the lived experience of Hispanic Americans the fulcrum for religious thought. Demographers also point to a far higher population growth rate in Central and South America (and in Africa and other areas south of the equator) than in the US. Global interconnectedness will increase the ties between American religious culture and lands to the south in the western hemisphere. So too the way Americans construct religious thought will become more Latino/a in nuance as these global connections are cemented.

Voices overlooked: gay and lesbian religious thought

Black theology, feminist religious thought, and Latino/a constructions were only the beginning of the theological revolution of the later twentieth century. In the summer of 1969, for example, a group of homosexuals, taking their cue from the non-violent resistance of the civil rights movement and from feminist calls for women's liberation, launched another movement. They spontaneously responded to a police raid in June 1969 on the Stonewall Inn, a gay bar in New York City's Greenwich Village, resisting arrest and rioting in the streets. The gay liberation movement was born. Several months earlier, in October 1968, Troy Perry (1940–), a former Pentecostal preacher, held the first worship service of what has become a global denomination ministering primarily to gays, lesbians, bisexuals, and transgender persons, the Universal Fellowship of Metropolitan Community Churches. Within a decade, theologians began producing works of religious thought based on the lived experience of gay men and lesbians.

Much gay and lesbian theology draws on feminist awareness that sexuality is critical to human experience and how one views the world. At the same time, it acknowledges that the oppression addressed by black theology and feminist thought still marginalized them because of their sexual identity. For gay men, responding to the HIV/AIDS pandemic in the 1980s added a different appreciation of suffering, leading many to turn to writings about the Holocaust and to wrestle with theodicy (a technical term that asks why God allows good people to suffer) in their search for a theological posture that spoke from and to the realities they encountered. At the same time, lesbians understood that their lived experience had dimensions not shared by gay men; society still privileged men and oppressed women. Out of this ferment came a host of efforts to rethink traditional doctrine and belief.

Several thinkers sustained the revolution in religious thought associated with gay male experience. John E. Fortunato's *Embracing the Exile* (1982) highlighted the psychological suffering experienced by gay men marginalized by religious communities; his later work addressed the dimension of suffering encountered by gay men because of the AIDS pandemic. In both, he found parallels to the notion of suffering central to much early African American theology. Connections between gay theology and liberation theology came to the forefront in *A Place to Start: Toward an Unapologetic Gay Liberation Theology* (1989) by J. Michael Clark (1953–). In other work, Clark

Figure 17.2 The Rev. Troy Perry, founder of the Universal Fellowship of Metropolitan
Community Churches, encouraged gay, lesbian, bisexual, and transgender
Christians to develop a theology that joined their sexuality with their faith.

© ZUMA Wire Service/Alamy

linked the lived experience of gay men to ecological and environmental concerns, as
did Daniel T. Spencer (1957–) in *God and Gaia* (1996). Another effort to filter the
broad Christian theological tradition through a Protestant gay male perspective came
in the work of Gary David Comstock (1945–). His *Gay Theology without Apology*
(1993) addressed many characteristic themes transmitted through the theological
tradition from a gay stance.

Gay Catholic theologians began challenging church teaching, offering alternative
ways to understand biblical texts thought to condemn homosexual practice and
traditional Catholic positions on homosexuality. Vatican II had given gay Catholics
hope that church teaching might be revised in light of newer insights into the nature
of homosexuality. John J. McNeill (1925–), one of the founders of the New York City
Dignity chapter in 1974, entered the fray with his book, *The Church and the
Homosexual* (1976). Soon he was ordered by Vatican authorities no longer to speak
publicly about homosexuality. In 1988, when McNeill refused to heed the order from
Cardinal Joseph Ratzinger (now Pope Benedict XVI) to stop his ministry with
homosexuals, he was expelled from the Jesuit order. Robert E. Goss, who left the
Jesuits in 1978, took more radical positions in his *Jesus Acted Up: A Gay Manifesto*
(1993) and *Queering Christ* (2002). In time, Goss left the Catholic fold, affiliating
with the Universal Fellowship of Metropolitan Community Churches.

Lesbian theologians, however, found that most writing by gay male theologians,
despite efforts to be inclusive, still made male experience the springboard for the

---

Box 17.3 Coming out as the experience of salvation

Gay theologian Gary David Comstock gave fresh interpretation to many traditional theological categories when he advanced a theological perspective starting with the lived experience of gay men. In the excerpt that follows, he likens the experience of "coming out" – of a person's unashamedly affirming a gay sexual identity – to the traditional experience of salvation. For Comstock, both endow the individual with new life, one that is complete and whole, for one no longer denies who one is, but accepts the self as loved by God:

> We know that our coming out affects other people, but we cannot control who will be affected or how they will be affected. Certain ways or actions do not guarantee certain effects. We cannot plan or shape our coming out to maximize its effect on others. We can only come out with regard for the talents, gifts, favor, [and] grace that have been entrusted to us. Only by living our individuality to the full, by anchoring ourselves in our own humanity, do we live for the good of others, become a bridge to others. And we do not always get to choose who those others may be or what form the goodness or bridge may take. We save and are saved by others when we insist on taking ourselves and others seriously. But we take ourselves and one another seriously without the purpose, expectation, or guarantee of saving others. We do this simply for the love of ourselves and the satisfaction of living fully among others. The moments of salvation come when most needed – not decided, planned, or arranged by us, but surprising, stretching, helping, changing, saving us.
>
> (From G.D. Comstock, *Gay Theology without Apology*,
> Cleveland, OH: Pilgrim, 1993, p. 134)

---

theological enterprise. The societal and religious power exerted by men, both heterosexual and homosexual, represented a major stumbling block for lesbians seeking to affirm their own identity as non-heterosexual women. Mainline Protestant theologian Carter Heyward (1945–) addressed issues of power from a lesbian perspective as early as the 1980s. Similar concerns lay behind writings informed by a more evangelical understanding that ignored women and oppressed lesbians. Virginia Ramey Mollenkott (1932–) articulated a lesbian theology shaped by evangelical understanding, insisting – much to the consternation of many male evangelical theologians – that a careful reading of scripture validated lesbian love. Catholic thinkers also made contributions, initially hoping, as had gay male Catholic thinkers, that the recasting of Catholic teaching prompted by Vatican II would open doors for lesbian Catholics to make their lived experience an accepted basis for Catholic thought. Much of the early work developing a Catholic perspective came from Mary E. Hunt (1951–). Other dimensions of the larger context for developing religious thought from a self-consciously gay and lesbian experience came under examination in Chapter 10.

If feminist religious thought made gender critical to the theological enterprise, gay and lesbian theology made sexuality central. Both efforts solidified the movement in religious thought away from doctrines and categories handed down over centuries. Black theology launched that shift to lived experience when it made race the starting point for the theological enterprise. Latino and Mujerista thinkers added ethnicity to the lived realities that theologians must take into account. By the second decade of the twenty-first century, religious thought in America had undergone a major refocusing, one that began in the 1960s. It seemed increasingly unlikely that anyone would again contemplate tackling a complete systematic theology along the lines of Paul Tillich's work that marked the 1950s and early 1960s. Experience had trumped tradition.

Key points you need to know

- The social ferment of the 1960s brought about major shifts in religious thought.
- Most important was a movement away from regarding theology as a received body of doctrine and instead looking to lived experience as the starting point.
- Some of the first efforts to make experience central led to black theology, building on the lived experience of African Americans from slavery through racism.
- A strong influence came from liberation theology originating in Latin America.
- Feminist thinkers began to challenge patriarchal assumptions and exclusive use of male-gendered language in traditional theology.
- African American women recognized that black theology and white feminist thought ignored their unique experience as black women, crafting Womanist theology in response.
- Others marginalized by a white male-dominated theological tradition developed their own theological works, based on their lived experience.
- Latino and Mujerista thinkers drew on their ethnic heritage to find fresh resources for theology.
- Gay males and lesbians made sexual identity central to religious thought.

Discussion questions

1 In what ways did black theology and Womanist theology speak to the unique experience of African American men and women? How and why is the idea of liberation central to both? Why did Womanist thinkers find black theology and white feminist theology inadequate?
2 How did feminist theology both build on and differ from the liberation theology that informed African American thought? What are the distinctive emphases of feminist thought?
3 What gave rise to the development of Latino and of Mujerista religious thought? How are they related to other newer theological currents such as African American theology and feminist religious thought?
4 What fresh contributions to religious thought came from gay and lesbian thinkers?

5   How and why has lived experience replaced received doctrine and categories as the basis for doing theology? What are the implications of this shift for the theological enterprise?

6   How do recent trends in American religious thought relate to changes and developments in the larger culture? How do thought and culture interact in a symbiotic relationship with each other?

Further reading

Cannon, K. (1988) *Black Womanist Ethics*, Atlanta: Scholars Press.

Comstock, G.D. (1993) *Gay Theology without Apology*, Cleveland, OH: Pilgrim.

Cone, J.H. and Wilmore, G.S. (eds.) (1992) *Black Theology: A Documentary History*, 2 vols., Maryknoll, NY: Orbis Books.

García-Rivera, A. (1999) *The Community of the Beautiful: A Theological Aesthetics*, Collegeville, MN: Liturgical Press.

Goizeuta, R.S. (1995) *Cominemos con Jesús: A Latino/a Theology of Accompaniment*, Maryknoll, NY: Orbis Books.

González, J. (1990) *Mañana: Christian Theology from a Hispanic Perspective*, Nashville, TN: Abingdon.

Heyward, C. (1984) *Our Passion for Justice: Images of Power, Sexuality, and Liberation*, New York: Pilgrim.

Isasi-Díaz, A.M. (1996) *Mujerista Theology: A Theology for the Twenty-First Century*, Maryknoll, NY: Orbis Books.

Mollenkott, V.R. (1992) *Sensuous Spirituality: Out from Fundamentalism*, New York: Crossroad.

Parsons, S.F. (ed.) (2002) *Cambridge Companion to Feminist Theology*, Cambridge: Cambridge University Press.

Ruether, R.R. (2007) *Feminist Theologies: Legacy and Prospect*, Minneapolis, MN: Fortress.

18 A new pluralism comes to America

In this chapter

This chapter examines the growth of religions such as Islam, Buddhism, and Hinduism. The first section looks at these religions in American life in the 1950s. Attention turns next to the impact of the 1960s, particularly the war in Vietnam and changes in immigration law. The increasing presence of Hinduism and Buddhism forms the focus for the third section, while the rise of Islam in America comes under analysis in the fourth. The last section suggests the consequences of this new pluralism, especially when joined with the expanding influence of Latino/a religious styles.

Major topics covered

- Intellectual interest in Asian religions in postwar America.
- How the civil rights movement and the Vietnam War kindled interest in Asian spirituality.
- The impact of immigration law changes in the 1960s.
- The "new religious pluralism" that challenges the dominance of the Judeo-Christian family.
- Issues these newer immigrant religions face in American culture.
- The consequences of the "new pluralism" for American religious culture.
- How and why it is easy to overlook the presence of some non-western religions.

Beyond the Judeo-Christian tradition in the 1950s

Prior to World War II, few Americans had more than a passing intellectual interest in the religions of Asia. When European empires expanded in the eighteenth century, scholars began to examine tests or scriptures held sacred by religions there and made them more generally available. In the nineteenth century, Christian missionaries disseminated additional information about these religions. Modest immigration from Japan and China had brought small Asian communities to some western states by the mid nineteenth century. But by the early 1880s, hostility to "Orientals" had led the US Congress to limit Asian immigration and, in some cases, prohibit it altogether. Such exclusion continued when a restrictive quota system became national policy after World War I.

An early breakthrough came in 1893 when the World's Parliament of Religions convened in Chicago. Held in conjunction with a world's fair marking the four-hundredth anniversary of Columbus's "discovery" of America, the gathering brought to the US representatives of major religious traditions from around the world. Some remained in the US for a time, lecturing in urban centers about their religions. A handful of new religious or quasi-religious movements resulted, but most attracted only a few with a purely intellectual interest in the new teachings, combining it with participation in other religious groups. The Theosophical Society and Vedanta Society are two examples.

Military efforts in the Pacific during World War II brought new exposure to Asian ways of life. Thousands of "war brides" joined spouses returning home after the war. American occupation of Japan, which lasted until 1952, spurred appreciation of Japanese culture, including approaches such as Zen that the Japanese adapted from Chinese forms.

Some awareness of Japanese Zen Buddhism resulted from the work of Japanese scholar D.T. Suzuki (1870–1966). Suzuki deftly explained Zen concepts in ways that Americans and other westerners could understand. He also connected Zen thinking to popular psychology. His *Introduction to Zen Buddhism*, first published in 1930, attracted a vast readership when an edition with a foreword by psychologist Carl Jung appeared in 1948. Writers of the "Beat Generation" also popularized Zen concepts. Among the more prominent were Jack Kerouac (1922–69) and Allen Ginsberg (1926–97). Philosopher Alan Watts (1915–73) and the prolific Joseph Campbell (1904–87) may have introduced even more Americans to Asian ways of being religious.

Watts, born in Britain, came to the US in 1938. He already had some contact with London Theosophical circles, heard Suzuki lecture, and experienced moments of ecstasy that he likened to both Zen notions and the mystical experiences described by some medieval Christians. After studying at an Episcopal seminary, Watts became a priest for a time. Consequently, he blended popular understandings of Christianity with Zen. Critics thought Watts oversimplified both, but for millions of Americans, Watts offered a heightened spiritual reality. Campbell exhibited similar abilities in his landmark studies of comparative mythology. Drawing on his training in art history, medieval studies, and philosophy, Campbell produced bestsellers that took readers through a maze of cultures, identifying similarities and differences among religions. At the end of the maze for Campbell lay absolute truth.

None, however, anticipated the fascination with Asian religiosity that swept across the US in the 1960s. Some emerged from the cultural disarray generated by the civil rights movement, and some from the Vietnam War. Much also stemmed from the "new immigration" after 1965.

Rediscovering the East

Pursuing Asian forms of spirituality with more than a cursory intellectual interest was one hallmark of American culture in the 1960s. Some of the intrigue came from popular culture. When the Beatles became associated with the Maharishi Mahesh Yogi (1917–2008), millions of Americans flocked to Transcendental Meditation (TM) centers to learn the Maharishi's technique. TM was tailor-made for Americans; it could be practiced anywhere at any time and for as little as ten or fifteen minutes. Nor did it require abandoning other religious affiliations or commitments. One simply added TM to whatever spiritual discipline one already found meaningful.

In 1965, His Grace Swami Bhaktivedanta Prabhupada (1896–1977) brought his message of Krishna to the US. In Chapter 13, we mentioned his International Society for Krishna Consciousness (ISKCON), or Hare Krisha as it was generally called after the mantra its devotees chanted. But this movement and a host of others differed from earlier Asian phenomena such as the Vedanta Society and the Theosophical Society. These newer groups actively sought American converts from among those alienated from a society torn apart by the civil rights movement, the Vietnam War, and other social issues. Converts did not just dabble with philosophical ideas, but practiced their new-found faith.

Part of the attraction of such groups was that they seemed divorced from the turmoil of American society. Traditional religion, including the mainline denominations, seemed complicit in the racism and hypocrisy that critics found everywhere. Asian religious alternatives appeared fresh and untainted by the issues cluttering American society. Mired in myriad social problems in Asia, they came across in the US as pure, a more viable way of providing meaning in life for those repulsed by the imperfections of American religious culture.

In 1965 came another harbinger of a future in which different religions would assume increasing importance. That year, President Lyndon Johnson signed the Immigration and Nationality Act, popularly called the Hart-Celler Act. The law overhauled immigration guidelines in place for more than forty years. Restrictions

Figure 18.1 When popular culture icons like the Beatles linked themselves to the Maharishi
             Mahesh Yogi, shown together here in this 1967 photo, interest in Transcendental
             Meditation soared

first enacted in the 1920s had been revamped several times, but the rationale behind them remained constant. Quotas on the total number of immigrants who could enter the country in any given year joined with quotas based on nation of origin to favor a modest immigration from northern and western Europe.

The greatest limits fell on immigration from Asia, Africa, and Latin America. Fewer persons from those areas were in the US in 1890, the year used to set figures for each nation. Exceptions were possible, but conditions for them limited. The rethinking in the 1960s resulted in part from an increase in exceptions for political refugees from Vietnam and other areas of Asia. Awareness that the policies in place were antiquated also encouraged change.

Johnson observed that the new law would make little difference to the fabric of American life. Neither he nor Congressional leaders envisioned what transpired. The law made possible a surge in immigration and major shifts in sources of immigrants. When the twenty-first century began, total numbers were surpassing those of the pre-World War I years, long the highpoint in immigration. The largest numbers, both documented and undocumented, came from Mexico, Central America, and South America. The numbers coming from Africa, the Near East, and Asia also increased dramatically.

Like earlier generations, these "new immigrants" brought their religions with them, an issue examined further in Chapter 19. So alongside groups like Krishna Consciousness, intent on seeking converts, hundreds of thousands of Hindus came from India, planting their own styles of Hindu devotion in the US. Asian Buddhists came to American shores, fusing ethnic identity and religious practice in their new home. Smaller numbers of Sikhs and Jains joined them. Equally stunning and vital for ongoing trends was the steady growth of Islam, reflecting the larger numbers of immigrants coming from Muslim nations in the Middle East, Asia, and Africa. Together, they created what historian of religion Diana Eck called "a new religious America."

The Pluralism Project at Harvard University, directed by Eck, has tracked the growth of these religious communities, recognizing that the numbers suggested are estimates. Some do not count members in the same way as, for example, mainline Protestants. Others represent groups so small that they meet in private homes, not in well-identified buildings. Consequently, they are easily overlooked or underestimated. Many Asian immigrants have ties to some form of Christianity, organizing their own congregations within their denominations or simply affiliating with existing churches.

Among Asian groups, Buddhism has shown the fastest rate of growth because of immigration. The Pluralism Project estimates that in 1970, just five years after immigration law changed, the US was home to only 200,000 Buddhists, of whom some were American converts or part-time practitioners. By 2010, there were around four million, or about double the number of Episcopalians in America. The number may be higher if one includes those Thomas Tweed dubbed "night-stand Buddhists." Tweed uses this term to refer to persons (virtually all non-Asians) who may have read casually about Buddhism or heard something about the character of the tradition and found something appealing about it, but are not part of any Buddhist institution even if they self-identify as Buddhists.

No single organizational structure embraces all American Buddhists. The Buddhist Churches of America, for example, has a name that sometimes leads outsiders to assume it is an umbrella organization for US Buddhists. This group, however, stems

---

Box 18.1 The Buddha and Buddhism

Buddhism emerged in India in the sixth century BCE from the teachings of Siddhartha Gautama, called the Buddha or the enlightened one. The Buddha's teachings built on the Hindu tradition, but sought to be more inclusive and less tied to the caste system. The Four Noble Truths summarize his main teachings. Buddhists often describe them as experiences central to human life rather than beliefs:

- Life is suffering.
- The cause of suffering is attachment to things, feelings or craving for what can never bring peace.
- That attachment can be ended and happiness (eternal bliss for some Buddhists) found.
- The way to do so is to follow an eight-fold path, whose mastery may take many lifetimes.

Buddhism spread quickly through much of south and east Asia, adapting to the cultures of areas it penetrated. Many Buddhist schools or sects developed. Three main families are Mahayana, which is the most expansive and inclusive; Theravada, which attempts to cling to the earliest Buddhist ways; and Vajrayana, which emerged primarily in Tibet.

---

from nineteenth-century immigrant Buddhists who migrated to the US via Hawaii. They adopted the name in order to look more American when everything Asian became suspect during World War II. Immigrants from Korea, Japan, and Taiwan tend to identify with forms of the Mahayana school within the Buddhist heritage; those from Sri Lanka, Cambodia, and Vietnam are more likely to align with the Theravada tradition. A third major strand includes those drawn to Tibetan Buddhism, given credibility because of the popularity of the Dalai Lama (1935–) in the US and its association with celebrities such as Richard Gere.

In every case, distinctive styles and practices reflect the place of practitioners' origins. Hence, pundits observe that no two Buddhists are alike in their beliefs and practices. For many Americans attracted to Buddhism, the practice of meditation remains basic; for many immigrant Buddhists, regardless of land of origin, the rigors of meditation are reserved for monks rather than laypersons. Buddhists are also not of one mind about whether to regard the Buddha as something like a deity. In daily life, most immigrant Buddhists, except those from the narrowest Theravada groups, look to the Buddha for guidance and strength, but may not worship him. By the second decade of the twenty-first century, virtually every American city had Buddhist temples. Some serve the immigrant faithful based on national origin and ethnicity; others cater primarily to American converts. Temple participation has never been as central to being Buddhist in the way that belonging to and participating in a congregation are central to most American Christians.

The Hindu tradition has also increased dramatically since immigration law changed. Except for a few thousand converts drawn to groups such as ISKCON, most US Hindus are recent immigrants and their descendants. Unlike Buddhism, Christianity, or Islam, Hinduism is not a proselytizing tradition – with the exception of new movements like ISKCON. That is, it never actively seeks converts, but sees itself as almost synonymous with being Indian. Being Hindu is thus usually a matter of birth.

Box 18.2 What is Hinduism?

With roots in the Indus river valley as early as the fourth century BCE, the Hindu tradition has no single founder. Rather it evolved along with Indian culture, adding layer after layer. Over the centuries, some distinguishing characteristics have surfaced:

- Although the divine may be One, deity takes countless forms, depending on situations, people, and place. Hindus often speak of three major manifestations: Brahma, Vishnu, and Siva. The familiar Krishna, for example, is an avatar or manifestation of Vishnu.
- All actions have consequences, though some may not be realized until a future life. Karma is the word describing actions; *samsara* refers to the seemingly endless cycle of birth and rebirth.
- That cycle can be ended if one truly does one's duty (*dharma*); that duty is contingent on the circumstances of one's birth, an idea that led to the development of the caste system. Caste sees different duty or dharma for different castes of people. Caste is not the same as socioeconomic class, although traditionally occupation is linked to caste.
- The religiosity of most ordinary Hindu folk is expressed in practices associated with *puja*, or devotion, that might include prayer and chanting at home, seeking a blessing from a priest at a temple, or making an offering to one's god(s).

Many regional variants mark the Hindu tradition in India. Different manifestations of deity are popular in different places; festivals and much mythology reflect the ethos of a particular region, with the form of the god(s) and stories about the god(s) echoing that ethos. Immigrants bring that cultural and religious baggage with them. However, in the US, Hindu temples often serve immigrant families from several regions, even if the majority comes from one; several gods may have images installed in them.

By 2010, most American cities had at least one Hindu temple. The temple in Chattanooga, TN, for example, served more than 700 families, primarily from the Indian state of Gujarat, where Mumbai is located. Organized in 1983 as the Gujarati Samaj of East Tennessee, the temple purchased its building from a Baptist congregation. When the temple opened in 1996, images of several Hindu deities were installed. Less than 175 miles away, the temple in Nashville, constructed in 1985, is dedicated to Ganesh, one of the most popular Hindu divine manifestations. Unlike temples in India, both are also cultural centers, offering programs to sustain an Indian American identity and a Hindu consciousness that go well beyond religion. Many American temples have this dual function. Consequently, Hindu families in the US may actually have greater association with a temple-cultural center than they would in India, where a Hindu aura infuses the entire society.

The expanding role of the Hindu temple in the American context echoes the changing role of the synagogue in American Judaism. For both traditions, spirituality centers on the home. Most Hindu homes have a space or even a room set aside for *puja* or devotion; images of the gods provide a focus for prayer and chanting. In India, one visits temples primarily to make an offering or receive a blessing. In Judaism, what transpires in the home is also foundational; synagogues emerged as places for studying Torah and for prayer. However, as American Jewish families became dispersed throughout the population, the social network supporting home-based practice weakened; synagogues became places of worship and often cultural centers, not just forums for study and prayer. In many places, several synagogues cooperated in organizing a Jewish community center that served all Jews, regardless of ethnicity or congregation. The synagogue and community center provided a link to the pre-immigrant past, just as Hindu temples help sustain an Indian identity.

The number of Hindus in the US remains rather modest. The Pluralism Project claims that around 100,000 Hindus lived in the US in 1970 and just over two million in 2010. The latter figure means, however, that there are more than three and a half times as many Hindus in America as there are members of the Disciples of Christ, a mainline Protestant denomination. In addition, the educational attainment of Indian immigrants is high; a disproportionately large number of Indian Hindu families is in the upper middle and upper economic classes. Immigration trends suggest that both Hinduism and Buddhism will grow at a more rapid rate than the general population. The same holds for two other religious groups with historical roots on the Indian subcontinent, Jainism and Sikhism, although their numbers remain small.

Figure 18.2 The Rajdhani Mandir temple in Chantilly, VA, serves hundreds of Hindu immigrant families in suburban Washington, DC

Courtesy of AFP/Getty Images

The growing Islamic presence in America

We have already noted how some African Americans identified with the Nation of Islam, especially in the era of the civil rights movement, and how some, following Malcolm X after his return from the pilgrimage to Mecca, came to affirm a non-separatist expression of Islam. But the stunning growth of Islam in the US since 1965 has come primarily from immigration, although analysts note a growing interest of African Americans in the Islamic tradition.

Like other immigrants, Muslims have tended to settle in areas where there is a Muslim presence, often earlier immigrants from the same place of origin. Dearborn, MI, for example, has boasted a significant Arab American population since the nineteenth century, persons of Arab descent accounting for nearly one-third of its population in 2010. Since most Arabs are Muslims, it is no surprise that the largest mosque in the US is in Dearborn.

Persons emigrating from Muslim nations span the socioeconomic spectrum, although many come from well-educated, professional backgrounds. Some left their lands of origin because of political turmoil there. For example, the Iranian Revolution in the late 1970s prompted many Westernized Iranians to come to America. So, too, continuing unrest in the Middle East has encouraged many Palestinian Muslims to immigrate to the US.

Much as Hinduism and Buddhism, Islam has faced challenges and had to adapt to the American environment. Like Hindu temples, mosques have often become Islamic cultural centers, drawing Muslims who might otherwise prefer separate facilities. For example, many American mosques embrace both Shi'ite and Sunni Muslims from a variety of national backgrounds; elsewhere they would remain separate. Participating in Friday prayer services is routine for Muslim men in an Islamic culture; in the US, many are unable to do so. Some communities have too few Muslims to sustain a mosque; many employers have yet to accommodate Muslims in terms of daily times of prayer and Friday services.

Muslim growth surged as second-wave feminism gripped hold in American culture. Images of Muslim women wearing a chador, a scarf-like fabric covering the head that is looped closed in the front, or a burqa, which covers the entire face and body, reinforce popular American perceptions that Islam subjugates women to a second-class status, denies them rights, and degrades their humanity. The Qur'an calls for respect for women, but presents visions of paradise, rewards for the faithful, and status within society that grant superior standing to men. But such do not necessarily denigrate women. The Qur'an grants women some rights, such as inheritance, denied to them in the Arab world of Muhammad's day. It also frowns on practices such as prostitution that shatter women's dignity.

Some American Muslim women insist that to presume Islam denigrates women is a mistake. Perhaps because American culture does not reinforce much Muslim tradition regarding gender roles, American Muslim women exhibit more diversity and freedom. Many see Islam as assuring that women are treated with dignity. Few wear a burqa, although many wear some head covering in public and accept male leadership within the family. Organizations such as the Association of Muslim Women in America are working to assure that Muslim women have full equality with men within Muslim communities, especially in terms of education. A few, however, still affirm traditional roles for American Muslim women.

Box 18.3 The face of Islam

Like Christianity and Judaism, Islam emerged in the Near East. Its founder, Muhammad (c. 570–632 CE) lived on the Arabian peninsula and received the core teachings of Islam in revelation received from God (Allah is the Arabic word for God) in the area around the city of Mecca. Those teachings form the basis of the Qur'an or holy/sacred book of Islam. The Five Pillars summarize Islam's foundational teachings:

Shahada: Belief that there is no God but God and that Muhammad is the prophet of God.
Salah: prayer five times daily facing in the direction of Mecca.
Zakat: charitable giving to help the poor and support the mosque.
Sawm: fasting during the daylight hours of the holy month of Ramadan.
Hajj: a pilgrimage to the holy city of Mecca at least once in one's lifetime.

As Islam developed, spreading throughout much of the Middle East, northern Africa, and even into Europe in the centuries after Muhammad's death, countless sects or branches emerged. *Sunni* Muslims comprise one large cluster today, although there are many varieties of Sunnis. The Five Pillars above are most closely associated with Sunni. The other large cluster is *Shia*. For Shi'ite Muslims, the Five Pillars are sometimes given as strict monotheism, belief in justice, affirmation that God (Allah) sends prophets to guide humanity, a conviction that leaders called imams now exercise the same leadership as the prophets, and an understanding that all face a final judgment by God.

Also central to Islam is a tradition of law or guidelines that govern daily life. For Muslims, no aspect of life lacks religious significance. In some nations where a large majority of the population embraces Islam, religious law and civil law are not distinct.

Most American Muslims support traditional Islamic teaching on homosexuality, believing that the Qur'an explicitly condemns it. Mosques and other Muslim organizations have marginalized or excluded gay and lesbian Muslims. Although many conservative Christians are wary of Islam, with some even insisting that it is not a legitimate religion, few attack Islam because of its hostility towards homosexuals; conservative Christians, as noted earlier, also likely believe that their sacred text, the Bible, condemns homosexual activity.

Historically, Islam, like Christianity has been a proselytizing religion. Convinced that it contains God's final revelation to humanity, Islam has sought to gain converts. In the US, however, circumstances have muted that effort. The widespread association of Islam with violence and terrorism has made Muslims reluctant to proselytize. Prompted by the terrorist attacks of 11 September 2001, millions of Americans harbor hostility toward Islam and toward all Muslims, echoing earlier anti-Catholicism and anti-Semitism and based on similar irrational fears. Some polls, for example, show that more than 40 per cent of non-Muslim Americans believe that Muslims are by definition terrorists and therefore never loyal citizens. They presume that all Muslims

Figure. 18.3 The Muslim faithful here fill the Los Angeles Convention Center for morning
prayer on Eid ul-Fitr, the holiday marking the end of the holy month of Ramadan

Courtesy of Kevork Djansezian/Getty Images

are extremists or fundamentalists, failing to see Islam as a faith operating just as other
traditions do.

The depth of anti-Muslim sentiment became evident in 2010 when Muslim leaders
announced plans to build a mosque and an Islamic community center near the former
World Trade Center. Opponents condemned not only the plan, but Islam itself. In
addition, in 2010, those outraged at the prospect of a mosque's being built in
Murfreesboro, TN, burned equipment in an effort to thwart construction. One group
sought to block further building in court, arguing that Islam was not a religion, but a
terrorist ideology. In late 2010, after authorities had arrested a young terrorist hoping
to disrupt a holiday ceremony in Portland, OR, by detonating what he thought was a
bomb, angry citizens burned a nearby mosque in retaliation. Scores of Muslims and
Muslim organizations report regularly receiving hate mail and other threats.

Also hindering aggressive proselytizing is awareness that few Americans understand
Islam's links to Judaism and Christianity. The level of ignorance challenges efforts to
gain converts. However, as the Islamic presence in the US has grown, even after 9/11,
efforts to convert Muslims to Christianity, especially by those inclined to conservative
evangelical views, have also grown. Occasionally, however, signs indicate that
Americans are slowly beginning to accept Muslims as part of the nation's religious
culture. For example, the White House has hosted celebrations marking Eid, the end
of Ramadan, since 1996, and Minnesotans in 2006 elected a Muslim to serve in the
US House of Representatives.

In time, Islam may grow in much the same way as Catholicism grew in the early
twentieth century, mitigating fear and bringing greater acceptance. The number of

American Muslims means that the tradition cannot be ignored. Figures from the Pluralism Project suggest that in 1970, approximately 800,000 Muslims lived in the US. By 2010, some analysts put that figure as high as six million; others claimed that four million was more accurate. Regardless, this rate of growth means that in the second decade of the twenty-first century Islam is among the ten largest religious groups in the nation and perhaps among the five largest.

Challenges to new immigrant religions

The new religious pluralism has added to the diversity of religious groups flourishing in the US. It has also influenced how Americans understand religion and ways of being religious. For those who compartmentalize religion, seeing it as only one aspect of life, both the Hindu and Muslim approaches are starkly different. Since Hinduism is virtually synonymous with Indian culture and Islam, like traditional Judaism, makes many civil or secular matters part of religious practice, the new pluralism encourages rethinking as to how religion relates to daily life.

Theological issues also complicate our understanding of religions whose growth depends on post-1965 immigration. School curricula offer one example. Textbooks designed for use in American schools, for example, frequently describe religion through categories appropriate to Christianity and Judaism – and perhaps Islam. Buddhism is one example of a religion that does not fit these categories. Since many Buddhists do not see the Buddha as divine or even posit belief in a god, school materials describing the Buddha as the "god" of this tradition distort the religion's essence. In addition, schools and businesses that close or excuse persons for being absent on religious holidays are challenged to accommodate different religious calendars. American society ignores a host of holidays and times for daily prayer in Islam, for example. Practitioners of religions thus marginalized raise issues of "free exercise" guarantee in the First Amendment to the Constitution when they experience such discrimination.

The American environment also forces adaptation and change, just as it did in the past with Catholicism and Judaism. In India, for example, where at least 80 per cent of the population identifies as Hindu, a Hindu aura pervades society as a whole. In the US, Hindus are one group among many; little in the culture nurtures a Hindu identity. The same holds true for Buddhists emigrating from nations where some style of Buddhism is part of the unconscious identity of the people and for Muslims coming from nations where Islamic law governs not only religious life, but also civic and public life. A pluralistic environment allows these groups to make their way into American life, but offers little support for a Muslim, Hindu, or Buddhist worldview.

It is sometimes easy to overlook the depth of the new pluralism because the numbers of adherents of some traditions remain small and their presence goes unnoticed outside of ethnic enclaves. Because many of those with Asian roots have never actively sought converts, they may escape notice. For example, except in larger cities, the Sikh and Jain communities are almost invisible, although immigrant families and their descendants may regularly gather for religious and social purposes. There are too few to attract public attention.

The full impact of this new pluralism requires including the Latino/a immigration discussed in earlier chapters and in Chapter 19. Not to be overlooked as well is the slow but steady growth of Eastern Orthodox Christian traditions. Although there was a Russian Orthodox presence in Alaska before the end of the eighteenth century, Orthodox Christianity's period of greatest growth, before the recent immigration, came in the major wave of immigration just prior to World War I. Since 1965, Orthodox Christian denominations have grown, with newer immigrants tending to come to areas where there were already stable communities of the same ethnic heritage.

Immigrants also brought the religious traditions that shaped earlier American culture. However, they came primarily from northern and western Europe. Consequently, the dominant religious influences maintained a European focus, and American religious communities often linked their own heritage with their European counterparts. The new immigration, however, undermines that European bias. Slowly, a more global perspective, one oriented to Asia, Latin America, and Africa, is replacing the Eurocentric understanding of religion that has long undergirded American life. In time, that may be the most significant impact of the new religious pluralism. It also raises questions about the extent to which it is appropriate to describe the US as a "Christian" nation, a matter discussed in greater detail in the next chapter.

Key points you need to know

- Until after World War II, most American interest in religions outside the Judeo-Christian tradition was intellectual, not focused on religious practice.
- In the 1950s, awareness increased, primarily in literary and academic circles.
- In the 1960s, popular culture icons lured some to probe Asian spirituality, as did religious movements such as the International Society for Krishna Consciousness.
- Such movements were attractive because they were not associated with the social problems facing American society.
- Major changes followed enactment of a new immigration law in 1965.
- Hundreds of thousands of Buddhists and Hindus have since come from Asia to the US.
- As with earlier immigrants, Asians accommodated their religious styles to their new cultural setting.
- Islam also experienced extraordinary growth, thanks to immigration from the Near East and Africa.
- Muslim Americans have encountered hostility because of perceptions that Islam fosters terrorism and because others lack understanding of Islam as a religion.
- The Muslim experience is also different because of the tradition's commitment to gaining converts.
- Many misconstrue how Islam views women, seeing it as anti-feminist.
- Issues of sexuality haunt Islam as they do other religious traditions.
- The new pluralism challenges how Americans think about religion and what it means to be religious.
- Pluralism raises new issues about how a culture accommodates unfamiliar groups.

Discussion questions

1   Describe how Americans understood religious traditions other than Christianity and Judaism before World War II.
2   How did the World's Parliament of Religions expand American awareness of global religious life?
3   Discuss how American involvement in World War II, the Korean conflict, and then the Vietnam War changed how Americans viewed Asian religions.
4   Explain the role of persons such as Alan Watts and Joseph Campbell in awakening new interest in world religions.
5   What in American culture in the 1960s made Asian religions and spirituality attractive alternatives to religions like Christianity?
6   Analyze the impact of changes in immigration law enacted in 1965 on American religion. Why does Diana Eck believe this law fashioned "a new religious America"?
7   Describe the character of Buddhism and Hinduism in America. In what ways are their American expressions similar to and different from their Asian expressions?
8   Compare and contrast the experience of immigrant Buddhists, Hindus, and Muslims with that of Catholic and Jewish immigrants coming to the US between the Civil War and World War I.
9   What religious and cultural influences shape the development of Islam in the US?
10 Why do many Americans misunderstand Islam as a religion?
11 What challenges do "new immigrants" face as they plant their religious styles on American soil?
12 How has the "new pluralism" changed the religious landscape of America?

Further reading

Cadge, W. (2004) *Heartwood: The First Generation of Theravada Buddhism in America*, Chicago: University of Chicago Press.

Coleman, J.W. (2001) *The New Buddhism: The Western Transformation of an Ancient Tradition*, New York: Oxford University Press.

Eck, D.L. (2001) *A New Religious America: How a "Christian Country" Has Become the World's Most Religiously Diverse Nation*, San Francisco: HarperOne.

Forsthoefel, T.A. and Humes, C.A. (eds.) (2005) *Gurus in America*, Albany: State University of New York Press.

Gregory, P.N. and Mrozik, S. (2008) *Women Practicing Buddhism: American Experiences*, Boston: Wisdom Publications.

Haddad, Y.Y. (2006) *Muslim Women in America: The Challenge of Islamic Identity Today*, New York: Oxford University Press.

Hammond, P. and Machacek, D. (1999) *Soka Gakkai in America: Accommodation and Conversion*, New York: Oxford University Press.

Nyang, S. (1999) *Islam in the United States of America*, Chicago: Kazi Publications.

Prebish, C. and Tanaka, K. (eds.) (1999) *The Faces of Buddhism in America*, Berkeley: University of California Press.

Smith, J.I. (2000) *Islam in America*, New York: Columbia University Press.

Tweed, T.A. (2002) "Who Is a Buddhist? Night-Stand Buddhists and Other Creatures," in C. Prebish and M. Baumann (eds.), *Westward Dharma: Buddhism Beyond Asia*, Berkeley: University of California Press.

Waghorne, J.P. (2004) *Diaspora of the Gods: Modern Hindu Temples in an Urban Middle Class World*, New York: Oxford University Press.

Williams, R.B. (1988) *Religions of Immigrants from India and Pakistan: New Threads in the American Tapestry*, Cambridge: Cambridge University Press.

19 Is America a Christian nation?

Religious pluralism in the twenty-first century

In this chapter

As described in the previous chapter, religious diversity and pluralism have brought profound changes to contemporary religious America. We open this chapter by looking at connections between religion and national identity. We then focus on immigrant religions and how immigration is changing American religion. Next, we examine the tension caused by increasing religious diversity in American life. Then we explore how these issues remain connected to American identity and democracy in the popular mind, paying close attention to the question: "Is America a Christian nation?" When directly asked the question, the majority of Americans believe that America is a Christian nation. However, research done by sociologists and other scholars of religion reveals that the answer is a more complicated one and depends on how the question is defined and understood. We also explore tensions that arise from an understanding of America as a Christian nation, including widespread negative attitudes toward non-Christian religions and, in particular, toward atheists and others with no religious belief. We conclude by arguing that these debates and tensions reveal much about the future of religion in contemporary America.

Main topics covered

- How religion, especially Christianity, shapes American national identity, which has a rich, but sometimes complicated history.
- The religions of immigrants demonstrate the power and limits of the American ways of being religious and organizing religion.
- Immigration has profoundly shaped American religion, but instances of tension between religious groups have again become an increasingly common feature of American life.
- The majority of Americans believe that America is a Christian nation and that it is a good thing it is a Christian nation.
- There are many different ways of defining, and answering, the question "Is America a Christian nation?"
- There is a general acceptance of religious diversity. However, many Americans, especially Christians, have negative views of specific religious minorities, particularly Muslims.

- Americans often view atheists and other "religious nones" as being immoral or anti-religious.
- America has been, and will continue to be, a land of both religious pluralism and religious tension.

Religion and national identity

At least since the arrival of the first European settlers in what became the US, religion and the identity of the American peoples have been intertwined. For some colonists, a desire for religious freedom propelled their migration to what was then a "new world." The English Puritans who settled in New England, for example, were eager to be free from the strictures of the Church of England, but they did not welcome those who disagreed with their way of being religious. They saw themselves as erecting a "city on a hill" that would be a model to the world, but wanted to protect it from contamination by those whose religious views were different. So early on, Puritan authorities banished folks like Roger Williams and Anne Hutchinson in order to preserve their own religious identity.

Throughout the colonial period, however, the territories that became the US exhibited an increasing religious diversity. Much of that reflected the way Protestant Christianity itself was taking a variety of forms. So Dutch Lutherans brought their brand of Christianity to New Netherland, Swedish Lutherans brought theirs to what became New Jersey, German sectarians and Quakers flocked to Pennsylvania. In the Southern colonies, Anglicans dominated, but in time evangelicals made inroads there as they did in New England, Calvinistic Huguenots with roots in France arrived, and gradually Presbyterians, Baptists, and then Methodists came south along the eastern slopes of the Appalachians. Then, too, in early Maryland (and in Pennsylvania especially), Roman Catholics sought a home. Of course, wherever the Spanish and French settled, they brought their own brand of Catholicism with them. By the eighteenth century, when white colonial Christians sought to convert those forced to migrate from Africa as slaves, they helped create yet other expressions of Christianity that fused the tribal ways of being religious with Christian practice.

And Christians were far from the only ones who settled what became the US. Native Americans had long had their own indigenous forms of spirituality, even if they were often ignored by Europeans. Some African slaves brought a Muslim identity. As early as the mid seventeenth century, Jewish immigrants were adding another dimension to the diverse texture of colonial religious life.

To be sure, the dominant influence came from Christianity, but there was no single expression of Christianity or any one Christian religious group that could claim a majority as adherents by the time of national independence. But a religious substratum buttressed national identity. Founders like Benjamin Franklin and George Washington believed that religion was vital as the force that created moral and ethical citizens; particulars of belief mattered little to them. Here we find some of the roots of the "civil religion" that we discussed in Chapter 4. But many also shared an aversion to having a direct link between government and religion; except for some Anglicans, most disliked the idea of having an established church, as it was called, or one in which tax monies supported one specially privileged religious group and marginalized all the rest. Political leaders did not want an established church trying to influence government, and religious leaders feared that political figures would attempt to control belief and practice if there were an established church.

Thus when delegates gathered in Philadelphia in 1787 to frame the US Constitution, they made no reference to religion in the original document, other than to state that there could be no religious test or requirement as a qualification to hold national political office. But the American people wanted more. Hence the First Amendment, to which we have referred many times, stated directly that there could be no national religious establishment and that government could not prohibit the free exercise of personal religion.

But that did not necessarily divorce religion from public life. People were still able to take positions on matters of public policy based on their own religious convictions. In the nineteenth century, anti-Catholic and anti-Semitic attitudes swelled, as many varieties of Protestants exhibited marked intolerance. Yet there have been times, like the Cold War era of the 1950s, which pitted a righteous America against godless communism, when religion colored national life and efforts to express common ground trumped differences in belief and practice. In addition, if Americans were all of a single mind religiously, the nation would not have seen so many cases coming to the Supreme Court attempting to determine just what separation of church and state denoted and just what limits there might be to the free exercise of religion.

On paper, then, the US is not officially a religious nation. But in reality, religion has infused the consciousness of Americans as they have struggled to understand for themselves just what it means to be an American. The ways in which that struggle continues to shape contemporary life finds evidence in the way continuing waves of immigration have challenged American national identity and enriched national religious diversity. It also lingers in the question that continues to haunt the popular mind: Is the US a Christian nation, and, if so, in just what sense. To those issues we now turn our attention.

Immigrant religions

The previous chapter described the remarkable increase in religious diversity caused by immigration in the contemporary US. In this section, we describe the sociological research on immigrant religions and how immigration is changing American religious experience. In the next section, we explore the religious tensions caused by increasing religious diversity, due both to the increase in those practicing non-Christian religions and those with no religious belief.

Immigrants bring their religions with them when they come to the US. However, immigrants face a new and different social context than the one they left. They have a choice to either conform to prevailing American religious norms or to try to hold onto the religious traditions of their home country. Research finds that immigrant religions quickly adopt the US congregational form described in Chapter 8. Immigrants of all religious faiths, including those usually practiced in the home, adopt the organizational features of Protestant churches and adapt their worship styles to American forms, including holding services on Sunday, making physical locations more "church-like," and conducting services in both a native language and English. For many, joining an immigrant congregation helps new immigrants to integrate into American society and the community. Finally, religion is often more important to immigrants in the US than it was in their country of origin due, at least in part, to the fact that the US is often more religious than their home nation. In addition, religion provides a place to go for comfort in a new and alienating world.

In other ways, immigrant religions try to hold onto the religious traditions of their home country. Immigrants often use their religious experiences to reaffirm and gain a stronger appreciation of their ethnic and national heritage. As such, involvement in an immigrant congregation offers nonreligious benefits to immigrants, such as integration into American society, and immigrant churches, temples, and mosques often serve as cultural centers. For example, Prema Kurien, in a study of twelve Hindu organizations, including temples, workshop groups, and student organizations, found that these organizations provided resources for members to be proud of their heritage, to network, to resist racism, and to become successful in multicultural America. Moreover, immigrant religions are often tightly integrated with the religious culture in their countries of origin, with religious ideas, practices, and norms being transmitted back and forth. Thus, immigrant religions both adapt to American religious culture and reinforce attachment to the homeland.

Figure 19.1 Immigrants of many faiths quickly integrate into American life, but also hold onto their religious and national heritage. Here, a Muslim immigrant from Pakistan celebrates during Pakistan Independence Day

© David Grossman/Alamy

This dualistic nature is not without internal conflict, often in relation to how much immigrant communities and congregations should integrate into American society. These conflicts often take the form of generational struggles within religious institutions or debates about the proper role of women in the community and religion. For example, there are often conflicts in immigrant churches regarding which language should be spoken during services, which customs to follow, and how much deference will be shown, with older generations favoring more traditional approaches and younger generations favoring more Americanized practices. A major flash point is the proper role of women, especially in the American Islamic community, with younger women wanting to take a more prominent public role in the community than is traditional.

We should not assume that all immigrant religions operate in the same way. Instead, the particular religion, the country of origin, and whether the religion was the religion of the majority in the home country and in America influence the experience of immigrants. Christian immigrants emigrating from a country where Christianity is a minority religion often come to the US to be free to practice their religion. They very quickly adopt US congregational forms, if they did not have them already. In turn, they are often regarded positively by native-born Americans. Immigrants who practice non-majority religions in the US, such as Buddhism, Hinduism, or Islam, often become more religious when they enter the US than they previously were, engaging in outreach and public relations efforts to explain their religion and dispel negative attitudes among native-born Americans. For example, Carolyn Chen studied two Taiwanese immigrant religious institutions, an evangelical Christian church and a Buddhist temple. She found that both groups see the world as a place to work for salvation and faced similar cultural and linguistic obstacles in enacting their mission outside their ethnic community. However, the Buddhist temple's status as a religious outsider put pressure on the faithful to engage in acts of public relations to both prove "Americanness" and remain representative Taiwanese. The evangelical church, on the other hand, was regarded with less suspicion.

Immigration has also had profound effects on American religion. As discussed in Chapter 6, the huge growth in immigration of Catholics from Latin American countries has been the sole reason for the growth of Catholicism in recent years and has led to changes in Catholic practices in the US. However, Catholic congregations are often strongly ethnically segregated. While white and Catholic parishioners often share the same building, they attend different masses, with Latinos attending a mass led in Spanish. Thus, it is nearly impossible to separate the ethnic and religious components of Catholic life. While evangelical Protestant churches are also racially segregated, the segregation is usually between whites and African Americans, with white evangelical Protestant congregations recruiting heavily among Spanish-speaking immigrants as well as from Korean and other Asian populations. A side effect of this new immigration on American religion is that, among white Americans of European origin, ethnicity has declined dramatically as a pivotal influence on religious life.

Religious diversity and tension in contemporary American life

As described throughout this volume, tensions about diversity in religious belief and practices are nothing new in American life. However, the period from 1965 onwards has seen a particularly sharp increase in religious diversity, which is associated with three trends. First, as described in Chapters 4, 5, 9, and 15, a recent stricter interpretation of the separation of church and state, especially with regard to schools and the regulation of reproduction, is associated with the decline of mainline Protestantism and the rise of fundamentalism and evangelical Protestantism in religious and public life. Second, as described in Chapter 8, the proportion of the religiously unaffiliated rose steadily during this period, especially among young adults. Third, as described in Chapter 18, changes to immigration law in 1965 increased the pace of immigration from Latin America, Asia, Africa, and the Middle East. Because immigrants bring their religion with them when they come into the US, there have been remarkable increases in the number of Hindus, Buddhists, and Muslims as a percentage of the population. In addition, as discussed in Chapter 6, American Catholicism has changed, as the majority of new Catholics in the US have a Latino heritage.

These changes in religious diversity have been a source of tension, bringing political and social polarization. Perceptions of the increased secularization of society and reactions to that secularization are at the root of the "culture wars" and polarized political behaviors, as documented in Chapter 9. In addition, the terrorist attacks on 9/11 and the resulting "war on terror," along with recent social controversies like the media attention to the mosque and cultural center being renovated near "Ground Zero," have led to increased religious tension surrounding non-Christian religions.

This tension often manifests itself in the form of vandalism, desecration, and destruction of Muslim, Hindu, Buddhist, and other facilities of minority religions in the US, with over 25,000 instances reported nationwide in 2008. In addition, members of minority religions who dress in distinctive ways – examples are the hijab worn by Muslim women, the turbans and beards of Sikh men, and the bindis (traditionally, the dot of red color applied in the center of the forehead close to the eyebrows) of Hindu women – are often the targets of hate speech or crimes. The most famous example is the murder of Balbir Singh Sodhi, a Sikh, four days after 9/11 by a person mistaking him for a Muslim. A recent study found that 83 per cent of Muslims, Sikhs, and Hindus report that they or someone they personally know has experienced a hate crime or incident, and another 64 per cent felt fear or danger for their family and themselves.

Is the United States a "Christian nation"?

Immigration of religious minority groups and the perceived increased secularization of the US raises tensions because it brings into question the country's national religious identity. A refrain still often heard in popular discourse is that the US is a Christian nation. A variety of surveys have asked how ordinary Americans respond to this statement. A 2005 Pew Research poll found that 71 per cent of American adults say that they "consider the United States a Christian nation." As shown in Table 19.1, the 2003 American Mosaic Project survey also found that two-thirds of American adults answered "yes" when asked if the "United States is a Christian nation." Further, the survey asked respondents to evaluate their response to that question, asking them if that is a good thing or a bad thing. Ninety-one per cent of those who responded that the US is a Christian nation consider that to be a good thing; on the other hand, 59 per cent of those who said the United States is not a Christian nation considered it to be a bad thing. Finally, the 1996 and 2004 General Social Surveys included an item

Table 19.1 Response to the "United States is a Christian Nation"

Is the United States a Christian nation?		That is a good thing	That is a bad thing
Yes	66%	91%	9%
No	34%	41%	59%

Source: 2003 American Mosaic Project Survey

that added a normative dimension to the question by asking whether it was important for one to be a Christian in order to truly be an American. In 2004, 50 per cent of adult Americans responded that it was very important to be Christian to truly be an American.

Using survey data, it is also possible to investigate precisely who responds in a particular way to the question of whether America is a Christian nation. An analysis of American Mosaic Survey data performed for this book by Eric Tranby on religious, demographic, and attitudinal differences in how people responded to this question are presented, in part, in Tables 19.2 and 19.3.

Table 19.2 demonstrates that Christians, those who regularly attend religious services, and those who report that religion is very important in their lives are more likely than others to agree with the statement that "It is a good thing that the US is a Christian nation" than those who say that "It is a bad thing that the US is a Christian nation." In addition, women, African Americans, Hispanics, those with less than a college degree, and Republicans are particularly likely to agree with the statement that "It is a good thing that the US is a Christian nation." Those who believe that the US is a Christian nation and that this is a good thing also believe that a white Christian cultural heritage is central to American identity and believe non-Christians to be

Table 19.2 Variations in Response to "The US is a Christian Nation and it is a Good Thing it is a Christian Nation" (Average: 91 per cent)

Religious characteristics	%	Demographics	%
Religion		*Gender*	
Mainline Protestants	94	Male	89
Evangelical Protestants	96	Female	93
Catholics	95		
Jews	70	*Race*	
Other religions	85	White	90
Religiously unaffiliated	50	Black	94
		Hispanic	96
Church attendance		Asian/native/multiracial	72
Never	68		
Less than once a month	85	*Education*	
Once a month	93	Less than college degree	93
Weekly	97	College degree or higher	85
More than once a week	98		
		Political affiliation	
Religious saliency		Republican	96
Very important	96	Democrat	85
Less than very important	82	Independent/other	89

Source: 2003 American Mosaic Project Survey

Table 19.3 Variations in Response to "The US is not a Christian nation and it is a good thing it is not" (Average: 41 per cent)

Religious characteristics		Demographics	
Religion	*%*	*Gender*	*%*
Mainline Protestants	40	Male	46
Evangelical Protestants	20	Female	35
Catholics	54		
Jews	92	*Race*	
Other religions	37	White	41
Religiously unaffiliated	70	Black	30
		Hispanic	48
Church attendance		Asian/native/multiracial	49
Never	58		
Less than once a month	57	*Education*	
Once a month	50	Less than college degree	38
Weekly	29	College degree or higher	50
More than once a week	12		
		Political affiliation	
Religious saliency		Republican	30
Very important	26	Democrat	46
Less than very important	64	Independent/other	43

Source: 2003 American Mosaic Project Survey

outside of that heritage. In particular, they are likely to believe that America should have a shared set of moral values, to think that the US is a white nation and that this is a good thing, to have negative attitudes towards new immigrants, Muslims, and homosexuals, and to disapprove if their child wanted to marry someone from a different religious background.

Comparisons between those who say that the United States is *not* a Christian nation and that this is a good thing and those who say that it is a bad thing that it is not a Christian nation are reported in Table 19.3. Jews and the religiously unaffiliated, those who do not attend religious services regularly, those who do not believe religion is important in their lives, men, those who have earned a college degree, and Democrats are more likely to believe that it is a good thing that the US is *not* a Christian nation. Those who agree with this statement are more likely to hold tolerant views of religious and racial diversity and to believe that religious minorities and those with no religion have been and are part of the American identity. In particular, those who say that the US is *not* a Christian nation and that this is a good thing also believe that diversity is a good thing. They value diversity in their neighborhood and friendship circles, believe that it is enough for everyone to follow the same rules, think that conservative Christians have too much power in contemporary society, and claim that public schools should teach about racial and religious diversity.

Over time, the percentage of Americans agreeing with statements that America is a Christian nation has increased. For example, in the mid 1990s, only 60 per cent of respondents to the Pew poll described above said that they "consider the United States a Christian nation." The percentage rose steadily to the peak year of 2005, when 71 per cent agreed with that statement. In 1996, only 38 per cent of respondents to the General Social Survey said that it was very important to be a Christian to truly be an American, compared to 50 per cent in 2004. Jeremy Brooke Straughn and Scott

L. Feld explore reasons for this increase, finding that it was driven entirely by Christians, with Christians who report regularly attending church services having the largest proportionate increase in saying that it is very important to be a Christian to truly be an American. They argue that this increase is a response to events such as 9/11 and to politicians emphasizing the religious and moral dimensions of issues such as abortion and same-sex marriage.

Statements like "America is a Christian nation" are not simply statements about demographic realities but are, instead, an attempt to align the boundaries of national belonging with membership in a particular community. Beliefs in a Christian America are especially prevalent among both white and African American evangelical Protestants. White evangelicals believe that their own doctrines and practices are more orthodox and more American than those of other Christian traditions. African American Protestants appear to define a Christian national identity as a strategy to combat social and symbolic exclusion. On the other hand, non-Christians, both believers and those with no religious affiliation, reject the notion that being "truly" American requires adherence to Christianity. This rejection represents a desire to downplay the symbolic importance of Christianity in defining American identity, in favor of religious pluralism and tolerance for diversity.

To this point, we have explored how everyday Americans answer questions about whether America is a Christian nation. Hugh Heclo, a political scientist, has carefully weighed a series of alternative ways of defining and answering the question. He argues the one could define the question as, first, one of demographic realties; second, as adherence to Christian morality, doctrines, and behaviors; or third, as a question of the extent to which Christianity is rooted in the larger culture.

Figure 19.2 Immigration and secularization have raised tensions about our national religious identity. Many Americans wonder whether the US is, or ever has been, a Christian nation

First, one could examine how Americans identify themselves religiously when asked about their religious affiliation. From this point of view, America is very clearly a Christian nation. In the 2007 Religious Landscape Survey, 78.6 per cent of the American adult population self-identified as Christian, with just over 50 per cent of the population claiming affiliation with one of the Protestant denominations. Examining reported beliefs and behaviors, about 40 per cent of Americans claim regular attendance at religious services and over 90 per cent believe in a God or universal spirit. One could also examine *changes* in Americans' religious affiliation. From this point of view, America is still a Christian nation, but less so than it has historically been. As discussed in Chapter 18, adherents of Buddhism, Islam, and Hindu religion (along with other world religions) made up about one-half of one per cent (0.5 per cent) of the population in 1970, but made up about 2 per cent of the US adult population by 2007. Moreover, the percentage of the population with no religious affiliation has increased from 5 per cent in 1972 to 16.1 per cent in 2007. Among Americans under the age of 35, one-quarter (25 per cent) claims no religious identity and perhaps as many as another quarter engage in "alternative" spiritual practices including occult/magical practices. However, as noted in Chapter 2, the percentage of those reporting that they regularly attend church services, believe in life after death, regard the Bible as the inspired word of God, and pray once a day has not significantly increased or decreased since the 1980s.

Second, one could define a Christian nation as one in which people, on average, adhere to Christian morality, doctrines, and behaviors. Based on this definition, America is not a profoundly Christian nation. The 2007 Pew Religious Landscape Survey finds that only 29 per cent of Americans and 35 per cent of American Christians report relying mainly on their religious beliefs for guidance regarding moral issues. Instead, 52 per cent say they rely primarily on practical experience and common sense for moral guidance. This finding is consistent with the literature on "lived religion" described in Chapter 2. Alan Wolfe, in a series of interviews with middle-class Americans, finds that people generally believe that each individual is the judge of what is right and wrong for that individual. The 2007 Pew Religious Landscape poll found that the majority of Christians agreed that many religions can lead to eternal life and that there is more than one true way to interpret the teachings of their religion. Both of these indicate a non-dogmatic approach to religion and Christianity. Finally, the majority of Americans do not engage in behaviors that one might consider to be Christian. While 39 per cent of Americans report attending church weekly and 17 per cent claim that they regularly tithe or donate to ministries, the likely rate is much lower and probably closer to 20 per cent and 6 per cent, respectively, for reasons described in Chapter 1. Other examples abound, including a survey in 2000 by the evangelical magazine *Christianity Today*, which found that 27 per cent of pastors said that they sought out pornography on the Internet, or the fact that 65 per cent of people who believe that extramarital sexual relationships are immoral have had extramarital sexual relations.

Third, American political and civic culture has certainly been heavily influenced by Christianity. As described in Chapter 9, the founders of the American political system rooted their thinking about church–state relations in a theological belief with both Enlightenment and Christian origins. More broadly, American culture carries the imprint of the nation's Christian heritage, particularly mainline Protestant theology and values. Included in this is the notion that America has a good, moral society in which justice and rights ordained by a higher power are the foundations of society. However, in contemporary society, visions of America as a good, moral society are generally religious in nature, but less exclusively focused on Christianity. For example, a 2001 Pew Forum on Religion and Public Life poll found that 70 per cent of Americans wanted to see religion's influence on American society grow, and the majority of Americans (53 per cent) said it did not matter which particular religion becomes more influential.

Acceptance and rejection of religious pluralism

As discussed above and in Chapter 18, questions about America as a Christian nation have taken on increasing salience due to religious diversity in the form of rising numbers of Hindus, Muslims, and Buddhists in the US. Sociologists have explored how Americans have responded to this. They have found that when asked about religious diversity in general, Americans are accepting of it. As described above, the 2007 Pew poll found that Americans have non-dogmatic views on religion, with 70 per cent of Americans saying that many religions can lead to eternal life and 68 per cent saying that there is more than one true way to interpret the teachings of their religion. The only two religious groups to have less than 50 per cent agreeing with those statements were Mormons and Jehovah's Witnesses. The 2002 Religion and Diversity Survey, funded by the Lilly Endowment, found that 89 per cent of Americans agree that religious diversity has been good for America. The 2003 American Mosaic Project Survey found that 73 per cent of Americans agreed that schools should teach about the religious diversity of the American people and 77 per cent believed that the government should guarantee equal treatment of all religions, including unpopular ones or religions that some people find offensive.

However, not all Americans have positive attitudes towards religious diversity, as evidenced by the vandalism and violence described above. In general, Americans are less comfortable with religious diversity when asked about specific religious groups. For example, less than a third of Americans would welcome a Hindu temple or Muslim mosque into their community, according to the Religion and Diversity Survey, and Jong Hyun Jung finds that Americans have less respect for Islam than for any other religion. In separate research, Stephen Merino, R. Khari Brown and Ronald E. Brown, and Jong Hyun Jung find that evangelical Protestants, as well as those who believe that Christianity is the only way to gain eternal life, those who believe that there is a conflict between Christians and non-Christians, and Christians who are more religiously involved are far more likely than other Americans to reject religious diversity. Stephen Merino finds that those who believe that the US is a Christian nation are less likely to include Muslims in community life. Related research by Penny Edgell and Eric Tranby estimates that about 25 per cent of the population holds these particularly negative views of religious minorities and believe that such persons are not part of the American cultural core.

On the other hand, some Americans have positive views of religious diversity, even when discussing specific minority religious groups. The development of positive attitudes towards specific groups is generally caused by contact with those groups. For example, Stephen Merino finds that having prior contact with non-Christians, and specifically with Hindus, Muslims, and Buddhists, is associated with being more willing to welcome a Hindu temple or Muslim mosque into the community. In addition, Jong Hyun Jung finds that more frequent contact with Muslims is associated with more respect for Islam. However, many Americans have little or no contact with members of these groups, with 50 per cent of adult Americans reporting no or almost no contact with Muslims and 65 per cent reporting no or almost no contact with Hindus and Buddhists, according to the Religion and Diversity Survey. Moreover, inter-group contact does not work to increase positive attitudes towards Muslims for white evangelical Christians. In related research, Penny Edgell and Eric Tranby estimate that about 30 per cent of the population holds positive attitudes about all groups and does not believe racial, religious, or social differences form a barrier to a shared national identity. This portion of the population tends to be less religiously involved, younger, and more educated than those who think otherwise.

Atheists as a religious other

Questions about America as a Christian nation have also taken on increasing salience due to the increase in those with no religious affiliation. As described earlier, 16 per cent of adult Americans considered themselves to have no religious affiliation in 2008, up from 9.2 per cent in 1994 and 5 per cent in 1972 (see Fig. 2.1 in Chapter 2). In the 2007 Pew Religious Landscape survey and as described in Chapter 6, 1.6 per cent identified as atheist and rejected a belief in God(s), the supernatural, or a higher power; 2.4 per cent are agnostics and view the truth of religious beliefs as unknown and unknowable; and 12.1 per cent are "nothing in particular" or indifferent toward religion.

Most sociological research on this sector of the population has focused on atheists and, in particular, Americans' attitudes towards atheists. Unlike the split response to religious diversity, the majority of Americans have negative views of atheists. Since 1958, the Gallup Poll has tracked the willingness of Americans to vote for presidential candidates who are also members of various groups. Atheists are consistently at the bottom of the list, with Americans reporting less willingness to vote for an atheist than for a homosexual, African American, Jew, or Catholic. Marcel Harper, in a study of college students in 2007, finds that many believe that nonreligious individuals are immoral, anti-Christian, prejudiced, and self-centered.

Table 19.4 presents information on the acceptance of various groups using two questions from the 2003 American Mosaic Project Survey. The first assesses agreement with the statement "This group does not at all agree with my vision of American society." This statement is about public cultural membership and moral solidarity with someone who does not share a vision of American society meaning someone who does not value the same things about America or understand in the same way what it means to be an American citizen. The second assesses agreement with the statement "I would disapprove if my child wanted to marry a member of this group." This question is about personal trust and acceptance of another as a worthy member of the family. Most Americans believe that atheists do not share their vision of American society and are less willing to accept intermarriage with atheists than any other group that was asked about. The gap between acceptance of atheists and acceptance of other religious and racial minorities is large and persistent across all measured demographic, religious, and racial groups, with the exception of those who are not religiously affiliated.

Table 19.4 Attitudes towards various groups

Groups	%
This group does not at all agree with my vision of American society	
Atheists	**39.6**
Muslims	26.3
Homosexuals	22.6
Conservative Christians	13.5
Recent Immigrants	12.5
Hispanics	7.6
Jews	7.4
Asian Americans	7
African Americans	4.6
White Americans	2.2
I would disapprove if my child wanted to marry a member of this group	
Atheist	**47.6**
Muslim	33.5
African American	27.2
Asian American	18.5
Hispanic	18.5
Jew	11.8
Conservative Christian	6.9
White	2.3

Source: American Mosaic Project Survey, 2003, N = 2,081

Penny Edgell, Doug Hartmann, and Joe Gerteis analyzed responses to these questions and found that Americans' willingness to exclude atheists is influenced by many of the same factors that are associated with the acceptance or rejection of religious pluralism. The religiously involved, evangelical Protestants, Catholics, and those who believe in a shared moral order built on God's laws are more likely to exclude atheists. On the other hand, the more educated, those who have contact with people from diverse religious and racial backgrounds, and those who are generally tolerant of other groups are less likely to exclude atheists.

Given the small proportion of atheists in the population, Edgell, Hartmann, and Gerteis argue that the exclusion of atheists from public and private life is not in reaction to actual atheists they have encountered, but instead, "the atheist" is a symbolic entity that draws boundaries of cultural membership. In private and public life, many Americans associate religiosity with morality, trustworthiness, a basis for citizenship, and a source of a common American identity. Thus, the exclusion of atheists from cultural membership is about the historic place of religion in providing the basis for American civic and public culture as a good, moral society. Atheists are not just a religious minority among many others in a sea of religious diversity; instead, for many Americans, atheists are the symbolic representation of those who reject the very basis of American society, regardless of the morality and patriotism of actual atheists.

Box 19.1 Attitudes toward atheists

Edgell, Gerteis, and Hartmann (2006) provide evidence from in-depth interviews about what people think atheists are like and what the label means. Respondents tended to view atheists as either cultural elites who threaten common values from above, or immoral people from the lower end of the status hierarchy, as illustrated in these two quotes:

> It's that same arrogance again. I'm an American, I can do anything I want, and to heck with the rest of the world. [Interviewer: Do you see religion fitting into it very well?] These people aren't very religious, you'll notice that. There's a real, "I'm an atheist" attitude among people with major money. You don't see this nice balance … I'll say it again, some religious belief, I don't care who or what you worship, just something to give you that stability. If you're going all through life, "I'm an atheist, I don't believe in anything except the almighty dollar," this is definitely a destructive attitude and the rest of the world sees it.
>
> (A Republican woman in her mid 60s)

> The prisons aren't filled with conservative Republican Christians. The prisons are probably filled with people who don't have any kind of a spiritual or religious core. So I don't have to worry about … a conservative Christian, you know, committing a crime against me, chances are.
>
> (A Republican man in his mid 40s)

The future of American religious life

The US has always been, and will continue to be, a land with a great deal of religious diversity and a great deal of tension caused by that religious diversity. Sociologists and historians are always cautious about predicting the future, but if current trends remain in force, religious diversity will continue to rise into the foreseeable future. While self-identified Christians will continue to be the majority of the population, Protestants will likely make up less than half of the population by 2015, and the number and percentage of religious minorities and the religiously unaffiliated as a proportion of the population will continue to rise, given the generational trends described in Chapters 15 and 16.

Tensions caused by religious diversity show no strong signs of abating in the future. Although the majority of Americans accept religious pluralism in general, they continue to see adherents of certain religious minority groups as being bad members of society. Yet as these minority religious groups grow, the frequency of contact that many Americans have with their adherents will increase. As noted above, the development of positive attitudes towards religious minority groups is generally caused by direct contact with those groups. Hence, as religious pluralism increases, tolerance is also likely to increase.

Strikingly negative views about atheists and those with no religious affiliation have also been a persistent finding in research. Although these views may moderate over time, religion remains central to the way that Americans draw symbolic boundaries and assess cultural membership. Religion has a historic place in American civic and political culture. Moreover, religion forms the basis for most Americans' understanding of the good, moral society and of citizenship. As the number of atheists and religiously unaffiliated grows, the question that may guide future debates about religion in American life may be not whether the US is a Christian nation but whether the US is even a "religious nation." The diversity and pluralism that shape contemporary life suggest that there may not be a single answer to that question. And if there is no single answer, then the American people themselves must engage in ongoing conversation, some of which may be contentious and difficult, about just what binds a diverse people into a single nation.

Key points you need to know

- Connections between religion and national identity have a long history in the US.
- Immigrant religions become Americanized and help people integrate in American society.
- Immigrant religious are also used to maintain the importance of, and contact with, the country of origin.
- Recently, the increase of immigrants with non-Christian religions and the increase of the religiously unaffiliated have highlighted religious diversity as a source of tension.
- The majority of Americans believe that the US is a Christian nation.
- There has been an increase in the number of Christians believing that the US is a Christian nation.
- A Christian nation can be defined as one where the majority of the population is Christian; as one in which people adhere to Christian morality, doctrine, or behaviors; or as one in which Christianity is rooted in the political and civic culture.
- In general, Americans are widely accepting of religious diversity.
- When asked about specific groups, some Americans hold negative views of Muslims, Hindus, and Buddhists, while others hold positive and pluralistic views of religious minorities.
- Negative views are high among evangelical Protestants, the religiously involved, and those who have a dogmatic approach to Christianity.
- Positive views are high among those who have had contact with religious minorities.
- Most Americans have negative views of atheists, seeing them as the symbolic representation of those who reject the very basis of American society.
- Religious diversity will continue to increase into the foreseeable future and tensions caused by that religious diversity also show no signs of abating, but they may be changing.

Discussion questions

1 What forces linked religion and American identity in the colonial period? How have they changed over time?
2 How are immigrant religions distinct from both the "home" and "American" religion?
3 Why are religious minorities the targets of hate crimes and speech?
4 Do you think America is a Christian nation?
5 How do you define a Christian nation?
6 Why are most Americans accepting of general religious diversity?
7 Why do some Americans reject religious pluralism when asked about specific groups, while others accept it?
8 Why do you think the number of religiously unaffiliated is growing?
9 Why do most Americans have negative views of atheists?
10 Do you think America is a religious nation, rather than a Christian one?
11 What do you think is the future of American religion in the twenty-first century?

Further reading

Backer, J.O. and Smith, B. (2009) "None Too Simple: Examining Issues of Religious Nonbelief and Nonbelonging in the United States," *Journal for the Scientific Study of Religion*, 48: 719–33.

Brekus, C. and Gilpin, W.C., (eds.) (2011) *American Christianities: A History of Dominance and Diversity*, Chapel Hill: University of North Carolina Press.

Brown, R.K. and Brown, R.E. (2011) "The Challenge of Religious Pluralism: The Association Between Interfaith Contact and Religious Pluralism," *Review of Religious Research*, 53: 323–40.

Chen, C. (2002) "The Religious Varieties of Ethnic Presence: A Comparison Between a Taiwanese Immigrant Buddhist Temple and an Evangelical Christian Church," *Sociology of Religion*, 63: 215–38.

Edgell, P. and Tranby, E. (2010) "Shared Visions? Diversity and Cultural Membership in American Life," *Social Problems*, 57: 175–204.

Edgell, P., Gerteis, J., and Hartmann, D. (2006), "Atheists As 'Other': Moral Boundaries and Cultural Membership in American Society," *American Sociological Review*, 71: 211–34.

Heclo, H. (2007), "Is America a Christian Nation?" *Political Science Quarterly*, 122: 59–87.

Jung, J.H. (2012), "Islamophobia? Religion, Contact with Muslims, and the Respect for Islam," *Review of Religious Research*, 54: 113–26.

Kurien, P. (2004) "Multiculturalism, Immigrant Religion and Diasporic Nationalism: The Development of an American Hinduism," *Social Problems*, 51: 362–85.

Merino, S.M. (2010) "Religious Diversity in a 'Christian Nation': The Effects of Theological Exclusivity and Interreligious Contact on the Acceptance of Religious Diversity," *Journal for the Scientific Study of Religion*, 49: 231–46.

Sherkat, D. (2008) "Beyond Belief: Atheism, Agnosticism, and Theistic Certainty in the United States," *Sociological Spectrum*, 28: 438–59.

Straugh, J.B. and Feld, S.L. (2010) "America as a 'Christian Nation'? Understand Religious Boundaries of National Identity in the United States," *Sociology of Religion*, 71: 280–306.

Yang, F. and Ebaugh, H.R. (2001) "Transformations in New Immigrant Religions," *American Sociological Review*, 66: 269–88.

Index